MW00676136

IF FOUND, please notify and arrange important study guide for the owner's c........ .... preparation.

Name: _____ Email: _____

Address: _____

City, State, ZIP: _____ Telephone: (___) _____

Additional copies of *Commercial Pilot PTS and Oral Exam Guide* are available from

Gleim Publications, Inc.
P.O. Box 12848 • University Station
Gainesville, Florida 32604

(352) 375-0772
(800) 87-GLEIM or (800) 874-5346
Fax: (352) 375-6940

www.gleim.com | avmarketing@gleim.com

The price is $15.95 (subject to change without notice). Orders must be prepaid. Order online or call us. Refer to the product listing at the back of the book for more information. Shipping and handling charges apply to all orders. Add applicable sales tax to shipments within Florida.

Gleim Publications, Inc., guarantees the immediate refund of all resalable texts, unopened and un-downloaded Test Prep Software, and unopened and un-downloaded audios returned within 30 days of purchase. Aviation Test Prep Online may be canceled within 30 days of purchase if no more than the first study unit has been accessed. Other Aviation online courses may be canceled within 30 days of purchase if no more than two study units have been accessed. This policy applies only to products that are purchased directly from Gleim Publications, Inc. No refunds will be provided on opened or downloaded Test Prep Software or audios, partial returns of package sets, or shipping and handling charges. Any freight charges incurred for returned or refused packages will be the purchaser's responsibility. Returns of books purchased from bookstores and other resellers should be made to the respective bookstore or reseller. For more information regarding the Gleim Return Policy, please contact our offices at (800) 874-5346.

For a listing of the Gleim aviation products, please visit
www.gleim.com/aviation/product_catalog.php

ii

REVIEWERS AND CONTRIBUTORS

Scott Krogh, CMEL, CFII, MEI, is the Gleim 141 Chief Flight Instructor and one of our aviation editors. Mr. Krogh researched questions, wrote and edited answer explanations, and incorporated revisions into the text.

Greg Hunsucker, ATP, CSEL, CFII–Gold Seal, AGI, is a Gleim Aviation Consultant. Mr. Hunsucker has accumulated over 3,500 hours in corporate business jets and cargo aircraft and over 800 hours instructing students from private to CFI. He researched questions, wrote and edited answer explanations, and incorporated revisions into the text.

The CFIs who have worked with us throughout the years to develop and improve our pilot training materials.

The many FAA employees who helped, in person or by telephone, primarily in Gainesville, Orlando, Oklahoma City, and Washington, DC.

The many pilots and student pilots who have provided comments and suggestions about our materials during the past several decades.

A PERSONAL THANKS

This manual would not have been possible without the extraordinary effort and dedication of Jacob Brunny, Julie Cutlip, Eileen Nickl, Teresa Soard, Justin Stephenson, Joanne Strong, Elmer Tucker, and Candace Van Doren, who typed the entire manuscript and all revisions and drafted and laid out the diagrams and illustrations in this book.

The authors also appreciate the production and editorial assistance of Ellen Buhl, Jessica Felkins, Chris Hawley, Jeanette Kerstein, Katie Larson, Diana Leon, Cary Marcous, Shane Rapp, Drew Sheppard, and Martha Willis.

Finally, we appreciate the encouragement, support, and tolerance of our families throughout this project.

FIRST EDITION

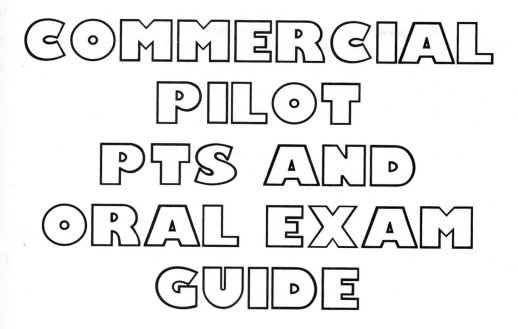

COMMERCIAL PILOT PTS AND ORAL EXAM GUIDE

by

Irvin N. Gleim, Ph.D., CFII

and

Garrett W. Gleim, CFII

ABOUT THE AUTHORS

Irvin N. Gleim earned his private pilot certificate in 1965 from the Institute of Aviation at the University of Illinois, where he subsequently received his Ph.D. He is a commercial pilot and flight instructor (instrument) with multi-engine and seaplane ratings, and is a member of the Aircraft Owners and Pilots Association, American Bonanza Society, Civil Air Patrol, Experimental Aircraft Association, National Association of Flight Instructors, and Seaplane Pilots Association. Dr. Gleim is the author of flight maneuvers and practical test prep books for the sport, private, instrument, commercial, and flight instructor certificates/ratings, and study guides for the sport, private/recreational, instrument, commercial, flight/ground instructor, fundamentals of instructing, airline transport pilot, and flight engineer FAA knowledge tests. Three additional pilot training books are *Pilot Handbook*, *Aviation Weather and Weather Services*, and *FAR/AIM*.

Dr. Gleim has also written articles for professional accounting and business law journals and is the author of widely used review materials for the CIA (Certified Internal Auditor), CMA (Certified Management Accountant), CPA (Certified Public Accountant), EA (IRS Enrolled Agent), and RTRP (Registered Tax Return Preparer) exams. He is Professor Emeritus, Fisher School of Accounting, University of Florida, and is a CFM, CIA, CMA, CPA, and RTRP.

Garrett W. Gleim earned his private pilot certificate in 1997 in a Piper Super Cub. He is a commercial pilot (single- and multi-engine), ground instructor (advanced and instrument), and flight instructor (instrument and multi-engine), and is a member of the Aircraft Owners and Pilots Association, National Association of Flight Instructors, and Society of Aviation and Flight Instructors. Mr. Gleim is the author of study guides for the sport, private/recreational, instrument, commercial, flight/ground instructor, fundamentals of instructing, and airline transport pilot FAA knowledge tests. He received a Bachelor of Science in Economics from The Wharton School, University of Pennsylvania. Mr. Gleim is also a CPA (not in public practice).

Gleim Publications, Inc.
P.O. Box 12848 · University Station
Gainesville, Florida 32604

(352) 375-0772
(800) 874-5346
Fax: (352) 375-6940

Internet: www.gleim.com
Email: admin@gleim.com

For updates to the first printing of the first edition of
Commercial Pilot PTS and Oral Exam Guide

Go To: www.gleim.com/updates

Or: Email update@gleim.com with **CPTS&OEG 1-1** in the subject
line. You will receive our current update as a reply.

Updates are available until the next edition is published.

ISSN Pending
ISBN 978-1-58194-473-0

First Printing: February 2014

This first edition is designed specifically for pilots who aspire to become
commercial pilots. Please email any corrections and suggestions for
subsequent editions to aviation@gleim.com.

SOURCES USED IN
COMMERCIAL PILOT PTS AND ORAL EXAM GUIDE

The abbreviated citations for the sources we used for the questions and answers in this book are below. These publications can be obtained from the FAA, the Government Printing Office, and aviation bookstores.

AC	Advisory Circular
ACL	Aeronautical Chart Legend
AFNA	Aerodynamics for Naval Aviators
AFH	*Airplane Flying Handbook*
AIM	*Aeronautical Information Manual*
A&PM PH	*Airframe and Powerplant Mechanics Powerplant Handbook*
AvW	*Aviation Weather*
AWBH	*Aircraft Weight and Balance Handbook*
AWS	*Aviation Weather Services*
FAR	Federal Aviation Regulations
Fl Comp	Flight Computer
IFH	*Instrument Flying Handbook*
NTSB	National Transportation Safety Board Regulations
PHAK	*Pilot's Handbook of Aeronautical Knowledge*

NOTE: ANSWER DISCREPANCIES and UPDATES

Our questions and answers have been carefully researched and reviewed. Inevitably, there will be differences with competitors' books and even the FAA. If necessary, we will develop an UPDATE for the *Commercial Pilot PTS and Oral Exam Guide*. Email update@gleim.com as described on page v or visit our website for the latest updates and information on all of our products. Updates for this first edition will be available until the next edition is published. To continue providing our customers with first-rate service, we request that questions about our materials be sent to us via email to aviation@gleim.com. The appropriate staff member will give each question thorough consideration and a prompt response. Questions concerning orders, prices, shipments, or payments will be handled via telephone by our competent and courteous customer service staff.

TABLE OF CONTENTS

*Includes only the multi-engine Tasks not covered in the single-engine Tasks.

INTRODUCING THE GLEIM
COMMERCIAL PILOT PTS AND ORAL EXAM GUIDE

All aspiring Commercial Pilots should bring the following resources to refer to during the oral section of their practical test: their personal logbook, the aircraft's logbook, POH, *Airport/Facility Directory*, the Practical Test Standards (PTS), VFR chart, *FAR/AIM*, and *Aviation Weather and Weather Services*. In addition, all students should have an Oral Exam Guide to prep for the assortment of questions they may face. Unlike most publishers, Gleim combines the PTS and the Oral Exam Guide into one convenient, easy-to-use book, the *Commercial Pilot PTS and Oral Exam Guide*.

The PTS portion comes first and includes a direct reprint of the most current version of the FAA Practical Test Standards at the time of print (February 2014). Gleim has removed references to seaplanes because the Gleim *Commercial Pilot PTS and Oral Exam Guide* is specific to single- and multi-engine land airplanes. Accordingly, tasks in this reprint are not always sequentially numbered because tasks that do not apply to single- and multi-engine land airplanes have been omitted. Gleim has made it easy to tell where the PTS portion begins and ends by darkening the edges of this section's pages.

The Oral Exam Guide comes after the PTS portion. Most flight schools and many CFIs recommend that pilots preparing for their practical test study an Oral Exam Guide. We agree: Your examiner will ask a wide-ranging series of questions during the oral portion of your practical test. Those questions may pertain to any subject or task included in the PTS for the commercial pilot certificate. Because most of the multi-engine tasks overlap with the single-engine tasks, we have included multi-engine-specific tasks separately at the end of the Oral Exam Guide. By studying the series of potential questions in this book, you will gain a significant advantage as you prepare for your testing experience.

The convenient table of contents in the Gleim Oral Exam Guide cross-references each question to the appropriate PTS Area of Operation, and Appendix A includes abbreviations and acronyms used by commercial pilots.

Think of this book as both a "PTS guide" and an "oral exam guide." It is a thoroughly researched tool that supports the entire Gleim system of oral and practical test preparation, which includes the following manuals: *Commercial Pilot FAA Knowledge Test, Commercial Pilot Flight Maneuvers, Commercial Pilot Syllabus, Aviation Weather and Weather Services, FAR/AIM*, and *Pilot Handbook*. These books contain all of the information you need to do well on your practical test.

Enjoy Flying -- Safely!

Irvin N. Gleim
Garrett W. Gleim
February 2014

FAA COMMERCIAL PILOT
PRACTICAL TEST STANDARDS REPRINTED
(FAA-S-8081-12C)

Except for in the Introduction, we have removed references to seaplanes because the Gleim *Commercial Pilot PTS and Oral Exam Guide* is specific to single- and multi-engine land airplanes. Accordingly, Tasks in this reprint are not always sequentially numbered because Tasks that do not apply to single- and multi-engine land airplanes have been omitted.

Introduction

General Information

The Flight Standards Service of the Federal Aviation Administration (FAA) has developed this practical test as the standard that shall be used by FAA examiners[1] when conducting commercial pilot–airplane practical tests. Instructors are expected to use this practical test standard (PTS) when preparing applicants for practical tests. Applicants should be familiar with this PTS and refer to these standards during their training.

Information considered directive in nature is described in this PTS in terms, such as "shall" and "must" indicating the actions are mandatory. Guidance information is described in terms, such as "should" and "may" indicating the actions are desirable or permissive, but not mandatory.

The FAA gratefully acknowledges the valuable assistance provided by many individuals and organizations throughout the aviation community who contributed their time and talent in assisting with the revision of these practical test standards.

This PTS may be purchased from the Superintendent of Documents, U.S. Government Printing Office (GPO), Washington, DC 20402-9325, or from http://bookstore.gpo.gov. This PTS is also available for download, in pdf format, from www.faa.gov.

This PTS is published by the U.S. Department of Transportation, Federal Aviation Administration, Airman Testing Standards Branch, AFS-630, P.O. Box 25082, Oklahoma City, OK 73125. Comments regarding this handbook should be sent, in e-mail form, to AFS630comments@faa.gov.

Practical Test Standard Concept

Title 14 of the Code of Federal Regulations (14 CFR) part 61 specifies the areas in which knowledge and skill must be demonstrated by the applicant before the issuance of a commercial pilot certificate or rating. The CFRs provide the flexibility to permit the FAA to publish practical test standards containing the Areas of Operation and specific Tasks in which pilot competency shall be demonstrated. The FAA will revise this PTS whenever it is determined that changes are needed in the interest of safety. **Adherence to the provisions of the regulations and the practical test standards is mandatory for the evaluation of commercial pilot applicants.**

---

[1] The word "examiner" denotes either the FAA inspector, FAA designated pilot examiner, or other authorized person who conducts the practical test.

Practical Test Book Description

This test book contains the following Commercial Pilot–Airplane Practical Test Standards:

Section 1: Airplane–Single-Engine Land and Sea
Section 2: Airplane–Multiengine Land and Sea

The Commercial Pilot–Airplane includes the Areas of Operation and Tasks for the issuance of an initial commercial pilot certificate and for the addition of category ratings and/or class ratings to that certificate.

Practical Test Standards Description

Areas of Operation are phases of the practical test arranged in a logical sequence within each standard. They begin with Preflight Preparation and end with Postflight Procedures. The examiner, however, **may conduct the practical test in any sequence that will result in a complete and efficient test; however, the ground portion of the practical test shall be accomplished before the flight portion**.

Tasks are titles of knowledge areas, flight procedures, or maneuvers appropriate to an Area of Operation. The abbreviation(s) within parentheses immediately following a Task refer to the category and/or class aircraft appropriate to that Task.* The meaning of each abbreviation is as follows.

ASEL: Airplane–Single-Engine Land
AMEL: Airplane–Multiengine Land
ASES: Airplane–Single-Engine Sea
AMES: Airplane–Multiengine Sea

NOTE: *When administering a test based on sections 1 and 2 of this PTS, the Tasks appropriate to the class airplane (ASEL, ASES, AMEL, or AMES) used for the test shall be included in the plan of action. The absence of a class indicates the Task is for all classes.*

NOTE is used to emphasize special considerations required in the Area of Operation or Task.

Reference identifies the publication(s) that describe(s) the Task. Descriptions of Tasks are not included in these standards because this information can be found in the current issue of the listed reference. Publications other than those listed may be used for references if their content conveys substantially the same meaning as the referenced publications.

*Authors' note: Gleim has removed these category and class indications from the Tasks because the Gleim *Commercial Pilot PTS and Oral Exam Guide* is specific to single- and multi-engine land airplanes. Seaplane Tasks are not included in this book, and therefore it is unnecessary to distinguish between land and sea categories and classes.

These practical test standards are based on the following references.

14 CFR part 39	Airworthiness Directives
14 CFR part 43	Maintenance, Preventive Maintenance, Rebuilding, and Alteration
14 CFR part 61	Certification: Pilots, Flight Instructors, and Ground Instructors
14 CFR part 91	General Operating and Flight Rules
14 CFR part 93	Special Air Traffic Rules
AC 00-6	Aviation Weather
AC 00-45	Aviation Weather Services
AC 61-65	Certification: Pilots and Flight Instructors
AC 61-67	Stall and Spin Awareness Training
AC 91-73	Part 91 and 135 Single-Pilot Procedures During Taxi Operations
AC 61-84	Role of Preflight Preparation
AC 90-48	Pilots' Role in Collision Avoidance
AC 90-66	Recommended Standard Traffic Patterns and Practices for Aeronautical Operations at Airports Without Operating Control Towers
AC 91-13	Cold Weather Operation of Aircraft
AC 91-55	Reduction of Electrical System Failures Following Aircraft Engine Starting
AC 91-69	Seaplane Safety for FAR Part 91 Operations
AC 120-51	Crew Resource Management Training
AC 120-74	Parts 91, 121, 125 and 135 Flightcrew Procedures During Taxi Operations
AC 150-5340-18	Standards for Airport Sign Systems
AIM	Aeronautical Information Manual
A/FD	Airport/Facility Directory
FAA-H-8083-1	Aircraft Weight and Balance Handbook
FAA-H-8083-2	Risk Management Handbook
FAA-H-8083-3	Airplane Flying Handbook
FAA-H-8083-6	Advanced Avionics Handbook
FAA-H-8083-15	Instrument Flying Handbook
FAA-H-8083-23	Seaplane, Skiplane, and Float/Ski Equipped Helicopter Operations Handbook
FAA-H-8083-25	Pilot's Handbook of Aeronautical Knowledge
FAA-P-8740-19	Flying Light Twins Safely
NOTAMs	Notices to Airmen
POH/AFM	Pilot Operating Handbook FAA-Approved Flight Manual
Other	Navigation Charts
	Navigation Equipment Operation Manuals
	Seaplane Supplement
	USCG Navigation Rules, International–Inland

The Objective lists the elements that must be satisfactorily performed to demonstrate competency in a Task. The Objective includes:

1. specifically what the applicant should be able to do;
2. conditions under which the Task is to be performed; and
3. acceptable performance standards.

Abbreviations

14 CFR	Title 14 of the Code of Federal Regulations
AC	Advisory Circular
ADM	Aeronautical Decision-Making
AGL	Above Ground Level
AMEL	Airplane Multiengine Land
AMES	Airplane Multiengine Sea
ATC	Air Traffic Control
CDL	Configuration Deviation List
CFIT	Controlled Flight into Terrain
CRM	Crew Resource Management
DA	Decision Altitude
DH	Decision Height
DP	Departure Procedure
FAA	Federal Aviation Administration
FAF	Final Approach Fix
FDC	Flight Data Center
FE	Flight Engineer
FMS	Flight Management System
FMSP	Flight Management System Procedures
FSB	Flight Standardization Board
FSD	Flight Simulation Device
FSDO	Flight Standards District Office
FTD	Flight Training Device
GLS	GNSS Landing System
GNSS	Global Navigation Satellite System
GPO	Government Printing Office
GPS	Global Positioning System
IAP	Instrument Approach Procedure
IFR	Instrument Flight Rules
ILS	Instrument Landing System
INS	Inertial Navigation System
LAHSO	Land and Hold Short Operations
LDA	Localizer-Type Directional Aid
LOC	ILS Localizer
MDA	Minimum Descent Altitude
MEL	Minimum Equipment List
NAVAID	Navigation Aid
NDB	Non-Directional Beacon
NOTAM	Notice to Airman
NWS	National Weather Service
POH	Pilot's Operating Handbook
PT	Procedure Turn
PTS	Practical Test Standard
RNAV	Area Navigation
SRM	Single-Pilot Resource Management
STAR	Standard Terminal Arrival
TAA	Terminal Arrival Area
V_1	Takeoff Decision Speed
V_2	Takeoff Safety Speed
VDP	Visual Descent Point
VFR	Visual Flight Rules
V_{MC}	Minimum Control Speed with Critical Engine Inoperative

VMC	Visual Meteorological Conditions
VOR	Very High Frequency Omnidirectional Range
V_R	Rotation Speed
V_{REF}	Reference Landing Approach Speed
V_{SSE}	Safe, Intentional, One-Engine Inoperative Speed
V_X	Best Angle of Climb Speed
V_Y	Best Rate of Climb Speed

Use of the Practical Test Standards

The FAA requires that all commercial pilot practical tests be conducted in accordance with the appropriate commercial practical test standards and the policies set forth in the INTRODUCTION. Applicants shall be evaluated in **ALL** Tasks included in each Area of Operation of the appropriate practical test standard, unless otherwise noted.

An applicant, who holds at least a commercial pilot certificate seeking an additional airplane category rating and/or class rating at the private pilot level, shall be evaluated in the Areas of Operation and Tasks listed in the Additional Rating Task Table. At the discretion of the examiner, an evaluation of the applicant's competence in the remaining Areas of Operation and Tasks may be conducted.

If the applicant holds two or more category or class ratings at least at the commercial level, and the ratings table indicates differing required Tasks, the "least restrictive" entry applies. For example, if "ALL" and "NONE" are indicated for one Area of Operation, the "NONE" entry applies. If "B" and "B, C" are indicated, the "B" entry applies.

In preparation for each practical test, the examiner shall develop a written "plan of action" for each practical test. The "plan of action" is a tool, for the sole use of the examiner, to be used in evaluating the applicant. The plan of action need not be grammatically correct or in any formal format. The plan of action must contain all of the required Areas of Operation and Tasks and any optional Tasks selected by the examiner. The plan of action will include a scenario that allows the evaluation of as many required Areas of Operation and Tasks as possible without disruption. During the mission, the examiner interjects problems and emergencies which the applicant must manage. It should be structured so that most of the Areas of Operation and Tasks are accomplished within the mission. The examiner is afforded the flexibility to change the plan to accommodate unexpected situations as they arise. Some Tasks (e.g., unusual attitudes) are not normally done during routine flight operations or may not fit into the scenario.

These maneuvers still must be demonstrated. It is preferable that these maneuvers be demonstrated after the scenario is completed. A practical test scenario can be suspended to do maneuvers, and then resumed if time and efficiency of the practical test so dictates. *Any Task selected for evaluation during a practical test shall be evaluated in its entirety.*

The examiner is expected to use good judgment in the performance of simulated emergency procedures. The use of the safest means for simulation is expected. Consideration must be given to local conditions, both meteorological and topographical, at the time of the test, as well as the applicant's workload, and the condition of the aircraft used. If the procedure being evaluated would jeopardize safety, it is expected that the applicant will simulate that portion of the maneuver.

Special Emphasis Areas

Examiners shall place special emphasis upon areas of aircraft operations considered critical to flight safety. Among these are:

1. Positive aircraft control,
2. Positive exchange of the flight controls procedure,
3. Stall/spin awareness,
4. Collision avoidance,
5. Wake turbulence avoidance,
6. LAHSO,
7. Runway incursion avoidance,
8. CFIT,
9. ADM and risk management,
10. Wire strike avoidance,
11. Checklist usage,
12. Temporary flight restrictions (TFRs),
13. Special use airspace (SUA),
14. Aviation security,
15. Single-Pilot Resource Management (SRM), and
16. Other areas deemed appropriate to any phase of the practical test.

A given special emphasis area may not be specifically addressed under a given Task. All areas are essential to flight and will be evaluated during the practice test.

Removal of the "Airplane Multiengine VFR Only" Limitation

The removal of the "Airplane Multiengine VFR Only" limitation, at the commercial pilot certificate level, requires an applicant to satisfactorily perform the following Area of Operation and Tasks from the commercial AMEL and AMES PTS in a multiengine airplane that has a manufacturer's published V_{MC} speed.

- Area of Operation X: Multiengine Operations
  - Task C: Engine Failure During Flight (By Reference to Instruments)
  - Task D: Instrument Approach–One Engine Inoperative (By Reference to Instruments)

Removal of the "Limited to Center Thrust" Limitation

The removal of the "Limited to Center Thrust" limitation at the commercial pilot certificate level requires an applicant to satisfactorily perform the following Areas of Operation and Tasks from the commercial AMEL and AMES PTS in a multiengine airplane that has a manufacturer's published V_{MC} speed. An applicant that holds an airplane instrument rating and has not demonstrated instrument proficiency in a multiengine airplane with a published V_{MC} shall complete the additional Tasks listed under Removal of the "Airplane Multiengine VFR Only" Limitation section.

- Area of Operation I: Preflight Preparation
  - Task H: Principles of Flight-Engine Inoperative
- Area of Operation VIII: Emergency Operations
  - Task B: Engine Failure During Takeoff Before V_{MC} (Simulated)
  - Task C: Engine Failure After Lift-Off (Simulated)
  - Task D: Approach and Landing with an Inoperative Engine (Simulated)
- Area of Operation X: Multiengine Operations
  - Task A: Maneuvering with One Engine Inoperative
  - Task B: V_{MC} Demonstration

Commercial Pilot–Airplane Practical Test Prerequisites

An applicant for the Commercial Pilot–Airplane Practical Test is required by 14 CFR part 61 to:

1. be at least 18 years of age;
2. be able to read, speak, write, and understand the English language. If there is a doubt, use AC 60-28, English Language Skill Standards;
3. possess a private pilot certificate if a commercial pilot certificate with an airplane rating is sought, or meet the flight experience required for a private pilot certificate (airplane rating) and pass the private airplane knowledge and practical test;
4. possess an instrument rating (airplane) or the following limitation shall be placed on the commercial pilot certificate: "Carrying passengers in airplanes for hire is prohibited at night or on cross-country flights of more than 50 nautical miles;"
5. have passed the appropriate commercial pilot knowledge test since the beginning of the 24th month before the month in which he or she takes the practical test;
6. have satisfactorily accomplished the required training and obtained the aeronautical experience prescribed;
7. possess at least a current third class medical certificate or, when a military pilot of the U.S. Armed Forces, can show and present evidence of an up-to-date medical examination authorizing pilot status issued by the U.S. Armed Forces;
8. receive and log ground training from an authorized instructor or complete a home-study course on the aeronautical knowledge areas of 14 CFR part 61.125 paragraph (b) that apply to the aircraft category and class rating sought; and have an endorsement from an authorized instructor certifying that the applicant has received and logged training time within 2 calendar months preceding the date of application in preparation for the practical test and is prepared for the practical test;
9. also have an endorsement certifying that the applicant has demonstrated satisfactory knowledge of the subject areas in which the applicant was deficient on the airman knowledge test (not required for power aircraft to power aircraft for additional category or class rating).

Aircraft and Equipment Required for the Practical Test

The commercial pilot–airplane applicant is required by 14 CFR section 61.45 to provide an airworthy, certificated aircraft for use during the practical test. This section further requires that the aircraft must:

1. be of U.S., foreign, or military registry of the same category, class, and type, if applicable, for the certificate and/or rating for which the applicant is applying;
2. have fully functioning dual controls, except as provided for in 14 CFR section 61.45(c) and (e);
3. be capable of performing all Areas of Operation appropriate to the rating sought and have no operating limitations which prohibit its use in any of the Areas of Operation required for the practical test; and
4. be a complex airplane furnished by the applicant, unless the applicant currently holds a commercial pilot certificate with a single-engine or multiengine class rating as appropriate, for the performance of takeoffs, landings, and appropriate emergency procedures. A complex landplane is one having retractable landing gear, flaps, and controllable propeller or turbine-powered. A complex seaplane is one having flaps and controllable propeller.

Use of FAA-Approved Flight Simulation Training Device (FSTD)

An airman applicant for Commercial Pilot-Airplane Certification is authorized to use a full flight simulator (FFS) qualified by the National Simulator Program as levels A-D and/or a flight training device (FTD) qualified by the National Simulator Program as levels 4-7 to complete certain flight Task requirements listed in this practical test standard.

In order to do so, such devices must be used pursuant to and in accordance with a curriculum approved for use at a 14 CFR part 141 pilot school or 14 CFR part 142 training center. Practical tests or portions thereof, when accomplished in an FSTD may only be conducted by FAA aviation safety inspectors, designees authorized to conduct such tests in FSTDs for part 141 pilot school graduates, or appropriately authorized part 142 Training Center Evaluators (TCE).

When flight Tasks are accomplished in an aircraft, certain Task elements may be accomplished through "simulated" actions in the interest of safety and practicality, but when accomplished in a flight simulator or flight training device, these same actions would not be "simulated." For example, when in an aircraft, a simulated engine fire may be addressed by retarding the throttle to idle, simulating the shutdown of the engine, simulating the discharge of the fire suppression agent, if applicable, simulating the disconnection of associated electrical, hydraulic, and pneumatics systems. However, when the same emergency condition is addressed in a FSTD, all Task elements must be accomplished as would be expected under actual circumstances.

Similarly, safety of flight precautions taken in the aircraft for the accomplishment of a specific maneuver or procedure (such as limiting altitude in an approach to stall or setting maximum airspeed for an engine failure expected to result in a rejected takeoff) need not be taken when a FSTD is used.

It is important to understand that, whether accomplished in an aircraft or FSTD, all Tasks and elements for each maneuver or procedure shall have the same performance standards applied equally for determination of overall satisfactory performance.

Training devices other than Flight Simulation Training Devices (FSTDs) may be used IAW AC-61-136.

Flight Instructor Responsibility

An appropriately rated flight instructor is responsible for training the commercial pilot applicant to acceptable standards in all subject matter areas, procedures, and maneuvers included in the Tasks within each Area of Operation in the appropriate commercial pilot practical test standard, even if the applicant is adding a category or class rating.

Because of the impact of their teaching activities in developing safe, proficient pilots, flight instructors should exhibit a high level of knowledge, skill, and the ability to impart that knowledge and skill to students.

Throughout the applicant's training, the flight instructor is responsible for emphasizing the performance of effective visual scanning and collision avoidance procedures, and the manufacturer's recommended procedures for the airplane flown and other areas deemed appropriate to the practical test.

Examiner Responsibility

The examiner conducting the practical test is responsible for determining that the applicant meets the acceptable standards of knowledge and skill of each Task within the appropriate practical test standard. Since there is no formal division between the "oral" and "skill" portions of the practical test, this becomes an ongoing process throughout the test. Oral questioning, to determine the applicant's knowledge of Tasks and related safety factors, should be used judiciously at all times, especially during the flight portion of the practical test. Examiners shall test to the greatest extent practicable the applicant's correlative abilities rather than mere rote enumeration of facts throughout the practical test.

If the examiner determines that a Task is incomplete, or the outcome uncertain, the examiner may require the applicant to repeat that Task, or portions of that Task. This provision has been made in the interest of fairness and does not mean that instruction, practice, or the repeating of an unsatisfactory Task is permitted during the certification process. When practical, the remaining Tasks of the practical test phase should be completed before repeating the questionable Task.

On multiengine practical tests, where the failure of the most critical engine after liftoff is required, the examiner must give consideration to local atmospheric conditions, terrain, and type of aircraft used. However, the failure of an engine shall not be simulated until attaining at least $V_{SSE}/V_{XSE}/V_{YSE}$ and at an altitude not lower than 400 feet AGL.

During simulated engine failures on multiengine practical tests, the examiner shall set zero thrust after the applicant has simulated feathering the propeller. The examiner shall require the applicant to demonstrate at least one landing with a simulated feathered propeller with the engine set to zero thrust. The feathering of one propeller shall be demonstrated in flight, unless the manufacturer prohibits the intentional feathering of the propellers during flight.

Throughout the flight portion of the practical test, the examiner shall evaluate the applicant's use of visual scanning and collision avoidance procedures.

Satisfactory Performance

Satisfactory performance to meet the requirements for certification is based on the applicant's ability to safely:

1. perform the Tasks specified in the Areas of Operation for the certificate or rating sought within the approved standards;
2. demonstrate mastery of the aircraft by performing each task successfully;
3. demonstrate satisfactory proficiency and competency within the approved standards;
4. demonstrate sound judgment and exercises aeronautical decision-making/risk management; and
5. demonstrate single-pilot competence if the aircraft is type certificated for single-pilot operations.

If the applicant satisfactorily performs the five items listed above, FAA Form 8060-4, Temporary Airman Certificate, or the appropriate IACRA form will be issued.

Unsatisfactory Performance

The tolerances represent the performance expected in good flying conditions. If, in the judgment of the examiner, the applicant does not meet the standards of performance of any Task performed, the associated Area of Operation is failed and therefore, the practical test is failed.

The examiner or applicant may discontinue the test at any time when the failure of an Area of Operation makes the applicant ineligible for the certificate or rating sought. The test may be continued ONLY with the consent of the applicant. If the test is discontinued, the applicant is entitled credit for only those Areas of Operation and their associated Tasks satisfactorily performed. However, during the retest, and at the discretion of the examiner, any Task may be reevaluated, including those previously passed.

Typical areas of unsatisfactory performance and grounds for disqualification are:

1. Any action or lack of action by the applicant that requires corrective intervention by the examiner to maintain safe flight.
2. Failure to use proper and effective visual scanning techniques to clear the area before and while performing maneuvers.
3. Consistently exceeding tolerances stated in the Objectives.
4. Failure to take prompt corrective action when tolerances are exceeded.

When a notice of disapproval is issued, the examiner shall record the applicant's unsatisfactory performance in terms of the Area of Operation and specific Task(s) not meeting the standard appropriate to practical test conducted. The Area(s) of Operation/Task(s) not tested and the number of practical test failures shall also be recorded. If the applicant fails the practical test because of a special emphasis area, the Notice of Disapproval shall indicate the associated task. i.e.: Area of Operation VIII, Maneuvering During Slow Flight, failure to use proper collision avoidance procedures.

Letter of Discontinuance

When a practical test is discontinued for reasons other than unsatisfactory performance (i.e., equipment failure, weather, illness), the FAA Form 8710-1, Airman Certificate and/or Rating Application, and, if applicable, the Airman Knowledge Test Report, is returned to the applicant. The examiner must then prepare, sign, and issue a Letter of Discontinuance to the applicant. The Letter of Discontinuance must identify the Areas of Operation and the associated Tasks of the practical test that were successfully completed. The applicant must be advised that the Letter of Discontinuance must be presented to the examiner, to receive credit for the items successfully completed, when the practical test is resumed, and made part of the certification file.

Single-Pilot Resource Management (SRM)

The examiner shall evaluate the applicant's ability throughout the practical test to use good aeronautical decision-making procedures in order to evaluate risks. The examiner shall accomplish this requirement by developing a scenario that incorporates as many Tasks as possible to evaluate the applicant's risk management in making safe aeronautical decisions. For example, the examiner may develop a scenario that incorporates weather decisions and performance planning.

The applicant's ability to utilize all the assets available in making a risk analysis to determine the safest course of action is essential for satisfactory performance. The scenario should be realistic and within the capabilities of the aircraft used for the practical test.

Single-Pilot Resource Management (SRM) is defined as the art and science of managing all the resources (both onboard the aircraft and from outside sources) available to a single-pilot (prior and during flight) to ensure that the successful outcome of the flight is never in doubt. SRM available resources can include human resources, hardware, and information. Human resources ". . . includes all other groups routinely working with the pilot who are involved in decisions that are required to operate a flight safely. These groups include, but are not limited to: dispatchers, weather briefers, maintenance personnel, and air traffic controllers." SRM is a set of skill competencies that must be evident in all Tasks in this practical test standard as applied to single-pilot operation.

The following six items are areas of SRM:

- **Aeronautical Decision-Making**

  References: FAA-H-8083-15, FAA-H-8083-25; AC 60-22.

  Objective: To determine that the applicant exhibits sound aeronautical decision-making during the planning and execution of the planned flight. The applicant should:

  1. Use a sound decision-making process, such as the DECIDE model, 3P model, or similar process when making critical decisions that will have an effect on the outcome of the flight. The applicant should be able to explain the factors and alternative courses of action that were considered while making the decision.
  2. Recognize and explain any hazardous attitudes that may have influenced any decision.
  3. Decide and execute an appropriate course of action to properly handle any situation that arises that may cause a change in the original flight plan in such a way that leads to a safe and successful conclusion of the flight.
  4. Explain how the elements of risk management, CFIT awareness, overall situational awareness, use of automation, and task management influenced the decisions made and the resulting course of action.

- **Risk Management**

  References: FAA-H-8083-25, FITS document, Managing Risk through Scenario Based Training, Single-Pilot Resource Management, and Learner Centered Grading.

  Objective: To determine that the applicant can utilize risk management tools and models to assess the potential risk associated with the planned flight during preflight planning and while in flight. The applicant should:

  1. Explain the four fundamental risk elements associated with the flight being conducted in the given scenario and how each one was assessed.
  2. Use a tool, such as the PAVE checklist, to help assess the four risk elements.
  3. Use a personal checklist, such as the I'MSAFE checklist, to determine personal risks.
  4. Use weather reports and forecasts to determine weather risks associated with the flight.
  5. Explain how to recognize risks and how to mitigate those risks throughout the flight.
  6. Use the 5P model to assess the risks associated with each of the five factors.

- **Task Management**

  Reference: FAA-H-8083-15.

  Objective: To determine that the applicant can prioritize the various tasks associated with the planning and execution of the flight. The applicant should:

  1. Explain how to prioritize tasks in such a way to minimize distractions from flying the aircraft.
  2. Complete all tasks in a timely manner considering the phase of flight without causing a distraction from flying.
  3. Execute all checklists and procedures in a manner that does not increase workload at critical times.

- **Situational Awareness**

  References: FAA-H-8083-15, FAA-H-8083-25.

  Objective: To determine that the applicant can maintain situational awareness during all phases of the flight. The applicant should:

  1. Explain the concept of situational awareness and associated factors.
  2. Explain the dangers associated with becoming fixated on a particular problem to the exclusion of other aspects of the flight.
  3. State the current situation at any time during the flight in such a way that displays an accurate assessment of the current and future status of the flight, including weather, terrain, traffic, ATC situation, fuel status, and aircraft status.
  4. Explain taxi operation planning procedures, such as recording taxi instructions, reading back taxi clearances, and reviewing taxi routes on the airport diagram.
  5. Explain procedures for steering, maneuvering, maintaining taxi, runway position, and situational awareness.
  6. Explain procedures for holding the pilot's workload to a minimum during taxi operations which should increase the pilot's awareness during taxiing.
  7. ATC communications and pilot operations before takeoff, before landing, and after landing at controlled and uncontrolled airports.
  8. Uses the navigation displays, traffic displays, terrain displays, weather displays, and other features of the aircraft to maintain a complete and accurate awareness of the current situation and any reasonably anticipated changes that may occur.

■   **Controlled Flight into Terrain Awareness**

References: *Controlled Flight Into Terrain Training Aid website:*
http://www.faa.gov/training_testing/training/media/cfit/volume1/
titlepg.pdf.

Objective: To determine that the applicant can accurately assess risks
associated with terrain and obstacles, maintain accurate
awareness of terrain and obstacles, and can use appropriate
techniques and procedures to avoid controlled flight into terrain or
obstacles by using all resources available. The applicant should:

1.   Use current charts and procedures during the planning of the flight to
     ensure the intended flight path avoids terrain and obstacles.
2.   Be aware of potential terrain and obstacle hazards along the intended
     route.
3.   Explain the terrain display, TAWS, and/or GPWS as installed in the
     aircraft.
4.   Use the terrain display, TAWS, and/or GPWS of the navigation displays
     as appropriate to maintain awareness and to avoid terrain and
     obstacles.
5.   Plan departures and arrivals to avoid terrain and obstacles.
6.   Alter flight as necessary to avoid terrain.
7.   Plan any course diversion, for whatever reason, in such a way to ensure
     proper terrain and obstruction clearance to the new destination.
8.   Explain and understand aircraft performance limitations associated with
     CFIT accidents.

■   **Automation Management**

References: FAA-H-8083-6, FAA-H-8083-15.

Objective: To determine that the applicant can effectively use the
automation features of the aircraft, including autopilot and flight
management systems, in such a way to manage workload and
can remain aware of the current and anticipated modes and
status of the automation. The applicant should:

1.   Explain how to recognize the current mode of operation of the autopilot/
     FMS.
2.   Explain how to recognize anticipated and unanticipated mode or status
     changes of the autopilot/FMS.
3.   State at any time during the flight the current mode or status and what
     the next anticipated mode or status will be.
4.   Use the autopilot/FMS to reduce workload as appropriate for the phase
     of flight, during emergency or abnormal operations.
5.   Recognize unanticipated mode changes in a timely manner and
     promptly return the automation to the correct mode.

Applicant's Use of Checklists

Throughout the practical test, the applicant is evaluated on the use of an approved manufacturer's checklist or equivalent. If no manufacturer's checklist is published, the appropriate FAA Handbook or equivalent checklist may be used. Proper use is dependent on the specific Task being evaluated. The situation may be such that the use of the checklist, while accomplishing elements of an Objective, would be either unsafe or impractical, especially in a single-pilot operation. In this case, a review of the checklist after the elements have been accomplished would be appropriate. Division of attention and proper visual scanning should be considered when using a checklist.

Use of Distractions During Practical Tests

Numerous studies indicate that many accidents have occurred when the pilot has been distracted during critical phases of flight. To evaluate the applicant's ability to utilize proper control technique while dividing attention both inside and/or outside the cockpit, the examiner shall cause realistic distractions during the flight portion of the practical test to evaluate the applicant's ability to divide attention while maintaining safe flight.

Positive Exchange of Flight Controls

During flight training, there must always be a clear understanding between students and flight instructors of who has control of the aircraft. Prior to flight, a briefing should be conducted that includes the procedure for the exchange of flight controls. A positive three-step process in the exchange of flight controls between pilots is a proven procedure and one that is strongly recommended.

When the instructor wishes the student to take control of the aircraft, he or she will say, "You have the flight controls." The student acknowledges immediately by saying, "I have the flight controls." The flight instructor again says, "You have the flight controls." When control is returned to the instructor, follow the same procedure. A visual check is recommended to verify that the exchange has occurred. There should never be any doubt as to who is flying the aircraft.

Stalls and Spin Awareness

During flight training, there must always be a clear understanding concerning stalls and spin awareness. All stalls at the commercial level will be in accordance with FAA policy. All stalls will be recovered no lower than 1,500 feet AGL for single-engine airplanes; 3,000 feet AGL for multiengine airplanes, unless the manufacturer recommends a higher altitude to initiate the recovery.

Section 1:
Commercial Pilot Airplane–
Single-Engine Land

Additional Rating Task Table:
Airplane Single-Engine Land

Addition of an Airplane Single-Engine Land Rating to an existing Commercial Pilot Certificate								
Required Tasks are indicated by either the Task letter(s) that apply(s) or an indication that all or none of the Tasks must be tested based on the notes in each Area of Operation.								
COMMERCIAL PILOT RATING(S) HELD								
AREAS OF OPERATION	ASES	AMEL	AMES	RH	RG	Glider	Balloon	Airship
I	F,G	F,G	F,G	F,G	F,G	F,G	F,G	F,G
II	D,F	D,F	D,F	A,C,D, F,G	A,D, F,G	A,B,C, D,F,G	A,B,C, D,F,G	A,B,C, D,F,G
III	C	NONE	C	B,C	NONE	B,C	B,C	B,C
IV	A,B,C, D,E,F, K	A,B,C, D,E,F, K	A,B,C, D,E,F, K	A,B,C, D,E,F, K,L	A,B,C, D,E,F, K,L	A,B,C, D,E,F, K,L	A,B,C, D,E,F, K,L	A,B,C, D,E,F, K,L
V	NONE	B,C,D	B,C,D	ALL	ALL	ALL	ALL	ALL
VI	NONE	ALL	ALL	ALL	ALL	ALL	ALL	ALL
VII	NONE	NONE	NONE	NONE	NONE	ALL	ALL	NONE
VIII	NONE	NONE	NONE	ALL	ALL	ALL	ALL	ALL
IX	A,B,C	A,B,C	A,B,C	ALL	ALL	ALL	ALL	ALL
X	NONE	NONE	NONE	ALL	ALL	ALL	ALL	ALL
XI	A	NONE	A	A	A	A	A	A

Applicant's Practical Test Checklist
Appointment with Examiner

Examiner's Name: _____

Location: _____

Date/Time: _____

Acceptable Aircraft
- ☐ Aircraft Documents:
  - ☐ Airworthiness Certificate
  - ☐ Registration Certificate
  - ☐ Operating Limitations
- ☐ Aircraft Maintenance Records:
  - ☐ Logbook Record of Airworthiness Inspections and AD Compliance
- ☐ Pilot's Operating Handbook, FAA-Approved Airplane Flight Manual

Personal Equipment
- ☐ View-Limiting Device
- ☐ Current Aeronautical Charts
- ☐ Computer and Plotter
- ☐ Flight Plan Form
- ☐ Flight Logs
- ☐ Current AIM, Airport Facility Directory, and Appropriate Publications

Personal Records
- ☐ Identification–Photo/Signature ID
- ☐ Pilot Certificate
- ☐ Current and Appropriate Medical Certificate
- ☐ Completed FAA Form 8710-1, Airman Certificate and/or Rating Application with Instructor's Signature (if applicable)
- ☐ Computer Test Report
- ☐ Pilot Logbook with appropriate Instructor Endorsements
- ☐ FAA Form 8060-5, Notice of Disapproval (if applicable)
- ☐ Approved School Graduation Certificate (if applicable)
- ☐ Examiner's Fee (if applicable)

Examiner's Practical Test Checklist
Airplane Single-Engine Land

Applicant's Name: _____

Location: _____

Date/Time: _____

I. Preflight Preparation
- ☐ **A.** Certificates and Documents
- ☐ **B.** Airworthiness Requirements
- ☐ **C.** Weather Information
- ☐ **D.** Cross-Country Flight Planning
- ☐ **E.** National Airspace System
- ☐ **F.** Performance and Limitations
- ☐ **G.** Operation of Systems
- ☐ **J.** Aeromedical Factors

II. Preflight Procedures
- ☐ **A.** Preflight Inspection
- ☐ **B.** Cockpit Management
- ☐ **C.** Engine Starting
- ☐ **D.** Taxiing
- ☐ **F.** Runway Incursion Avoidance
- ☐ **G.** Before Takeoff Check

III. Airport Operations
- ☐ **A.** Radio Communications and ATC Light Signals
- ☐ **B.** Traffic Patterns
- ☐ **C.** Airport, Runway, and Taxiway Signs, Markings, and Lighting

IV. Takeoffs, Landings, and Go-Arounds
- ☐ **A.** Normal and Crosswind Takeoff and Climb
- ☐ **B.** Normal and Crosswind Approach and Landing
- ☐ **C.** Soft-Field Takeoff and Climb
- ☐ **D.** Soft-Field Approach and Landing
- ☐ **E.** Short-Field Takeoff and Maximum Performance Climb
- ☐ **F.** Short-Field Approach and Landing
- ☐ **K.** Power-Off 180° Accuracy Approach and Landing
- ☐ **L.** Go-Around/Rejected Landing

V. Performance Maneuvers
- ☐ **A.** Steep Turns
- ☐ **B.** Steep Spiral
- ☐ **C.** Chandelles
- ☐ **D.** Lazy Eights

VI. Ground Reference Maneuver
- ☐ **A.** Eights on Pylons

VII. Navigation
- ☐ **A.** Pilotage and Dead Reckoning
- ☐ **B.** Navigation Systems and Radar Services
- ☐ **C.** Diversion
- ☐ **D.** Lost Procedures

VIII. Slow Flight and Stalls
- ☐ **A.** Maneuvering During Slow Flight
- ☐ **B.** Power-Off Stalls
- ☐ **C.** Power-On Stalls
- ☐ **D.** Accelerated Stalls
- ☐ **E.** Spin Awareness

IX. Emergency Operations
- ☐ **A.** Emergency Descents
- ☐ **B.** Emergency Approach and Landing (Simulated)
- ☐ **C.** Systems and Equipment Malfunctions
- ☐ **D.** Emergency Equipment and Survival Gear

X. High Altitude Operations
- ☐ **A.** Supplemental Oxygen
- ☐ **B.** Pressurization

XI. Postflight Procedures
- ☐ **A.** After Landing, Parking, and Securing

Areas of Operation:

I. Preflight Preparation

NOTE: The examiner shall develop a scenario based on real time weather to evaluate Tasks C and D.

Task A: Certificates and Documents

References: 14 CFR parts 39, 43, 61, 91; FAA-H-8083-3, FAA-H-8083-25; POH/AFM.

Objective: To determine that the applicant exhibits satisfactory knowledge of the elements related to certificates and documents by:

1. Explaining–
   a. commercial pilot certificate privileges, limitations, and recent flight experience requirements.
   b. medical certificate class and duration.
   c. pilot logbook or flight records.
2. Locating and explaining–
   a. airworthiness and registration certificates.
   b. operating limitations, placards, instrument markings, and POH/AFM.
   c. weight and balance data and equipment list.

Task B: Airworthiness Requirements

References: 14 CFR parts 39, 91; FAA-H-8083-25.

Objective: To determine that the applicant exhibits satisfactory knowledge of the elements related to airworthiness requirements by:

1. Explaining–
   a. required instruments and equipment for day/night VFR.
   b. procedures and limitations for determining airworthiness of the airplane with inoperative instruments and equipment with and without an MEL.
   c. requirements and procedures for obtaining a special flight permit.
2. Locating and explaining–
   a. airworthiness directives.
   b. compliance records.
   c. maintenance/inspection requirements.
   d. appropriate record keeping.

Task C: Weather Information

References: 14 CFR part 91; AC 00-6, AC 00-45; AC 61-84; FAA-H-8083-25; AIM.

Objective: To determine that the applicant:

1. Exhibits satisfactory knowledge of the elements related to weather information by analyzing weather reports, charts, and forecasts from various sources with emphasis on–
   a. METAR, TAF, and FA.
   b. surface analysis chart.
   c. radar summary chart.
   d. winds and temperature aloft chart.
   e. significant weather prognostic charts.
   f. convective outlook chart.
   g. AWOS, ASOS, and ATIS reports.
   h. SIGMETs and AIRMETs.
   i. PIREPs.
   j. windshear reports.
   k. icing and freezing level information.
2. Makes a competent "go/no-go" decision based on available weather information.

Task D: Cross-Country Flight Planning

References: 14 CFR part 91; FAA-H-8083-25; AC 61-84; Navigation Charts; AFD; AIM; NOTAMS.

Objective: To determine that the applicant:

1. Exhibits satisfactory knowledge of the elements related to cross-country flight planning by presenting and explaining a pre-planned VFR cross-country flight, as previously assigned by the examiner. On the day of the practical test, the final flight plan shall be to the first fuel stop, based on maximum allowable passengers, baggage, and/or cargo loads using real-time weather.
2. Uses appropriate and current aeronautical charts.
3. Properly identifies airspace, obstructions, and terrain features.
4. Selects easily identifiable en route checkpoints.
5. Selects most favorable altitudes considering weather conditions and equipment capabilities.
6. Computes headings, flight time, and fuel requirements.
7. Selects appropriate navigation system/facilities and communication frequencies.
8. Applies pertinent information from AFD, NOTAMs, and NOTAMS relative to airport, runway and taxiway closures, and other flight publications.
9. Completes a navigation log and simulates filing a VFR flight plan.

Task E: National Airspace System

References: 14 CFR parts 71, 91, 93; Navigation Charts; AIM.

Objective: To determine that the applicant exhibits satisfactory knowledge of the elements related to the National Airspace System by explaining:

1. Basic VFR weather minimums—for all classes of airspace.
2. Airspace classes—their operating rules, pilot certification, and airplane equipment requirements for the following—

    a. Class A.
    b. Class B.
    c. Class C.
    d. Class D.
    e. Class E.
    f.   Class G.

3. Special use, special flight rules areas, and other airspace areas.

Task F: Performance and Limitations

References: FAA-H-8083-1, FAA-H-8083-25; AC 61-84; POH/AFM.

Objective: To determine that the applicant:

1. Exhibits satisfactory knowledge of the elements related to performance and limitations by explaining the use of charts, tables, and data to determine performance and the adverse effects of exceeding limitations.
2. Computes weight and balance. Determines the computed weight and center of gravity are within the airplane's operating limitations and if the weight and center of gravity will remain within limits during all phases of flight.
3. Demonstrates use of the appropriate manufacturer's performance charts, tables, and data.
4. Describes the effects of atmospheric conditions on the airplane's performance.

Task G: Operation of Systems

References: FAA-H-8083-25; POH/AFM.

Objective: To determine that the applicant exhibits satisfactory knowledge of the elements related to the operation of systems on the airplane provided for the flight test by explaining at least three of the following systems.

1. Primary flight controls and trim.
2. Flaps, leading edge devices, and spoilers.
3. Powerplant and propeller.
4. Landing gear.
5. Fuel, oil, and hydraulic.
6. Electrical.
7. Avionics.
8. Pitot-static, vacuum/pressure, and associated flight instruments.
9. Environmental.
10. Deicing and anti-icing.

Task J: Aeromedical Factors

References: FAA-H-8083-25; AIM.

Objective: Satisfactory knowledge of the elements related to aeromedical factors by explaining:

1. The symptoms, causes, effects, and corrective actions of at least three of the following–
   a. hypoxia.
   b. hyperventilation.
   c. middle ear and sinus problems.
   d. spatial disorientation.
   e. motion sickness.
   f. carbon monoxide poisoning.
   g. stress and fatigue.
   h. dehydration.
2. The effects of alcohol, drugs, and over-the-counter medications.
3. The effects of excess nitrogen during scuba dives upon a pilot or passenger in flight.

II. Preflight Procedures

Task A: Preflight Inspection

References: FAA-H-8083-3; POH/AFM.

Objective: To determine that the applicant:

1. Exhibits satisfactory knowledge of the elements related to preflight inspection. This shall include which items must be inspected, the reasons for checking each item, and how to detect possible defects.
2. Inspects the airplane with reference to an appropriate checklist.
3. Verifies the airplane is in condition for safe flight.

Task B: Cockpit Management

References: FAA-H-8083-3; POH/AFM.

Objective: To determine that the applicant:

1. Exhibits satisfactory knowledge of the elements related to cockpit management procedures.
2. Ensures all loose items in the cockpit and cabin are secured.
3. Organizes material and equipment in an efficient manner so they are readily available.
4. Briefs occupants on the use of safety belts, shoulder harnesses, doors, and emergency procedures.

Task C: Engine Starting

References: FAA-H-8083-3, FAA-H-8083-25; AC 91-13, AC 91-55; POH/AFM.

Objective: To determine that the applicant:

1. Exhibits satisfactory knowledge of the elements related to recommended engine starting procedures. This shall include the use of an external power source, hand propping safety, and starting under various atmospheric conditions.
2. Positions the airplane properly considering structures, surface conditions, other aircraft, and the safety of nearby persons and property.
3. Utilizes the appropriate checklist for starting procedure.

Task D: Taxiing

References: FAA-H-8083-3; POH/AFM.

Objective: To determine that the applicant:

1. Exhibits satisfactory knowledge of the elements related to safe taxi procedures at towered and non-towered airports.
2. Performs a brake check immediately after the airplane begins moving.
3. Positions the flight controls properly for the existing wind conditions.
4. Controls direction and speed without excessive use of brakes.
5. Exhibits procedures for steering, maneuvering, maintaining taxiway, runway position, and situational awareness to avoid runway incursions.
6. Exhibits proper positioning of the aircraft relative to hold lines.
7. Exhibits procedures to insure clearances/instructions are received and recorded/read back correctly.
8. Exhibits situational awareness/taxi procedures in the event the aircraft is on a taxiway that is between parallel runways.
9. Uses a taxi chart during taxi.
10. Complies with airport/taxiway markings, signals, ATC clearances, and instructions.
11. Utilizes procedures for eliminating pilot distractions.
12. Taxiing to avoid other aircraft/vehicles and hazards.

Task F: Runway Incursion Avoidance

References: FAA-H-8083-3, FAA-H-8083-25; AC 91-73, AC 150-5340-18; AIM.

Objective: To determine that the applicant exhibits knowledge of the elements of runway incursion avoidance by:

1. Exhibiting distinct challenges and requirements during taxi operations not found in other phases of flight operations.
2. Exhibiting procedures for appropriate cockpit activities during taxiing including taxi route planning, briefing the location of HOT SPOTS, communicating and coordinating with ATC.
3. Exhibiting procedures for steering, maneuvering, maintaining taxiway, runway position, and situational awareness.
4. Knowing the relevance/importance of hold lines.

5. Exhibiting procedures to ensure the pilot maintains strict focus to the movement of the aircraft and ATC communications, including the elimination of all distractive activities (i.e. cell phone, texting, conversations with passengers) during aircraft taxi, takeoff and climb out to cruise altitude.
6. Utilizing procedures for holding the pilot's workload to a minimum during taxi operations.
7. Utilizing taxi operation planning procedures, such as recording taxi instructions, reading back taxi clearances, and reviewing taxi routes on the airport diagram.
8. Utilizing procedures to insure that clearance or instructions that are actually received are adhered to rather than the ones expected to be received.
9. Utilizing procedures to maintain/enhance situational awareness when conducting taxi operations in relation to other aircraft operations in the vicinity as well as to other vehicles moving on the airport.
10. Exhibiting procedures for briefing if a landing rollout to a taxiway exit will place the pilot in close proximity to another runway which can result in a runway incursion.
11. Conducting appropriate after landing/taxi procedures in the event the aircraft is on a taxiway that is between parallel runways.
12. Knowing specific procedures for operations at an airport with an operating air traffic control tower, with emphasis on ATC communications and runway entry/crossing authorizations.
13. Utilizing ATC communications and pilot actions before takeoff, before landing, and after landing at towered and non-towered airports.
14. Knowing procedures unique to night operations.
15. Knowing operations at non-towered airports.
16. Knowing the use of aircraft exterior lighting.
17. Knowing the hazards of Low visibility operations.

Task G: Before Takeoff Check

References: FAA-H-8083-3; POH/AFM.

Objective: To determine that the applicant:

1. Exhibits satisfactory knowledge of the elements related to the before takeoff check. This shall include the reasons for checking each item and how to detect malfunctions.
2. Positions the airplane properly considering other aircraft/vessels, wind, and surface conditions.
3. Divides attention inside and outside the cockpit.
4. Ensures that engine temperature(s) and pressure(s) are suitable for runup and takeoff.
5. Accomplishes the before takeoff checklist and ensures the airplane is in safe operating condition as recommended by the manufacturer.
6. Reviews takeoff performance, such as airspeeds, takeoff distances, departure, and emergency procedures.
7. Avoids runway incursions and ensures no conflict with traffic prior to taxiing into takeoff position.

III. Airport Operations

Task A: Radio Communications and ATC Light Signals

References: 14 CFR part 91; FAA-H-8083-25; AIM.

Objective: To determine that the applicant:

1. Exhibits satisfactory knowledge of the elements related to radio communications and ATC light signals.
2. Selects appropriate frequencies.
3. Transmits using AIM specified phraseology and procedures.
4. Acknowledges radio communications and complies with instructions.

Task B: Traffic Patterns

References: FAA-H-8083-3, FAA-H-8083-25; AC 90-66; AIM.

Objective: To determine that the applicant:

1. Exhibits satisfactory knowledge of the elements related to traffic patterns. This shall include procedures at airports with and without operating control towers, prevention of runway incursions, collision avoidance, wake turbulence avoidance, and wind shear.
2. Properly identifies and interprets airport runways, taxiway signs, markings, and lighting.
3. Complies with proper traffic pattern procedures.
4. Maintains proper spacing from other aircraft.
5. Corrects for wind drift to maintain the proper ground track.
6. Maintains orientation with the runway/landing area in use.
7. Maintains traffic pattern altitude, ±100 feet, and the appropriate airspeed, ±10 knots.

Task C: Airport, Runway, and Taxiway Signs, Markings, and Lighting

References: FAA-H-8083-25; AIM; AFD; AC 91-73, AC 150-5340-18.

Objective: To determine that the applicant:

1. Exhibits satisfactory knowledge of the elements related to airport, runway, and taxiway operations with emphasis on runway incursion avoidance.
2. Properly identifies and interprets airport, runway, and taxiway signs, markings, and lighting, with emphasis on runway incursion avoidance.

IV. Takeoffs, Landings, and Go-Arounds

Task A: Normal and Crosswind Takeoff and Climb

NOTE: If a crosswind condition does not exist, the applicant's knowledge of crosswind elements shall be evaluated through oral testing.

References: FAA-H-8083-3; POH/AFM.

Objective: To determine that the applicant:

1. Utilizes procedures before taxiing onto the runway or takeoff area to ensure runway incursion avoidance. Verify ATC clearance/no aircraft on final at non-towered airports before entering the runway, and ensure that the aircraft is on the correct takeoff runway.

2. Exhibits satisfactory knowledge of the elements related to a normal and crosswind takeoff, climb operations, and rejected takeoff procedures.
3. Ascertains wind direction with or without visible wind direction indicators.
4. Calculates/determines if crosswind component is above his or her ability or that of the aircraft's capability.
5. Positions the flight controls for the existing wind conditions.
6. Clears the area, taxies onto the takeoff surface, and aligns the airplane on the runway center/takeoff path.
7. Advances the throttle smoothly to takeoff power.
8. Rotates and lifts off at the recommended airspeed and accelerates to V_Y.
9. Establishes a pitch attitude that will maintain V_Y, ±5 knots.
10. Retracts the landing gear, if appropriate, and flaps after a positive rate of climb is established.
11. Maintains takeoff power and V_Y ±5 knots to a safe maneuvering altitude.
12. Maintains directional control, proper wind-drift correction throughout the takeoff and climb.
13. Complies with responsible environmental practices, to include noise abatement procedures.
14. Completes appropriate checklists.

Task B: *Normal and Crosswind Approach and Landing*

NOTE: *If a crosswind condition does not exist, the applicant's knowledge of crosswind elements shall be evaluated through oral testing.*

References: FAA-H-8083-3; POH/AFM.

Objective: To determine that the applicant:

1. Exhibits satisfactory knowledge of the elements related to a normal and crosswind approach and landing.
2. Considers the wind conditions, landing surface, obstructions, and selects a suitable touchdown point.
3. Establishes the recommended approach and landing configuration and airspeed, and adjusts pitch attitude and power as required.
4. Maintains a stabilized approach and recommended airspeed or in its absence, not more than 1.3 V_{SO}, ±5 knots, with wind gust factor applied.
5. Makes smooth, timely, and correct control application during the round out and touchdown.
6. Touches down smoothly at approximate stalling speed.
7. Touches down within the available runway, within 200 feet beyond a specified point with no drift, and with the airplane's longitudinal axis aligned with and over the runway center/landing path.
8. Maintains crosswind correction and directional control throughout the approach and landing sequence.
9. Executes a timely go-around decision when the approach cannot be made within the tolerance specified above.
10. Utilizes after landing runway incursion avoidance procedures.
11. Completes the appropriate checklist.

Task C: Soft-Field Takeoff and Climb

References: FAA-H-8083-3; POH/AFM.

Objective: To determine that the applicant:

1. Utilizes procedures before taxiing onto the runway or takeoff area to ensure runway incursion avoidance. Verify ATC clearance/no aircraft on final at non-towered airports before entering the runway, and ensure that the aircraft is on the correct takeoff runway.
2. Exhibits satisfactory knowledge of the elements related to a soft-field takeoff and climb.
3. Positions the flight controls for existing conditions and to maximize lift as quickly as possible.
4. Clears the area; taxies onto takeoff surface at a speed consistent with safety and aligns the airplane without stopping while advancing the throttle smoothly to takeoff power.
5. Establishes and maintains a pitch attitude that will transfer the weight of the airplane from the wheels to the wings as rapidly as possible.
6. Rotates and lifts off at the lowest possible airspeed and remains in ground effect while accelerating to V_X or V_Y, as appropriate.
7. Establishes a pitch attitude for V_X or V_Y, as appropriate, and maintains selected airspeed ±5 knots during the climb.
8. Retracts the landing gear, if appropriate, and flaps after clear of any obstacles or as recommended by the manufacturer.
9. Maintains takeoff power and V_X or V_Y ±5 knots to a safe maneuvering altitude.
10. Maintains directional control and proper wind-drift correction throughout the takeoff and climb.
11. Completes appropriate checklist.

Task D: Soft-Field Approach and Landing

References: FAA-H-8083-3; POH/AFM.

Objective: To determine that the applicant:

1. Exhibits satisfactory knowledge of the elements related to a soft-field approach and landing.
2. Considers the wind conditions, landing surface, and obstructions, and selects the most suitable touchdown area.
3. Establishes the recommended approach and landing configuration and airspeed; adjusts pitch attitude and power as required.
4. Maintains a stabilized approach and manufacturer's recommended airspeed, or in its absence, not more than 1.3 V_{SO}, ±5 knots, with wind gust factor applied.
5. Makes smooth, timely, and correct control application during the round out and touchdown.
6. Touches down softly, with no drift, and with the airplane's longitudinal axis aligned with the runway/landing path.
7. Maintains crosswind correction and directional control throughout the approach and landing sequence.
8. Maintains proper position of the flight controls and sufficient speed to taxi on the soft surface.
9. Utilizes after landing runway incursion avoidance procedures.
10. Completes appropriate checklist.

Task E: Short-Field Takeoff and Maximum Performance Climb

References: FAA-H-8083-3; POH/AFM.

Objective: To determine that the applicant:

1. Utilizes procedures before taxiing onto the runway or takeoff area to ensure runway incursion avoidance. Verify ATC clearance/no aircraft on final at non-towered airports before entering the runway, and ensure that the aircraft is on the correct takeoff runway.
2. Exhibits satisfactory knowledge of the elements related to a short-field takeoff and maximum performance climb.
3. Positions the flight controls for the existing wind conditions, sets flaps as recommended.
4. Clears the area; taxies into takeoff position utilizing maximum available takeoff area and aligns the airplane on the runway center/takeoff path.
5. Applies brakes (if appropriate) while advancing the throttle smoothly to takeoff power.
6. Rotates and lifts off at the recommended airspeed, and accelerates to recommended obstacle clearance airspeed, or V_X.
7. Establishes a pitch attitude that will maintain the recommended obstacle clearance airspeed, or V_X,+5/-0 knots, until the obstacle is cleared, or until the airplane is 50 feet above the surface.
8. After clearing the obstacle, establishes the pitch attitude for V_Y, accelerates to V_Y, and maintains V_Y, ±5 knots, during the climb.
9. Retracts the landing gear, if appropriate, and flaps after clear of any obstacles or as recommended by manufacturer.
10. Maintains takeoff power and V_Y ±5 knots to a safe maneuvering altitude.
11. Maintains directional control and proper wind-drift correction throughout the takeoff and climb.
12. Completes appropriate checklist.

Task F: Short-Field Approach and Landing

References: FAA-H-8083-3; POH/AFM.

Objective: To determine that the applicant:

1. Exhibits satisfactory knowledge of the elements related to a short-field approach and landing.
2. Considers the wind conditions, landing surface, obstructions, and selects the most suitable touchdown point.
3. Establishes the recommended approach and landing configuration and airspeed; adjusts pitch attitude and power.
4. Maintains a stabilized approach and recommended approach airspeed, or in its absence, not more than 1.3 V_{SO}, ±5 knots, with wind gust factor applied.
5. Makes smooth, timely, and correct control application during the round out and touchdown.
6. Touches down smoothly at minimum control airspeed.
7. Touches down within the available runway, at or within 100 feet beyond a specified point, with no side drift, minimum float, and with the airplane's longitudinal axis aligned with and over the runway center/landing path.

8. Maintains crosswind correction and directional control throughout the approach and landing sequence.
9. Applies brakes, as necessary, to stop in the shortest distance consistent with safety.
10. Utilizes after landing runway incursion avoidance procedures.
11. Completes appropriate checklist.

Task K: Power-Off 180° Accuracy Approach and Landing

Reference: FAA-H-8083-3.

Objective: To determine that the applicant:

1. Exhibits satisfactory knowledge of the elements related to a power-off 180° accuracy approach and landing.
2. Considers the wind conditions, landing surface, obstructions, and selects an appropriate touchdown point.
3. Positions airplane on downwind leg, parallel to landing runway, and not more than 1,000 feet AGL.
4. Completes final airplane configuration.
5. Touches down in a normal landing attitude, at or within 200 feet beyond the specified touchdown point.
6. Completes appropriate checklist.

Task L: Go-Around/Rejected Landing

References: FAA-H-8083-3; POH/AFM.

Objective: To determine that the applicant:

1. Exhibits satisfactory knowledge of the elements related to a go-around/ rejected landing, with emphasis on factors that contribute to landing conditions that may require a go-around.
2. Makes a timely decision to discontinue the approach to landing.
3. Applies takeoff power immediately and transitions to climb pitch attitude for V_X or V_Y as appropriate +10/−5 knots and/or appropriate pitch attitude.
4. Retracts flaps as appropriate.
5. Retracts the landing gear if appropriate after a positive rate of climb is established.
6. Maneuvers to the side of runway/landing area to clear and avoid conflicting traffic.
7. Maintains takeoff power and V_Y ±5 knots to a safe maneuvering altitude.
8. Maintains directional control and proper wind-drift correction throughout the climb.
9. Completes the appropriate checklist.

V. Performance Maneuvers

NOTE: *The examiner shall at least select either Task A or B, and either C or D.*

Task A: Steep Turns

References: FAA-H-8083-3; POH/AFM.

Objective: To determine that the applicant:

1. Exhibits satisfactory knowledge of the elements related to steep turns.
2. Establishes the manufacturer's recommended airspeed or if one is not stated, a safe airspeed not to exceed V_A.
3. Rolls into a coordinated 360° steep turn with at least a 50° bank, followed by a 360° steep turn in the opposite direction.
4. Divides attention between airplane control and orientation.
5. Maintains the entry altitude, ±100 feet, airspeed, ±10 knots, bank, ±5°; and rolls out on the entry heading, ±10°.

Task B: Steep Spiral

Reference: FAA-H-8083-3.

Objective: To determine that the applicant:

1. Exhibits satisfactory knowledge of the elements related to a steep spiral, not to exceed 60° angle of bank to maintain a constant radius about a point.
2. Selects an altitude sufficient to continue through a series of at least three 360° turns.
3. Selects a suitable ground reference point.
4. Applies wind-drift correction to track a constant radius circle around selected reference point with bank not to exceed 60° at steepest point in turn.
5. Divides attention between airplane control and ground track, while maintaining coordinated flight.
6. Maintains the specified airspeed, ±10 knots, rolls out toward object or specified heading, ±10°.

Task C: Chandelles

Reference: FAA-H-8083-3.

Objective: To determine that the applicant:

1. Exhibits satisfactory knowledge of the elements related to chandelles.
2. Selects an altitude that will allow the maneuver to be performed no lower than 1,500 feet AGL.
3. Establishes the recommended entry configuration, power, and airspeed.
4. Establishes the angle of bank at approximately 30°.
5. Simultaneously applies power and pitch to maintain a smooth, coordinated climbing turn to the 90° point, with a constant bank.
6. Begins a coordinated constant rate rollout from the 90° point to the 180° point maintaining power and a constant pitch attitude.
7. Completes rollout at the 180° point, ±10° just above a stall airspeed, and maintaining that airspeed momentarily avoiding a stall.
8. Resumes straight-and-level flight with minimum loss of altitude.

Task D: Lazy Eights

Reference: FAA-H-8083-3.

Objective: To determine that the applicant:

1. Exhibits satisfactory knowledge of the elements related to lazy eights.
2. Selects an altitude that will allow the task to be performed no lower than 1,500 feet AGL.
3. Establishes the recommended entry configuration, power, and airspeed.
4. Maintains coordinated flight throughout the maneuver.
5. Achieves the following throughout the maneuver–
   a. approximately 30° bank at the steepest point.
   b. constant change of pitch and roll rate.
   c. altitude tolerance at 180° point, ±100 feet from entry altitude.
   d. airspeed tolerance at the 180° point, plus ±10 knots from entry airspeed.
   e. heading tolerance at the 180° point, ±10°.
6. Continues the maneuver through the number of symmetrical loops specified and resumes straight-and-level flight.

VI. Ground Reference Maneuver

Task D: Eights on Pylons

Reference: FAA-H-8083-3.

Objective: To determine that the applicant:

1. Exhibits satisfactory knowledge of the elements related to eights on pylons.
2. Determines the approximate pivotal altitude.
3. Selects suitable pylons that will permit straight-and-level flight between the pylons.
4. Enters the maneuver at the appropriate altitude and airspeed and at a bank angle of approximately 30° to 40° at the steepest point.
5. Applies the necessary corrections so that the line-of-sight reference line remains on the pylon.
6. Divides attention between accurate coordinated airplane control and outside visual references.
7. Holds pylon using appropriate pivotal altitude avoiding slips and skids.

VII. Navigation

Task A: Pilotage and Dead Reckoning

References: FAA-H-8083-25; Navigation Chart.

Objective: To determine that the applicant:

1. Exhibits satisfactory knowledge of the elements related to pilotage and dead reckoning.
2. Follows the preplanned course by reference to landmarks.
3. Identifies landmarks by relating surface features to chart symbols.
4. Navigates by means of precomputed headings, groundspeeds, and elapsed time.

5. Demonstrates the use of magnetic compass in navigation, to include turns to new headings.
6. Corrects for and records differences between preflight groundspeed and heading calculations and those determined en route.
7. Verifies the airplane's position within 2 nautical miles of flight planned route.
8. Arrives at the en route checkpoints within 3 minutes of the initial or revised ETA and provides a destination estimate.
9. Maintains appropriate altitude, ±100 feet, and headings, ±10°.

Task B: Navigation Systems and Radar Services

References: FAA-H-8083-3, FAA-H-8083-25; Navigation Equipment Operation Manuals; AIM; FAA-H-8083-2.

Objective: To determine that the applicant:

1. Exhibits satisfactory knowledge of the elements related to navigation systems and radar services.
2. Demonstrates the ability to use an airborne electronic navigation system.
3. Locates the airplane's position using the navigation system.
4. Intercepts and tracks a given course, radial, or bearing as appropriate.
5. Recognizes and describes the indication of station passage if appropriate.
6. Recognizes signal loss and takes appropriate action.
7. Uses proper communication procedures when utilizing radar services.
8. Maintains the appropriate altitude, ±100 feet and heading, ±10°.

Task C: Diversion

References: FAA-H-8083-25; AIM; Navigation Chart.

Objective: To determine that the applicant:

1. Exhibits satisfactory knowledge of the elements related to diversion.
2. Selects an appropriate alternate airport and route.
3. Makes an accurate estimate of heading, groundspeed, arrival time, and fuel consumption to the alternate airport.
4. Maintains the appropriate altitude, ±100 feet, and heading, ±10°.

Task D: Lost Procedures

References: FAA-H-8083-25; AIM; Navigation Chart.

Objective: To determine that the applicant:

1. Exhibits satisfactory knowledge of the elements related to lost procedures.
2. Selects an appropriate course of action.
3. Maintains an appropriate heading and climbs, if necessary.
4. Identifies prominent landmarks.
5. Uses navigation systems/facilities and/or contacts an ATC facility for assistance, as appropriate.

VIII. Slow Flight and Stalls

NOTE: *In accordance with FAA policy, all stalls for the Commercial Certificate/ Rating will be taken to the "onset" (buffeting) stall condition.*

Task A: Maneuvering During Slow Flight

References: FAA-H-8083-3; POH/AFM.

Objective: To determine that the applicant:

1. Exhibits satisfactory knowledge of the elements related to maneuvering during slow flight.
2. Selects an entry altitude that will allow the task to be completed no lower than 1,500 feet AGL.
3. Establishes and maintains an airspeed at which any further increase in angle of attack, increase in load factor, or reduction in power, would result in an immediate stall.
4. Accomplishes coordinated straight-and-level flight, turns, climbs, and descents with landing gear and flap configurations specified by the examiner.
5. Divides attention between airplane control and orientation.
6. Maintains the specified altitude, ±50 feet; specified heading, ±10°; airspeed +5/-0 knots; and specified angle of bank, ±5°.

Task B: Power-Off Stalls

References: FAA-H-8083-3; AC 61-67; POH/AFM.

NOTE: *When published, the aircraft manufacturer's procedures for the specific make/mode/series aircraft take precedent over the identification and recovery procedures described in paragraphs 6, 7, and 8 below.*

Objective: To determine that the applicant:

1. Exhibits satisfactory knowledge of the elements related to power-off stalls.
2. Selects an entry altitude that allows the task to be completed no lower than 1,500 feet (460 meters) AGL.
3. Establishes a stabilized descent approximating a 3 degree final approach or landing descent rate in the landing configuration, as specified by the examiner.
4. Transitions smoothly from the approach or landing attitude to a pitch attitude that will induce a stall.
5. Maintains a specified heading, ±10°, if in straight flight; maintains a specified angle of bank, not to exceed 20°, ±5°, if in turning flight while inducing the stall.
6. Recognizes and recovers promptly at the "onset" (buffeting) stall condition.

NOTE: *Evaluation criteria for a recovery from an approach to stall should not mandate a predetermined value for altitude loss and should not mandate maintaining altitude during recovery. Proper evaluation criteria should consider the multitude of external and internal variables which affect the recovery altitude.*

7. Retracts the flaps to the recommended setting, retracts the landing gear if retractable after a positive rate of climb is established.
8. Accelerates to V_x or V_y speed before the final flap retraction; returns to the normal climb attitude, airspeed, and configuration or an altitude, heading, and airspeed specified by the examiner.

Task C: Power-On Stalls

NOTE: *In some high performance airplanes, the power setting may have to be reduced below the practical test standards guideline power setting to prevent excessively high pitch attitudes (greater than 30° nose up).*

References: FAA-H-8083-3; POH/AFM.

Objective: To determine that the applicant:

1. Exhibits satisfactory knowledge of the elements related to power-on stalls.
2. Selects an entry altitude that allows the task to be completed no lower than 1,500 feet (460 meters) AGL.
3. Establishes the takeoff or departure configuration as specified by the examiner. Sets power to no less than 65 percent available power.
4. Transitions smoothly from the takeoff or departure attitude to a pitch attitude that will induce a stall.
5. Maintains a specified heading ±10°, in straight flight; maintains a specified angle of bank, not to exceed a 20°, ±10°, in turning flight, while inducing the stall.
6. Recognizes and recovers promptly at the "onset" (buffeting) stall condition.

NOTE: *Evaluation criteria for a recovery from an approach to stall should not mandate a predetermined value for altitude loss and should not mandate maintaining altitude during recovery. Proper evaluation criteria should consider the multitude of external and internal variables which affect the recovery altitude.*

7. Retracts flaps to the recommended setting, retracts the landing gear, if retractable, after a positive rate of climb is established.
8. Accelerates to V_x or V_y speed before the final flap retraction; returns to the normal climb attitude, airspeed, and configuration or an altitude, heading, and airspeed specified by the examiner.

Task D: Accelerated Stalls

References: FAA-H-8083-3; AC 61-67; POH/AFM.

Objective: To determine that the applicant:

1. Exhibits satisfactory knowledge of the elements related to accelerated (power on or power off) stalls.
2. Selects an entry altitude that allows the task to be completed no lower than 3,000 feet AGL.
3. Establishes the airplane in a steady flight condition, airspeed below V_A, 20 knots above unaccelerated stall speed or the manufacturer's recommendations.
4. Transitions smoothly from the cruise attitude to the angle of bank of approximately 45° that will induce a stall.
5. Maintains coordinated turning flight, increasing elevator back pressure steadily and firmly to induce the stall.
6. Recognizes and recovers promptly at the "onset" (buffeting) stall condition.
7. Returns to the altitude, heading, and airspeed specified by the examiner.

Task E: Spin Awareness

References: FAA-H-8083-3; AC 61-67; POH/AFM.

Objective: To determine that the applicant exhibits satisfactory knowledge of the elements related to spin awareness by explaining:

1. Aerodynamic factors related to spins.
2. Flight situations where unintentional spins may occur.
3. Procedures for recovery from unintentional spins.

IX. Emergency Operations

Task A: Emergency Descent

References: FAA-H-8083-3; POH/AFM.

Objective: To determine that the applicant:

1. Exhibits satisfactory knowledge of the elements related to an emergency descent.
2. Recognizes situations, such as depressurization, cockpit smoke and/or fire that require an emergency descent.
3. Establishes the appropriate airspeed, ±10 knots, and configuration for the emergency descent.
4. Exhibits orientation, division of attention, and proper planning.
5. Maintains positive load factors during the descent.
6. Maintains appropriate airspeed, +0/–10 knots, and levels off at specified altitude, ±100 feet.
7. Completes appropriate checklists.

Task B:　Emergency Approach and Landing (Simulated)

References: FAA-H-8083-3; POH/AFM.

Objective:　To determine that the applicant:

1. Exhibits satisfactory knowledge of the elements related to emergency approach and landing procedures.
2. Analyzes the situation and selects an appropriate course of action.
3. Establishes and maintains the recommended best glide airspeed, ±10 knots.
4. Selects a suitable landing area.
5. Plans and follows a flight pattern to the selected landing area considering altitude, wind, terrain, and obstructions.
6. Prepares for landing, or go-around, as specified by the examiner.
7. Follows the appropriate checklist.

Task C:　Systems and Equipment Malfunctions

References: FAA-H-8083-3; POH/AFM.

Objective:　To determine that the applicant:

1. Exhibits satisfactory knowledge of the elements related to systems and equipment malfunctions appropriate to the airplane provided for the practical test.
2. Analyzes the situation and takes appropriate action for simulated emergencies appropriate to the airplane provided for the practical test for at least three of the following:
   a. partial or complete power loss.
   b. engine roughness or overheat.
   c. carburetor or induction icing.
   d. loss of oil pressure.
   e. fuel starvation.
   f. electrical malfunction.
   g. vacuum/pressure, and associated flight instruments malfunction.
   h. pitot/static system malfunction.
   i. landing gear or flap malfunction.
   j. inoperative trim.
   k. inadvertent door or window opening.
   l. structural icing.
   m. smoke/fire/engine compartment fire.
   n. any other emergency appropriate to the airplane.
3. Follows the appropriate checklist or procedure.

Task D:　Emergency Equipment and Survival Gear

References: FAA-H-8083-3; POH/AFM.

Objective:　To determine that the applicant:

1. Exhibits satisfactory knowledge of the elements related to emergency equipment and survival gear appropriate to the airplane and environment encountered during flight. Identifies appropriate equipment that should be aboard the airplane.

X. High Altitude Operations

Task A: Supplemental Oxygen

References: 14 CFR part 91; FAA-H-8083-25; AC 61-107; AIM; POH/AFM.

Objective: To determine that the applicant exhibits satisfactory knowledge of the elements related to supplemental oxygen by explaining:

1. Supplemental oxygen requirements for flight crew and passengers when operating non-pressurized airplanes.
2. Identification and differences between "aviator's breathing oxygen" and other types of oxygen.
3. Operational characteristics of continuous flow, demand, and pressure-demand oxygen systems.

Task B: Pressurization

References: FAA-H-8083-3, FAA-H-8083-25A; AC 61-107; AIM; POH/AFM.

Objective: To determine that the applicant:

1. Exhibits satisfactory knowledge of the elements related to pressurization by explaining–
    a. fundamental concept of cabin pressurization.
    b. supplemental oxygen requirements when operating airplanes with pressurized cabins.
    c. flight and decompression.

NOTE: *Element 2 applies only if the airplane provided for the practical test is equipped for pressurized flight operations.*

2. Operates the pressurization system properly, and reacts appropriately to simulated pressurization malfunctions.

XI. Postflight Procedures

Task A: After Landing, Parking, and Securing

NOTE: *The examiner shall select Task A.*

References: FAA-H-8083-3; POH/AFM.

Objective: To determine that the applicant:

1. Exhibits satisfactory knowledge of the elements related to after landing, parking, and securing procedures.
2. Maintains directional control after touchdown while decelerating to an appropriate speed.
3. Observes runway hold lines and other surface control markings and lighting.
4. Parks in an appropriate area, considering the safety of nearby persons and property.
5. Follows the appropriate procedure for engine shutdown.
6. Completes the appropriate checklist.
7. Conducts an appropriate post flight inspection and secures the aircraft.

Appendix 1: Task vs. Simulation Device Credit

Airplane Single-Engine Land

Task vs. Simulation Device Credit

Examiners conducting the Commercial Pilot–Airplane Practical Tests with flight simulation devices should consult appropriate documentation to ensure that the device has been approved for training, testing, or checking. The documentation for each device should reflect that the following activities have occurred:

1. The device must be evaluated, determined to meet the appropriate standards, and assigned the appropriate qualification level by the National Simulator Program Manager. The device must continue to meet qualification standards through continuing evaluations as outlined in the appropriate advisory circular (AC) or 14 CFR part 60. For airplane flight training devices (FTDs), AC 120-45 (as amended), Airplane Flight Training Device Qualifications, will be used. For simulators, AC 120-40 (as amended), Airplane Simulator Qualification, or part 60 will be used.
2. The FAA must approve the device for training, testing, and checking the specific flight Tasks listed in this appendix.
3. The device must continue to support the level of student or applicant performance required by the PTS.

NOTE: *Users of the following chart are cautioned that use of the chart alone is incomplete. The description and objective of each Task as listed in the body of the PTS, including all notes, must also be incorporated for accurate simulation device use.*

Use of Chart

X Creditable.
A Creditable if appropriate systems are installed and operating.
  * Asterisk items require use of FTD or Simulator visual reference.

NOTES:

1. Use of Level 1, 2 or Level 3 FTDs is not authorized for the practical test required by this PTS.
2. For practical tests, not more than 50% of the maneuvers may be accomplished in an FTD or simulator UNLESS:

   a. each maneuver has been satisfactorily accomplished for an instructor, in the appropriate airplane, not less than three (3) times,

OR

   b. the applicant has logged not less than 500 hours of flight time as a pilot in airplanes.

3. Not all Areas of Operation (AOO) and Tasks required by this PTS are listed in the appendix. The remaining AOO and Tasks must be accomplished in an airplane.

Flight Simulation Device Level

Areas of Operation	Flight Simulation Device Level							
	4	5	6	7	A	B	C	D
II. Preflight Procedures								
A. Preflight Inspection (Cockpit Only)	A	A	X	X	X	X	X	X
B. Cockpit Management	A	A	X	X	X	X	X	X
C. Engine Starting	A	A	X	X	X	X	X	X
D. Taxiing	—	—	—	—	—	—	X	X
G. Before Takeoff Check	A	A	X	X	X	X	X	X
IV. Takeoffs, Landings, and Go-Arounds								
A. Normal and Crosswind Takeoff and Climb	—	—	—	—	—	—	X	X
B. Normal and Crosswind Approach and Landing	—	—	—	—	—	—	X	X
E. Short-Field Takeoff and Climb	—	—	—	—	X	X	X	X
F. Short-Field Approach and Landing	—	—	—	—	—	—	X	X
L. Go-Around*/Rejected Landing	—	—	X	X	X	X	X	X
V. Performance Maneuvers								
A. Steep Turns	—	—	X	X	X	X	X	X
VII. Navigation*								
A. Navigation Systems and Radar Services	—	A	X	X	X	X	X	X
B. Diversion	—	A	X	X	X	X	X	X
C. Lost Procedures	—	A	X	X	X	X	X	X
VIII. Slow Flight and Stalls								
A. Maneuvering During Slow Flight	—	—	X	X	X	X	X	X
IX. Emergency Operations								
A. Emergency Descent	—	—	X	X	X	X	X	X
B. Emergency Approach and Landing	—	—	—	—	—	—	X	X
C. Systems and Equipment Malfunctions	A	A	X	X	X	X	X	X
X. High Altitude Operations								
B. Pressurization	A	A	X	X	X	X	X	X
XI. Postflight Procedures								
A. After Landing, Parking, and Securing	A	A	X	X	X	X	X	X

Section 2:
Commercial Pilot Airplane–
Multiengine Land

Additional Rating Task Table:
Airplane Multiengine Land

	Addition of an Airplane Multiengine Land Rating to an existing Commercial Pilot Certificate							
	Required Tasks are indicated by either the Task letter(s) that apply(s) or an indication that all or none of the Tasks must be tested based on the notes in each Area of Operation.							
	COMMERCIAL PILOT RATING(S) HELD							
AREAS OF OPERATION	ASEL	ASES	AMES	RH	RG	Glider	Balloon	Airship
I	F,G,H	F,G,H	F,G	F,G,H	F,G,H	F,G,H	F,G,H	F,G,H
II	ALL	ALL	D,F	ALL	ALL	ALL	ALL	ALL
III	NONE	C	C	B,C	NONE	B,C	B,C	B,C
IV	A,B,C, D	A,B,C, D	A,B,C, D	A,B,C, D,I	A,B,C, D,I	A,B,C, D,I	A,B,C, D,I	A,B,C, D,I
V	ALL	ALL	NONE	ALL	ALL	ALL	ALL	ALL
VI	NONE	NONE	NONE	NONE	NONE	ALL	ALL	NONE
VII	ALL	ALL	NONE	ALL	ALL	ALL	ALL	ALL
VIII	ALL	ALL	B,D,E	ALL	ALL	ALL	ALL	ALL
IX	NONE	NONE	NONE	ALL	ALL	ALL	ALL	ALL
X	ALL	ALL	NONE	ALL	ALL	ALL	ALL	ALL
XI	NONE	A	A	A	A	A	A	A

Applicant's Practical Test Checklist
Appointment with Examiner

Examiner's Name: _____

Location: _____

Date/Time: _____

Acceptable Aircraft
- ☐ Aircraft Documents:
  - ☐ Airworthiness Certificate
  - ☐ Registration Certificate
  - ☐ Operating Limitations
- ☐ Aircraft Maintenance Records:
  - ☐ Logbook Record of Airworthiness Inspections and AD Compliance
- ☐ Pilot's Operating Handbook, FAA-Approved Airplane Flight Manual

Personal Equipment
- ☐ View-Limiting Device
- ☐ Current Aeronautical Charts
- ☐ Computer and Plotter
- ☐ Flight Plan Form
- ☐ Flight Logs
- ☐ Current AIM, Airport Facility Directory, and Appropriate Publications

Personal Records
- ☐ Identification–Photo/Signature ID
- ☐ Pilot Certificate
- ☐ Current and Appropriate Medical Certificate
- ☐ Completed FAA Form 8710-1, Airman Certificate and/or Rating Application with Instructor's Signature (If applicable)
- ☐ Computer Test Report
- ☐ Pilot Logbook with appropriate Instructor Endorsements
- ☐ FAA Form 8060-5, Notice of Disapproval (if applicable)
- ☐ Approved School Graduation Certificate (if applicable)
- ☐ Examiner's Fee (if applicable)

Examiner's Practical Test Checklist
Airplane Multiengine Land

Applicant's Name: _____

Location: _____

Date/Time: _____

I. Preflight Preparation
- ☐ **A.** Certificates and Documents
- ☐ **B.** Airworthiness Requirements
- ☐ **C.** Weather Information
- ☐ **D.** Cross-Country Flight Planning
- ☐ **E.** National Airspace System
- ☐ **F.** Performance and Limitations
- ☐ **G.** Operation of Systems
- ☐ **H.** Principles of Flight–Engine Inoperative
- ☐ **K.** Aeromedical Factors

II. Preflight Procedures
- ☐ **A.** Preflight Inspection
- ☐ **B.** Cockpit Management
- ☐ **C.** Engine Starting
- ☐ **D.** Taxiing
- ☐ **F.** Runway Incursion Avoidance
- ☐ **G.** Before Takeoff Check

III. Airport Operations
- ☐ **A.** Radio Communications and ATC Light Signals
- ☐ **B.** Traffic Patterns
- ☐ **C.** Airport, Runway, and Taxiway Signs, Markings, and Lighting

IV. Takeoffs, Landings, and Go-Arounds
- ☐ **A.** Normal and Crosswind Takeoff and Climb
- ☐ **B.** Normal and Crosswind Approach and Landing
- ☐ **C.** Short-Field Takeoff and Maximum Performance Climb
- ☐ **D.** Short-Field Approach and Landing
- ☐ **I.** Go-around/Rejected Landing

V. Performance Maneuver
- ☐ **A.** Steep Turns

VI. Navigation
- ☐ **A.** Pilotage and Dead Reckoning
- ☐ **B.** Navigation Systems and Radar Services
- ☐ **C.** Diversion
- ☐ **D.** Lost Procedures

VII. Slow Flight and Stalls
- ☐ **A.** Maneuvering During Slow Flight
- ☐ **B.** Power-Off Stalls
- ☐ **C.** Power-On Stalls
- ☐ **D.** Accelerated Stalls
- ☐ **E.** Spin Awareness

VIII. Emergency Operations
- ☐ **A.** Emergency Descent
- ☐ **B.** Engine Failure During Takeoff Before V_{MC} (Simulated)
- ☐ **C.** Engine Failure After Lift-Off (Simulated)
- ☐ **D.** Approach and Landing with an Inoperative Engine (Simulated)
- ☐ **E.** Systems and Equipment Malfunctions
- ☐ **F.** Emergency Equipment and Survival Gear

IX. High Altitude Operations
- ☐ **A.** Supplemental Oxygen
- ☐ **B.** Pressurization

X. Multiengine Operations
- ☐ **A.** Maneuvering with One Engine Inoperative
- ☐ **B.** V_{MC} Demonstration
- ☐ **C.** Engine Failure During Flight (by Reference to Instruments)
- ☐ **D.** Instrument Approach–One Engine Inoperative (by Reference to Instruments)

XI. Postflight Procedures
- ☐ **A.** After Landing, Parking, and Securing

Areas of Operation:

I. Preflight Preparation

NOTE: *The examiner shall develop a scenario based on real time weather to evaluate Tasks C and D.*

Task A: Certificates and Documents

References: 14 CFR parts 39, 43, 61, 91; FAA-H-8083-3, FAA-H-8083-25; POH/AFM.

Objective: To determine that the applicant exhibits satisfactory knowledge of the elements related to certificates and documents by:

1. Explaining–
   a. commercial pilot certificate privileges, limitations, and recent flight experience requirements.
   b. medical certificate class and duration.
   c. pilot logbook or flight records.
2. Locating and explaining–
   a. airworthiness and registration certificates.
   b. operating limitations, placards, instrument markings, and POH/AFM.
   c. weight and balance data and equipment list.

Task B: Airworthiness Requirements

References: 14 CFR parts 39, 91; FAA-H-8083-25.

Objective: To determine that the applicant exhibits satisfactory knowledge of the elements related to airworthiness requirements by:

1. Explaining–
   a. required instruments and equipment for day/night VFR.
   b. procedures and limitations for determining airworthiness of the airplane with inoperative instruments and equipment with and without an MEL.
   c. requirements and procedures for obtaining a special flight permit.
2. Locating and explaining–
   a. airworthiness directives.
   b. compliance records.
   c. maintenance/inspection requirements.
   d. appropriate record keeping

Task C: Weather Information

References: 14 CFR part 91; AC 00-6, AC 00-45, AC 61-84; FAA-H-8083-25; AIM.

Objective: To determine that the applicant:

1. Exhibits satisfactory knowledge of the elements related to weather information by analyzing weather reports, charts, and forecasts from various sources with emphasis on—

    a. METAR, TAF, and FA.
    b. surface analysis chart.
    c. radar summary chart.
    d. winds and temperature aloft chart.
    e. significant weather prognostic charts.
    f. convective outlook chart.
    g. AWOS, ASOS, and ATIS reports.
    h. SIGMETs and AIRMETs.
    i. PIREPs.
    j. windshear reports.
    k. icing and freezing level information.

2. Makes a competent "go/no-go" decision based on available weather information.

Task D: Cross-Country Flight Planning

References: 14 CFR part 91; FAA-H-8083-25; AC 61-84; Navigation Charts; AFD; AIM; NOTAMS.

Objective: To determine that the applicant:

1. Exhibits satisfactory knowledge of the elements related to cross-country flight planning by presenting and explaining a pre-planned VFR cross-country flight, as previously assigned by the examiner. On the day of the practical test, the final flight plan shall be to the first fuel stop, based on maximum allowable passengers, baggage, and/or cargo loads using real-time weather.
2. Uses appropriate and current aeronautical charts.
3. Properly identifies airspace, obstructions, and terrain features.
4. Selects easily identifiable en route checkpoints.
5. Selects most favorable altitudes considering weather conditions and equipment capabilities.
6. Computes headings, flight time, and fuel requirements.
7. Selects appropriate navigation system/facilities and communication frequencies.
8. Applies pertinent information from AFD, NOTAMs, and NOTAMS relative to airport, runway and taxiway closures, and other flight publications.
9. Completes a navigation log and simulates filing a VFR flight plan.

Task E: National Airspace System

References: 14 CFR parts 71, 91, 93; Navigation Charts; AIM.

Objective: To determine that the applicant exhibits satisfactory knowledge of the elements related to the National Airspace System by explaining:

1. Basic VFR weather minimums—for all classes of airspace.
2. Airspace classes—their operating rules, pilot certification, and airplane equipment requirements for the following—
   a. Class A.
   b. Class B.
   c. Class C.
   d. Class D.
   e. Class E.
   f. Class G.
3. Special use, special flight rules areas, and other airspace areas.

Task F: Performance and Limitations

References: FAA-H-8083-1, FAA-H-8083-25; AC 61-84; POH/AFM.

Objective: To determine that the applicant:

1. Exhibits satisfactory knowledge of the elements related to performance and limitations by explaining the use of charts, tables, and data to determine performance and the adverse effects of exceeding limitations.
2. Computes weight and balance. Determines the computed weight and center of gravity are within the airplane's operating limitations and if the weight and center of gravity will remain within limits during all phases of flight.
3. Demonstrates use of the appropriate manufacturer's performance charts, tables, and data.
4. Describes the effects of atmospheric conditions on the airplane's performance.

Task G: Operation of Systems

References: FAA-H-8083-25; POH/AFM.

Objective: To determine that the applicant exhibits satisfactory knowledge of the elements related to the operation of systems on the airplane provided for the flight test by explaining at least three of the following systems.

1. Primary flight controls and trim.
2. Flaps, leading edge devices, and spoilers.
3. Powerplant and propeller.
4. Landing gear.
5. Fuel, oil, and hydraulic.
6. Electrical.
7. Avionics.
8. Pitot-static, vacuum/pressure, and associated flight instruments.
9. Environmental.
10. Deicing and anti-icing.

Task H: Principles of Flight–Engine Inoperative

References: FAA-H-8083-3, FAA-H-8083-25, FAA-P-8740-19; POH/AFM.

Objective: To determine that the applicant exhibits satisfactory knowledge of the elements related to engine inoperative principles of flight by explaining the:

1. meaning of the term "critical engine."
2. effects of density altitude on the V_{MC} demonstration.
3. effects of airplane weight and center of gravity on control.
4. effects of angle of bank on V_{MC}.
5. relationship of V_{MC} to stall speed.
6. reasons for loss of directional control.
7. indications of loss of directional control.
8. importance of maintaining the proper pitch and bank attitude, and the proper coordination of controls.
9. loss of directional control recovery procedure.
10. engine failure during takeoff including planning, decisions, and single-engine operations.

Task K: Aeromedical Factors

References: FAA-H-8083-25; AIM.

Objective: To determine that the applicant exhibits satisfactory knowledge of the elements related to aeromedical factors by explaining:

1. The symptoms, causes, effects, and corrective actions of at least 4 of the following–

   a. hypoxia.
   b. hyperventilation.
   c. middle ear and sinus problems.
   d. spatial disorientation.
   e. motion sickness.
   f. carbon monoxide poisoning.
   g. stress and fatigue.
   h. dehydration.

2. The effects of alcohol, drugs, and over-the-counter medications.
3. The effects of excess nitrogen during scuba dives upon a pilot or passenger in flight.

II.   Preflight Procedures

Task A: Preflight Inspection

References: FAA-H-8083-3; POH/AFM.

Objective: To determine that the applicant:

1. Exhibits satisfactory knowledge of the elements related to preflight inspection. This shall include which items must be inspected, the reasons for checking each item, and how to detect possible defects.
2. Inspects the airplane with reference to an appropriate checklist.
3. Verifies the airplane is in condition for safe flight.

Task B: Cockpit Management

References: FAA-H-8083-3; POH/AFM.

Objective: To determine that the applicant:
1. Exhibits satisfactory knowledge of the elements related to cockpit management procedures.
2. Ensures all loose items in the cockpit and cabin are secured.
3. Organizes material and equipment in an efficient manner so they are readily available.
4. Briefs occupants on the use of safety belts, shoulder harnesses, doors, and emergency procedures.

Task C: Engine Starting

References: FAA-H-8083-3, FAA-H-8083-25; AC 91-13, AC 91-55; POH/AFM.

Objective: To determine that the applicant:
1. Exhibits knowledge of the elements related to recommended engine starting procedures. This shall include the use of an external power source, and starting under various atmospheric conditions.
2. Positions the airplane properly considering structures, surface conditions, other aircraft, and the safety of nearby persons and property.
3. Utilizes the appropriate checklist for starting procedure.

Task D: Taxiing

References: FAA-H-8083-3; POH/AFM.

Objective: To determine that the applicant:
1. Exhibits satisfactory knowledge of the elements related to safe taxi procedures at towered and non-towered airports.
2. Performs a brake check immediately after the airplane begins moving.
3. Positions the flight controls properly for the existing wind conditions.
4. Controls direction and speed without excessive use of brakes.
5. Exhibits procedures for steering, maneuvering, maintaining taxiway, runway position, and situational awareness to avoid runway incursions.
6. Exhibits proper positioning of the aircraft relative to hold lines.
7. Exhibits procedures to insure clearances/instructions are received and recorded/read back correctly.
8. Exhibits situational awareness/taxi procedures in the event the aircraft is on a taxiway that is between parallel runways.
9. Uses a taxi chart during taxi.
10. Complies with airport/taxiway markings, signals, ATC clearances, and instructions.
11. Utilizes procedures for eliminating pilot distractions.
12. Taxiing to avoid other aircraft/vehicles and hazards.

Task F: *Runway Incursion Avoidance*

References: FAA-H-8083-3, FAA-H-8083-25; AC 91-73, AC 150-5340-18; AIM.

Objective: To determine that the applicant exhibits knowledge of the elements of runway incursion avoidance by:

1. Exhibiting distinct challenges and requirements during taxi operations not found in other phases of flight operations.
2. Exhibiting procedures for appropriate cockpit activities during taxiing including taxi route planning, briefing the location of HOT SPOTS, communicating and coordinating with ATC.
3. Exhibiting procedures for steering, maneuvering, maintaining taxiway, runway position, and situational awareness.
4. Knowing the relevance/importance of hold lines.
5. Exhibiting procedures to ensure the pilot maintains strict focus to the movement of the aircraft and ATC communications, including the elimination of all distractive activities (i.e. cell phone, texting, conversations with passengers) during aircraft taxi, takeoff and climb out to cruise altitude.
6. Utilizing procedures for holding the pilot's workload to a minimum during taxi operations.
7. Utilizing taxi operation planning procedures, such as recording taxi instructions, reading back taxi clearances, and reviewing taxi routes on the airport diagram.
8. Utilizing procedures to insure that clearance or instructions that are actually received are adhered to rather than the ones expected to be received.
9. Utilizing procedures to maintain/enhance situational awareness when conducting taxi operations in relation to other aircraft operations in the vicinity as well as to other vehicles moving on the airport.
10. Exhibiting procedures for briefing if a landing rollout to a taxiway exit will place the pilot in close proximity to another runway which can result in a runway incursion.
11. Conducting appropriate after landing/taxi procedures in the event the aircraft is on a taxiway that is between parallel runways.
12. Knowing specific procedures for operations at an airport with an operating air traffic control tower, with emphasis on ATC communications and runway entry/crossing authorizations.
13. Utilizing ATC communications and pilot actions before takeoff, before landing, and after landing at towered and non-towered airports.
14. Knowing procedures unique to night operations.
15. Knowing operations at non-towered airports.
16. Knowing the use of aircraft exterior lighting.
17. Knowing the hazards of Low visibility operations.

Task G: Before Takeoff Check

References: FAA-H-8083-3; POH/AFM.

Objective: To determine that the applicant:

1. Exhibits satisfactory knowledge of the elements related to the before takeoff check. This shall include the reasons for checking each item and how to detect malfunctions.
2. Positions the airplane properly considering other aircraft/vessels, wind, and surface conditions.
3. Divides attention inside and outside the cockpit.
4. Ensures that engine temperatures and pressure are suitable for run-up and takeoff.
5. Accomplishes the before takeoff checklist and ensures the airplane is in safe operating condition as recommended by the manufacturer.
6. Reviews takeoff performance, such as airspeeds, takeoff distances, departure, and emergency procedures.
7. Avoids runway incursions and ensures no conflict with traffic prior to taxiing into takeoff position.

III. Airport Operations

Task A: Radio Communications and ATC Light Signals

References: 14 CFR part 91; FAA-H-8083-25; AIM.

Objective: To determine that the applicant:

1. Exhibits satisfactory knowledge of the elements related to radio communications and ATC light signals.
2. Selects appropriate frequencies.
3. Transmits using AIM specified phraseology and procedures.
4. Acknowledges radio communications and complies with instructions.

Task B: Traffic Patterns

References: FAA-H-8083-3, FAA-H-8083-25; AC 90-66; AIM.

Objective: To determine that the applicant:

1. Exhibits satisfactory knowledge of the elements related to traffic patterns. This shall include procedures at airports with and without operating control towers, prevention of runway incursions, collision avoidance, wake turbulence avoidance, and wind shear.
2. Complies with proper traffic pattern procedures.
3. Maintains proper spacing from other aircraft.
4. Corrects for wind drift to maintain the proper ground track.
5. Maintains orientation with the runway/landing area in use.
6. Maintains traffic pattern altitude, ±100 feet, and the appropriate airspeed, ±10 knots.

Task C: Airport, Runway, and Taxiway Signs, Markings, and Lighting

References: FAA-H-8083-25; AIM; AFD; AC 91-73, AC 150-5340-18.

Objective: To determine that the applicant:

1. Exhibits satisfactory knowledge of the elements related to airport, runway, and taxiway operations with emphasis on runway incursion avoidance.
2. Properly identifies and interprets airport, runway, and taxiway signs, markings, and lighting, with emphasis on runway incursion avoidance.

IV. Takeoffs, Landings, and Go-Arounds

Task A: Normal and Crosswind Takeoff and Climb

NOTE: *If a crosswind condition does not exist, the applicant's knowledge of crosswind elements shall be evaluated through oral testing.*

References: FAA-H-8083-3, FAA-P-8740-19; POH/AFM.

Objective: To determine that the applicant:

1. Utilizes procedures before taxiing onto the runway or takeoff area to ensure runway incursion avoidance. Verify ATC clearance/no aircraft on final at non-towered airports before entering the runway, and ensure that the aircraft is on the correct takeoff runway.
2. Exhibits satisfactory knowledge of the elements related to a normal and crosswind takeoff, climb operations, and rejected takeoff procedures.
3. Ascertains wind direction with or without visible wind direction indicators.
4. Calculates/determines if crosswind component is above his or her ability or that of the aircraft's capability.
5. Positions the flight controls for the existing wind conditions.
6. Clears the area, taxies onto the takeoff surface, and aligns the airplane on the runway center/takeoff path.
7. Advances the throttle smoothly to takeoff power.
8. Rotates and lifts off at the recommended airspeed and accelerates to V_Y.
9. Establishes a pitch attitude that will maintain V_Y, ±5 knots.
10. Retracts the landing gear, if appropriate, and flaps after a positive rate of climb is established.
11. Maintains takeoff power and V_Y ±5 knots to a safe maneuvering altitude.
12. Maintains directional control, proper wind-drift correction throughout the takeoff and climb.
13. Complies with responsible environmental practices, including noise abatement procedures.
14. Completes appropriate checklists.

Task B: Normal and Crosswind Approach and Landing

NOTE: *If a crosswind condition does not exist, the applicant's knowledge of crosswind elements shall be evaluated through oral testing.*

References: FAA-H-8083-3; POH/AFM.

Objective: To determine that the applicant:

1. Exhibits satisfactory knowledge of the elements related to a normal and crosswind approach and landing with emphasis on proper use and coordinating of flight controls.

2. Considers the wind conditions, landing surface, obstructions, and selects a suitable touchdown point.
3. Establishes the recommended approach and landing configuration and airspeed, and adjusts pitch attitude and power as required.
4. Maintains a stabilized approach and recommended airspeed established by the manufacturer, or in its absence, not more than 1.3 V_{SO}, +10/-5 knots, with wind gust factor applied.
5. Makes smooth, timely, and correct control application during the round out and touchdown.
6. Touches down smoothly at approximate stalling speed.
7. Touches down within the first one-third of the available runway, within 200 feet beyond a specified point, with no drift, and with the airplane's longitudinal axis aligned with and over the runway center/landing path.
8. Maintains crosswind correction and directional control throughout the approach and landing sequence.
9. Executes a timely go-around decision when the approach cannot be made within the tolerance specified above.
10. Utilizes after landing runway incursion avoidance procedures.
11. Completes the appropriate checklist.

Task C: Short-Field Takeoff and Maximum Performance Climb

References: FAA-H-8083-3, FAA-P-8740-19; POH/AFM.

Objective: To determine that the applicant:

1. Utilizes procedures before taxiing onto the runway or takeoff area to ensure runway incursion avoidance. Verify ATC clearance/no aircraft on final at non-towered airports before entering the runway, and ensure that the aircraft is on the correct takeoff runway.
2. Exhibits satisfactory knowledge of the elements related to a short-field takeoff and maximum performance climb.
3. Positions the flight controls for the existing wind conditions, sets flaps as recommended.
4. Clears the area, taxies into takeoff position utilizing maximum available takeoff area, and aligns the airplane on the runway center/takeoff path.
5. Applies brakes, if appropriate, while advancing the throttles smoothly to takeoff power.
6. Rotates and lifts off at the recommended airspeed, and accelerates to recommended obstacle clearance airspeed, or V_X.
7. Establishes a pitch attitude that will maintain the recommended obstacle clearance airspeed, or V_X, +5/-0 knots, until the obstacle is cleared, or until the airplane is 50 feet above the surface.
8. After clearing the obstacle, establishes the pitch attitude for V_Y, accelerates to V_Y, and maintains V_Y, ±5 knots, during the climb.
9. Retracts the landing gear, if appropriate, and flaps after clear of any obstacles or as recommended by manufacturer.
10. Maintains takeoff power and V_Y ±5 knots to a safe maneuvering altitude.
11. Maintains directional control and proper wind-drift correction throughout the takeoff and climb.
12. Completes appropriate checklist.

Task D: Short-Field Approach and Landing

References: FAA-H-8083-3; POH/AFM.

Objective: To determine that the applicant:

1. Exhibits satisfactory knowledge of the elements related to a short-field approach and landing.
2. Considers the wind conditions, landing surface, obstructions, and selects the most suitable touchdown point.
3. Establishes the recommended approach and landing configuration and airspeed; adjusts pitch attitude and power as required.
4. Maintains a stabilized approach and recommended approach airspeed, or in its absence, not more than 1.3 V_{so}, ±5 knots, with wind gust factor applied.
5. Makes smooth, timely, and correct control application during the round out and touchdown.
6. Touches down smoothly at minimum control airspeed.
7. Touches down at or within 100 feet beyond a specified point, with no side drift, minimum float, and with the airplane's longitudinal axis aligned with and over the runway center/landing path.
8. Maintains crosswind correction and directional control throughout the approach and landing sequence.
9. Applies brakes, as necessary, to stop in the shortest distance consistent with safety.
10. Utilizes after landing runway incursion avoidance procedures.
11. Completes appropriate checklist.

Task I: Go-Around/Rejected Landing

References: FAA-H-8083-3; POH/AFM.

Objective: To determine that the applicant:

1. Exhibits satisfactory knowledge of the elements related to a go-around/ rejected landing, with emphasis on factors that contribute to landing conditions that may require a go-around.
2. Makes a timely decision to discontinue the approach to landing.
3. Applies takeoff power immediately and transitions to climb pitch attitude for V_x or V_y as appropriate +10/–5 knots and/or appropriate pitch attitude.
4. Retracts flaps, as appropriate.
5. Retracts the landing gear if appropriate after a positive rate of climb is established.
6. Maneuvers to the side of runway/landing area to clear and avoid conflicting traffic.
7. Maintains takeoff power and V_y ±5 knots to a safe maneuvering altitude.
8. Maintains directional control and proper wind-drift correction throughout the climb.
9. Completes the appropriate checklist.

V. Performance Maneuver

Task A: Steep Turns

References: FAA-H-8083-3; POH/AFM.

Objective: To determine that the applicant:

1. Exhibits satisfactory knowledge of the elements related to steep turns.
2. Establishes the manufacturer's recommended airspeed or if one is not stated, a safe airspeed not to exceed V_A.
3. Rolls into a coordinated 360° steep turn with at least a 50° bank, followed by a 360° steep turn in the opposite direction.
4. Divides attention between airplane control and orientation.
5. Maintains the entry altitude, ±100 feet, airspeed, ±10 knots, bank, ±5°; and rolls out on the entry heading, ±10°.

VI. Navigation

Task A: Pilotage and Dead Reckoning

References: FAA-H-8083-25; 14 CFR Part 61; Navigation Chart.

Objective: To determine that the applicant:

1. Exhibits satisfactory knowledge of the elements related to pilotage and dead reckoning.
2. Follows the preplanned course by reference to landmarks.
3. Identifies landmarks by relating surface features to chart symbols.
4. Navigates by means of precomputed headings, groundspeed, and elapsed time.
5. Demonstrates use of magnetic compass in navigation, to include turns to new headings.
6. Corrects for and records differences between preflight groundspeed, fuel consumption, and heading calculations and those determined en route.
7. Verifies the airplane's position within 2 nautical miles of flight planned route.
8. Arrives at the en route checkpoints within 3 minutes of the initial or revised ETA and provides a destination estimate.
9. Maintains appropriate altitude, ±100 feet and heading, ±10°.

Task B: Navigation Systems and Radar Services

References: FAA-H-8083-3, FAA-H-8083-6, FAA-H-8083-25; Navigation Equipment Operation Manuals; AIM.

Objective: To determine that the applicant:

1. Exhibits satisfactory knowledge of the elements related to navigation systems and radar services.
2. Demonstrates the ability to use an airborne electronic navigation system.
3. Locates the airplane's position using the navigation system.
4. Intercepts and tracks a given course, radial, or bearing, as appropriate.
5. Recognizes and describes the indication of station passage, if appropriate.
6. Recognizes signal loss and takes appropriate action.
7. Uses proper communication procedures when utilizing radar services.
8. Maintains the appropriate altitude, ±100 feet and heading, ±10°.

Task C: Diversion

References: FAA-H-8083-25; AIM; Navigation Chart.

Objective: To determine that the applicant:

1. Exhibits satisfactory knowledge of the elements related to diversion.
2. Selects an appropriate alternate airport and route.
3. Makes an accurate estimate of heading, groundspeed, arrival time, and fuel consumption to the alternate airport.
4. Maintains the appropriate altitude, ±100 feet, and heading, ±10°.

Task D: Lost Procedures

References: FAA-H-8083-25; AIM; Navigation Chart.

Objective: To determine that the applicant:

1. Exhibits satisfactory knowledge of the elements related to lost procedures.
2. Selects an appropriate course of action.
3. Maintains an appropriate heading and climbs, if necessary.
4. Identifies prominent landmarks.
5. Uses navigation systems/facilities and/or contacts an ATC facility for assistance, as appropriate.

VII. Slow Flight and Stalls

NOTE: *In accordance with FAA policy, all stalls for the Commercial Certificate/ Rating will be taken to the "onset" (buffeting) stall condition.*

Task A: Maneuvering During Slow Flight

References: FAA-H-8083-3; POH/AFM.

Objective: To determine that the applicant:

1. Exhibits satisfactory knowledge of the elements related to maneuvering during slow flight.
2. Selects an entry altitude that will allow the task to be completed no lower than 3,000 feet AGL.
3. Establishes and maintains an airspeed at which any further increase in angle of attack, increase in load factor, or reduction in power, would result in an immediate stall.
4. Accomplishes coordinated straight-and-level flight, turns, climbs, and descents with landing gear and flap configurations specified by the examiner.
5. Divides attention between airplane control and orientation.
6. Maintains the specified altitude, ±50 feet; specified heading, ±10°; airspeed +5/-0 knots, and specified angle of bank, ±5°.

Task B: Power-Off Stalls

References: FAA-H-8083-3; AC 61-67; POH/AFM.

Objective: To determine that the applicant:

1. Exhibits satisfactory knowledge of the elements related to power-off stalls.
2. Selects an entry altitude that allows the task to be completed no lower than 3,000 feet AGL.

3. Establishes a stabilized descent approximating a 3 degree final approach glidepath or landing descent rate in the approach or landing configuration, as specified by the examiner.
4. Transitions smoothly from the approach or landing attitude to a pitch attitude that will induce a stall.
5. Maintains a specified heading, ±10°, in straight flight; maintains a specified angle of bank, not to exceed 20°, ±5°, in turning flight while inducing the stall.
6. Recognizes and recovers promptly at the "onset" (buffeting) stall condition.

NOTE: *Evaluation criteria for a recovery from an approach to stall should not mandate a predetermined value for altitude loss and should not mandate maintaining altitude during recovery. Proper evaluation criteria should consider the multitude of external and internal variables which affect the recovery altitude.*

7. Retracts the flaps to the recommended setting, retracts the landing gear, if retractable, after a positive rate of climb is established.
8. Accelerates to V_x or V_y speed before the final flap retraction; returns to the maneuvering speed for the configuration or altitude, heading, and airspeed specified by the examiner.

Task C: Power-On Stalls

References: FAA-H-8083-3; AC 61-67; POH/AFM.

NOTE: *In some high performance airplanes as defined by 14 CFR part 61, the power setting may have to be reduced below the practical test standards guideline power setting to prevent excessively high pitch attitudes (greater than 30° nose up).*

Objective: To determine that the applicant:

1. Exhibits satisfactory knowledge of the elements related to power-on stalls.
2. Selects an entry altitude that allows the task to be completed no lower than 3,000 feet AGL.
3. Establishes the takeoff or departure configuration. Sets power to no less than 65 percent available power.
4. Transitions smoothly from the takeoff or departure attitude to a pitch attitude that will induce a stall.
5. Maintains a specified heading ±10°, in straight flight; maintains a specified angle of bank, not to exceed a 20°, ±10° in turning flight, while inducing the stall.
6. Recognizes and recovers promptly at the "onset" (buffeting) stall condition.

NOTE: *Evaluation criteria for a recovery from an approach to stall should not mandate a predetermined value for altitude loss and should not mandate maintaining altitude during recovery. Proper evaluation criteria should consider the multitude of external and internal variables which affect the recovery altitude.*

7. Retracts the flaps to the recommended setting, retracts the landing gear, if retractable, after a positive rate of climb is established.
8. Accelerates to V_x or V_y speed before the final flap retraction; returns to the normal climb attitude, airspeed, and configuration or an altitude, heading, and airspeed specified by the examiner.

Task D: Accelerated Stalls

References: FAA-H-8083-3; AC 61-67; POH/AFM.

Objective: To determine that the applicant:

1. Exhibits satisfactory knowledge of the elements related to accelerated (power on or power off) stalls.
2. Selects an entry altitude that allows the task to be completed no lower than 3,000 feet AGL.
3. Establishes a steady flight condition and recommended airspeed established by the manufacturer, or in it's absence, not more than 1.2 V_S.
4. Transitions smoothly from the cruise attitude to the angle of bank of approximately 45° that will induce a stall.
5. Maintains coordinated turning flight, increasing elevator back pressure steadily and firmly to induce the stall.
6. Recognizes and recovers promptly at the "onset" (buffeting) stall condition.
7. Returns to the altitude, heading, and airspeed specified by the examiner.

Task E: Spin Awareness

References: FAA-H-8083-3; AC 61-67; POH/AFM.

Objective: To determine that the applicant exhibits knowledge of the elements related to spin awareness by explaining:

1. Aerodynamic factors related to spins.
2. Flight situations where unintentional spins may occur.
3. Procedures for recovery from unintentional spins.

VIII. Emergency Operations

NOTE: Examiners shall select an entry altitude that will allow the single engine demonstrations Task to be completed no lower than 3,000 feet AGL or the manufacturer's recommended altitude, whichever is higher. At altitudes lower than 3,000 feet AGL, engine failure shall be simulated by reducing throttle to idle and then establishing zero thrust.

Task A: Emergency Descent

References: FAA-H-8083-3; POH/AFM.

Objective: To determine that the applicant:

1. Exhibits satisfactory knowledge of the elements related to an emergency descent.
2. Recognizes situations, such as depressurization, cockpit smoke, and/or fire that require an emergency descent.
3. Establishes the appropriate airspeed and configuration for the emergency descent.
4. Exhibits orientation, division of attention, and proper planning.
5. Maintains positive load factors during the descent.
6. Completes appropriate checklists.
7. Maintains appropriate airspeed, +0/−10 knots, and levels off at specified altitude, ±100 feet.

Task B: Engine Failure During Takeoff Before V_{MC} (Simulated)

References: FAA-H-8083-3; POH/AFM.

NOTE: *Engine failure (simulated) shall be accomplished before reaching 50 percent of the calculated V_{MC}.*

Objective: To determine that the applicant:

1. Exhibits satisfactory knowledge of the elements related to the procedure used for engine failure during takeoff prior to reaching V_{MC}.
2. Closes the throttles smoothly and promptly when simulated engine failure occurs.
3. Maintains directional control and applies brakes, as necessary.

Task C: Engine Failure After Lift-Off (Simulated)

NOTE: *Simulated engine failure of the most critical engine shall be demonstrated after liftoff. However, the failure of an engine shall not be simulated until attaining at least $V_{SSE}/V_{XSE}/V_{YSE}$ and at an altitude not lower than 400 feet AGL.*

References: FAA-H-8083-3, FAA-P-8740-19; POH/AFM.

Objective: To determine that the applicant:

1. Exhibits satisfactory knowledge of the elements related to the procedure used for engine failure after lift-off.
2. Recognizes a simulated engine failure promptly, maintains control, and utilizes appropriate manufacturer's emergency procedures.
3. Reduces drag, identifies and verifies the inoperative engine after simulated engine failure.
4. Simulates feathering the propeller on the inoperative engine. Examiner shall then establish zero-thrust on the inoperative engine.
5. Establishes V_{YSE}; if obstructions are present, establishes V_{XSE} or V_{MC} +5 knots, whichever is greater, until obstructions are cleared. Then transitions to V_{YSE}.
6. Banks toward the operating engine as required for best performance.
7. Monitors operating engine and makes adjustments, as necessary.
8. Recognizes the airplane's performance capabilities. If a climb is not possible at V_{YSE}, maintain V_{YSE} and return to the departure airport for landing, or initiates an approach to the most suitable landing area available.
9. Simulates securing the inoperative engine.
10. Maintains heading, ±10°, and airspeed, ±5 knots.
11. Completes appropriate emergency checklist.

Task D: *Approach and Landing with an Inoperative Engine (Simulated)*

References: FAA-H-8083-3, FAA-P-8740-19; POH/AFM.

Objective: To determine that the applicant:

1. Exhibits satisfactory knowledge of the elements related to an approach and landing with an engine inoperative to include engine failure on final approach.
2. Recognizes engine failure and takes appropriate action, maintains control, and utilizes manufacturer's recommended emergency procedures.
3. Banks toward the operating engine, as required, for best performance.
4. Monitors the operating engine and makes adjustments as necessary.
5. Maintains the manufacturer's recommended approach airspeed ±5 knots, and landing configuration with a stabilized approach, until landing is assured.
6. Makes smooth, timely, and correct control applications during round out and touchdown.
7. Touches down on the first one-third of available runway, with no drift and the airplane's longitudinal axis aligned with and over the runway center/landing path.
8. Maintains crosswind correction and directional control throughout the approach and landing sequence.
9. Completes appropriate checklists.

Task E: *Systems and Equipment Malfunctions*

References: FAA-H-8083-3; POH/AFM.

Objective: To determine that the applicant:

1. Exhibits knowledge of the elements related to systems and equipment malfunctions appropriate to the airplane provided for the practical test.
2. Analyzes the situation and takes appropriate action for simulated emergencies appropriate to the airplane provided for the practical test for at least three of the following–

   a. partial or complete power loss.
   b. engine roughness or overheat.
   c. carburetor or induction icing.
   d. loss of oil pressure.
   e. fuel starvation.
   f. electrical malfunction.
   g. vacuum/pressure, and associated flight instruments malfunction.
   h. pitot/static system malfunction.
   i. landing gear or flap malfunction.
   j. inoperative trim.
   k. inadvertent door or window opening.
   l. structural icing.
   m. smoke/fire/engine compartment fire.
   n. any other emergency appropriate to the airplane.

3. Follows the appropriate checklist or procedure.

Task F: Emergency Equipment and Survival Gear

References: FAA-H-8083-3; POH/AFM.

Objective: To determine that the applicant:

1. Exhibits knowledge of the elements related to emergency equipment and survival gear appropriate to the airplane and environment encountered during flight. Identifies appropriate equipment that should be onboard the airplane.

IX.   High Altitude Operations

Task A: Supplemental Oxygen

References: 14 CFR part 91; FAA-H-8083-3, FAA-H-8083-25; AC 61-107; AIM; POH/AFM.

Objective: To determine that the applicant exhibits satisfactory knowledge of the elements related to supplemental oxygen by explaining:

1. Supplemental oxygen requirements for flight crew and passengers when operating non-pressurized airplanes.
2. Identification and differences between "aviator's breathing oxygen" and other types of oxygen.
3. Operational characteristics of continuous flow, demand, and pressure-demand oxygen systems.

Task B: Pressurization

References: FAA-H-8083-3, FAA-H-8083-25; AC 61-107; AIM; POH/AFM.

Objective: To determine that the applicant:

1. Exhibits knowledge of the elements related to pressurization by explaining–
    a. fundamental concept of cabin pressurization.
    b. supplemental oxygen requirements when operating airplanes with pressurized cabins.
    c. physiological hazards associated with high altitude flight and decompression.

NOTE: *Element 2 applies only if the airplane provided for the practical test is equipped for pressurized flight operations.*

2. Operates the pressurization system properly, and reacts appropriately to simulated pressurization malfunctions.

X. Multiengine Operations

NOTE: *If the applicant does not hold an instrument rating airplane, Tasks C and D need not to be accomplished. All other tasks need to be completed.*

Task A: *Maneuvering with One Engine Inoperative*

References: *FAA-H-8083-3, FAA-P-8740-19; POH/AFM.*

NOTE: *The feathering of one propeller shall be demonstrated in flight, unless the manufacturer prohibits the intentional feathering of the propellers during flight. The maneuver shall be performed at altitudes above 3,000 feet AGL or the manufacturer's recommended altitude, whichever is higher, and positions where safe landings on established airports can be readily accomplished. In the event a propeller cannot be unfeathered during the practical test, it shall be treated as an emergency.*

Objective: To determine that the applicant:

1. Exhibits satisfactory knowledge of the elements related to maneuvering with one engine inoperative.
2. Recognizes engine failure and maintains control.
3. Sets the engine controls, reduces drag, identifies and verifies the inoperative engine, and feathers appropriate propeller.
4. Establishes and maintains a bank toward the operating engine as required for best performance in straight-and-level flight.
5. Follows the manufacturer's prescribed checklists to verify procedures for securing the inoperative engine.
6. Monitors the operating engine and makes necessary adjustments.
7. Demonstrates coordinated flight with one engine inoperative (propeller feathered).
8. Restarts the inoperative engine using manufacturer's appropriate restart procedures.
9. Maintains altitude ±100 feet or minimum sink, as appropriate, and heading ±10°.
10. Completes the appropriate checklists.

Task B: V_{MC} *Demonstration*

References: *FAA-H-8083-3, FAA-P-8740-19; POH/AFM.*

NOTE: *An applicant seeking an airplane–multiengine land (AMEL) rating, "Limited to Center Thrust," is not required to be evaluated on this Task.*

NOTE: *Airplanes with normally aspirated engines will lose power as altitude increases because of the reduced density of the air entering the induction system of the engine. This loss of power will result in a V_{MC} lower than the stall speed at higher altitudes. Therefore, recovery should be made at the first indication of loss of directional control, stall warning, or buffet. Do not perform this maneuver by increasing the pitch attitude to a high angle with both engines operating and then reducing power on the critical engine. This technique is hazardous and may result in loss of airplane control.*

Objective: To determine that the applicant:

1. Exhibits satisfactory knowledge of the elements related to V_{MC} by explaining the causes of loss of directional control at airspeeds less than V_{MC}, the factors affecting V_{MC}, and safe recovery procedures.
2. Configures the airplane in accordance with the manufacturer's recommendation, in the absence of the manufacturer's recommendations, then at V_{SSE}/V_{YSE}, as appropriate–
   a. Landing gear retracted.
   b. Flaps set for takeoff.
   c. Cowl flaps set for takeoff.
   d. Trim set for takeoff.
   e. Propellers set for high RPM.
   f. Power on critical engine reduced to idle.
   g. Power on operating engine set to takeoff or maximum available power.
3. Establishes a single-engine climb attitude with the airspeed at approximately 10 knots above V_{SSE} or V_{YSE}, as appropriate.
4. Establishes a bank toward the operating engine, as required for best performance and controllability.
5. Increases the pitch attitude slowly to reduce the airspeed at approximately 1 knot per second while applying rudder pressure to maintain directional control until full rudder is applied.
6. Recognizes indications of loss of directional control, stall warning, or buffet.
7. Recovers promptly by simultaneously reducing power sufficiently on the operating engine while decreasing the angle of attack as necessary to regain airspeed and directional control. Recovery SHOULD NOT be attempted by increasing the power on the simulated failed engine.
8. Recovers within 20° of the entry heading.
9. Advances power smoothly on operating engine and accelerates to V_{XSE}/V_{YSE}, as appropriate, ±5 knots, during the recovery.

Task C: *Engine Failure During Flight (By Reference to Instruments)*

References: 14 CFR part 61; FAA-H-8083-3, FAA-H-8083-15.

Objective: To determine that the applicant:

1. Exhibits satisfactory knowledge of the elements by explaining the procedures used during instrument flight with one engine inoperative.
2. Recognizes engine failure, sets the engine controls, reduces drag, identifies, and verifies the inoperative engine, and simulates feathering appropriate engine propeller.
3. Establishes and maintains a bank toward the operating engine as required for best performance in straight-and-level.
4. Follows the prescribed manufacturer's checklists to verify procedures for securing the inoperative engine.
5. Monitors the operating engine and makes necessary adjustments.
6. Demonstrates coordinated flight with one engine inoperative.
7. Maintains altitude ±100 feet or minimum sink, as appropriate, and heading ±10°, bank ±5°, and levels off from climbs and descents within ±100 feet.

Task D: *Instrument Approach–One Engine Inoperative (By Reference to Instruments)*

References: 14 CFR part 61; FAA-H-8083-3, FAA-S-8081-4; AC 61-27.

Objective: To determine that the applicant:

1. Exhibits satisfactory knowledge of the elements by explaining the procedures used during a published instrument approach with one engine inoperative.
2. Recognizes engine failure, sets the engine controls, reduces drag, identifies and verifies the simulated inoperative engine, and simulates feathering the appropriate engine propeller.
3. Establishes and maintains a bank toward the operating engine, as required, for best performance in straight-and-level.
4. Follows the manufacturer's prescribed checklists to verify procedures for securing the inoperative engine.
5. Monitors the operating engine and makes necessary adjustments.
6. Requests and receives an actual or a simulated ATC clearance for an instrument approach.
7. Follows the actual or a simulated ATC clearance for an instrument approach.
8. Maintains altitude within 100 feet, the airspeed within ±10 knots if within the aircraft's capability, and heading ±10°.
9. Establishes a rate of descent that will ensure arrival at the MDA or DH/DA, with the airplane in a position from which a descent to a landing, on the intended runway can be made, either straight in or circling as appropriate.
10. On final approach segment, no more than three-quarter-scale deflection of the CDI/glide slope indicator. For RMI or ADF indicators, within 10° of the course.
11. Avoids loss of aircraft control, or attempted flight contrary to the engine-inoperative operating limitations of the aircraft.
12. Complies with the published criteria for the aircraft approach category when circling.
13. Completes landing and manufacturer's appropriate checklists.

XI. Postflight Procedures

Task A: *After Landing, Parking, and Securing*

NOTE: *The examiner shall select Task A.*

References: FAA-H-8083-3; POH/AFM.

Objective: To determine that the applicant:

1. Exhibits satisfactory knowledge of the elements related to after landing, parking, and securing procedures.
2. Maintains directional control after touchdown while decelerating to an appropriate speed.
3. Observes runway hold lines and other surface control markings and lighting.
4. Parks in an appropriate area, considering the safety of nearby persons and property.
5. Follows the appropriate procedure for engine shutdown.
6. Completes the appropriate checklist.
7. Conducts an appropriate postflight inspection and secures the aircraft.

Appendix 2: Task vs. Simulation Device Credit

Airplane Multiengine Land

Task vs. Simulation Device Credit

Examiners conducting the Commercial Pilot–Airplane Practical Tests with flight simulation devices should consult appropriate documentation to ensure that the device has been approved for training, testing, or checking. The documentation for each device should reflect that the following activities have occurred:

1. The device must be evaluated, determined to meet the appropriate standards, and assigned the appropriate qualification level by the National Simulator Program Manager. The device must continue to meet qualification standards through continuing evaluations as outlined in the appropriate advisory circular (AC) or 14 CFR part 60. For airplane flight training devices (FTDs), AC 120-45 (as amended), Airplane Flight Training Device Qualifications, will be used. For simulators, AC 120-40 (as amended), Airplane Simulator Qualification, or part 60 will be used.
2. The FAA must approve the device for training, testing, and checking the specific flight Tasks listed in this appendix.
3. The device must continue to support the level of student or applicant performance required by the PTS.

NOTE: *Users of the following chart are cautioned that use of the chart alone is incomplete. The description and objective of each Task as listed in the body of the PTS, including all notes, must also be incorporated for accurate simulation device use.*

Use of Chart

X   Creditable.

A   Creditable if appropriate systems are installed and operating.

*   Asterisk items require use of FTD or Simulator visual reference.

NOTES:

1. Use of Level 1, 2 or Level 3 FTDs is not authorized for the practical test required by this PTS.
2. For practical tests, not more than 50% of the maneuvers may be accomplished in an FTD or simulator UNLESS:

   a. each maneuver has been satisfactorily accomplished for an instructor, in the appropriate airplane, not less than three (3) times,

OR

   b. the applicant has logged not less than 500 hours of flight time as a pilot in airplanes.

3. Not all Areas of Operation (AOO) and Tasks required by this PTS are listed in the appendix. The remaining AOO and Tasks must be accomplished in an airplane.

Flight Simulation Device Level

Areas of Operation	4	5	6	7	A	B	C	D
II. Preflight Procedures								
A. Preflight Inspection (Cockpit Only)	A	A	X	X	X	X	X	X
B. Cockpit Management	A	A	X	X	X	X	X	X
C. Engine Starting	A	A	X	X	X	X	X	X
D. Taxiing	_	_	_	_			X	X
G. Before Takeoff Check	A	A	X	X	X	X	X	X
IV. Takeoffs, Landings, and Go-Arounds								
A. Normal and Crosswind Takeoff and Climb	_	_	_	_			X	X
B. Normal and Crosswind Approach and Landing	_	_	_	_			X	X
E. Short-Field Takeoff and Climb	_	_	_	_	X	X	X	X
F. Short-Field Approach and Landing	_	_	_	_			X	X
L. Go-Around*/Rejected Landing	_	_	X	X	X	X	X	X
V. Performance Maneuvers								
A. Steep Turns	_	_	X	X	X	X	X	X
VI. Navigation*								
A. Navigation Systems and Radar Services	_	A	X	X	X	X	X	X
B. Diversion	_	A	X	X	X	X	X	X
C. Lost Procedures	_	A	X	X	X	X	X	X
VII. Slow Flight and Stalls								
A. Maneuvering During Slow Flight	_	_	X	X	X	X	X	X
VIII. Emergency Operations								
A. Emergency Descent	_	_	X	X	X	X	X	X
B. Engine Failure During Takeoff Before V_{MC}	_	_	_	_	X	X	X	X
C. Engine Failure After Liftoff (Simulated)	_	_	_	_	X	X	X	X
D. Approach and Landing with Inoperative Engine (Simulated)	_	_	_	_				_
E. Systems and Equipment Malfunctions	A	A	X	X	X	X	X	X
IX. High Altitude Operations								
B. Pressurization	A	A	X	X	X	X	X	X
X. Multiengine Operations								
C. Engine Failure During Flight (By Reference to Instruments)	_	_	X	X	X	X	X	X
D. Instrument Approach – One Engine Inoperative (By Reference to Instruments)	_	_	_	_	X	X	X	X
XI. Postflight Procedures								
A. After Landing, Parking, and Securing	A	A	X	X	X	X	X	X

AIRCRAFT INFORMATION

AIRPLANE MAKE/MODEL _____

WEIGHT   ## AIRSPEEDS

Gross ____ V_{SO} ____

Empty ____ V_{S1} ____

Pilot/Pasngrs ____ V_X ____

Baggage ____ V_Y ____

Fuel (gal × 6) ____ V_A ____

                    V_{NO} ____

CENTER OF GRAVITY V_{NE} ____

Fore Limit ____ V_{FE} ____

Aft Limit ____ V_{LO} ____

Current CG ____ V_R ____

(Instrument panel: ASI, AI, ALT, TC, HI, VSI)

PRIMARY vs. SECONDARY INSTRUMENTS

(IFR maneuvers) -- instruments:
AI, ASI, ALT, TC, HI, VSI, RPM and/or MP
(most relevant to instrument instruction)

	PITCH	BANK	POWER
ENTRY			
primary	____	____	____
supporting	____	____	____
ESTABLISHED			
primary	____	____	____
supporting	____	____	____

FUEL

Capacity   L ___ gal   R ___ gal

Current Estimate L ___ gal   R ___ gal

Endurance (Hr.) ____

Fuel-Flow -- Cruise (GPH) ____

PERFORMANCE DATA

	Airspeed	Power* MP	RPM
Takeoff Rotation	____	____	____
Climbout	____	____	____
Cruise Climb	____	____	____
Cruise Level	____	____	____
Cruise Descent	____	____	____
Approach**	____	____	____
Approach to Land (Visual)	____	____	____
Landing Flare	____	____	____

* If you do not have a constant-speed propeller, ignore manifold pressure (MP).
**Approach speed is for holding and performing instrument approaches.

AIRCRAFT MAINTENANCE RECORDS

Date of Most Recent Annual Inspection [91.409(a)] _____

Date of Most Recent 100-Hour Inspection [91.409(b)] _____

Tachometer Time at Most Recent 100-Hour Inspection _____

Current Tachometer Time _____ Date _____

Date of Most Recent ATC Transponder Tests and Inspections (91.413) _____

Date of Most Recent ELT Inspection [91.207(d)] _____

FAA COMMERCIAL PILOT
ORAL EXAM GUIDE

Aircraft Information

The previous page has a blank form for you to write in information pertaining to the aircraft you will specifically use during the practical test. This page helps you (1) put this information into your long-term memory and (2) get organized and know if your aircraft is airworthy.

Sample Examiner Questions

The following pages contain questions that may be asked by your designated examiner during the oral exam portion of your commercial pilot practical test. We present these questions in the order their associated subjects are listed in the Commercial Pilot Practical Test Standards. However, your designated examiner may ask these questions (or questions that are very similar) in any order (s)he wishes. Because most of the multi-engine Tasks overlap with the single-engine Tasks, we have included multi-engine-specific Tasks separately at the end of the Oral Exam Guide. Starting below is a listing of the Tasks and the pages on which the related questions start. Gleim has removed the seaplane Tasks because the Gleim *Commercial Pilot PTS and Oral Exam Guide* is specific to single- and multi-engine land airplanes.

From PTS Introduction: Page*

Single-Pilot Resource Management (SRM)
1. Aeronautical Decision Making 70
2. Risk Management 73
3. Task Management 77
4. Situational Awareness 78
5. Controlled Flight Into Terrain Awareness 80
6. Automation Management 81

From PTS ASEL Areas of Operation:

I. **Preflight Preparation**
  A. Certificates and Documents - Oral 82
  B. Airworthiness Requirements - Oral 90
  C. Weather Information - Oral 98
  D. Cross-Country Flight Planning - Oral 107
  E. National Airspace System - Oral 115
  F. Performance and Limitations - Oral 121
  G. Operation of Systems - Oral................................. 125
  J. Aeromedical Factors - Oral................................. 140
NOTE: Tasks H and I are Seaplane Tasks.

II. **Preflight Procedures**
  A. Preflight Inspection - Flight 145
  B. Cockpit Management - Flight 147
  C. Engine Starting - Flight 148
  D. Taxiing - Flight 150
  F. Runway Incursion Avoidance - Flight 153
  G. Before Takeoff Check - Flight 155
NOTE: Task E is a Seaplane Task.

*Page number on which questions for Task begin.

The questions in this oral exam guide cover primarily the oral tasks listed in the PTS. Be confident; you will do fine. You can never be totally prepared. If you have studied this book, you will pass with confidence. This book contains the answer to virtually every question, issue, and requirement that is possible on the oral exam portion of the commercial pilot practical test. GOOD LUCK!

Single-Pilot Resource Management (SRM)

1. Aeronautical Decision Making

1.	What are the components of the 3P model used in aeronautical decision making?	Perceive, process, and perform are the three components of the 3P model.
2.	How would the 3P model come into play if you suspected an instrument failure in flight?	Perceive; I would recognize if a conflict existed between supporting instruments that suggested a potential failure. Process; I would determine how significant an effect this potential failure would have on flight safety. For instance, if the failure is in the VSI, it would be a minor issue, but if the failure is of the altimeter, that would be significantly more important. Perform; I would verify the failure and implement the best possible course of action to either continue the flight safely or terminate the flight early in the interest of safety.
3.	The 3P model is associated with another acronym, PAVE. What does PAVE indicate?	PAVE is a reminder for the pilot to evaluate the various aspects that make up a successful flight. PAVE is a means of evaluating the Pilot, Aircraft, enVironment, and External Pressures associated with the flight in an organized manner.

4.	In respect to PAVE, what is the question we want to ask ourselves as it pertains to each point?	For each element of PAVE, the pilot should ask, "What could hurt me, my passengers, or my aircraft?" PAVE is a defensive tool.
5.	What is the rule of thumb when working with the processing phase of the 3P model?	If you find yourself thinking that you'll probably be okay on a given flight, that is a good indication that you really need to take time out for a reality check. "Probably" being okay is not a good starting point for any flight, nor is it an effective approach to risk management.
6.	Is there a reminder associated with the Perform element of the 3P model?	Yes, it's ME. That stands for Mitigate (or eliminate) the risk, then Evaluate the outcome of your actions.
7.	How would you describe the DECIDE model of aeronautical decision making?	The DECIDE model is a six-step process that allows the pilot to use a logical progression when involved in aeronautical decision making.
8.	What are the six elements of the DECIDE model?	Detect, Estimate, Choose, Identify, Do, and Evaluate.
9.	Can you explain the function of each element of the DECIDE model?	Detect recognizes that the pilot in command has detected that a change has occurred. Estimate acknowledges the PIC's need to react to the change. Choose suggests the PIC should select a desirable outcome for the flight. Identify deals with the PIC identifying the steps necessary to successfully deal with the change. Do is the action step, where the PIC actually performs the steps necessary for the situation. And Evaluate is the point where the PIC will evaluate the result of his or her actions.
10.	Does the DECIDE model scenario end with Evaluate?	No, DECIDE is a looping process of thoughts and actions that repeats. After completing the Evaluate element, the PIC would typically run through the process again, starting with Detect each time a change is recognized.
11.	How many recognized hazardous attitudes do pilots need to concern themselves with?	There are five hazardous attitudes that have been identified. They are anti-authority, impulsivity, invulnerability, macho, and resignation.
12.	What is resignation?	That is a passive hazardous attitude. If the pilot takes the attitude, "What's the use?," (s)he will not deal with problems effectively or in a timely manner.

13.	Explain the macho attitude.	The catch phrase is, "I can do it." This is the belief that above all odds, regardless of how significant the issue, I can rise above the problem and save the day. This attitude is dangerous because the pilot assumes (s)he is better than any other pilot, which may lead to taking unnecessary risks.
14.	Are female pilots immune from the macho attitude?	No, the term "macho" is not literal; it merely describes a thought process. Women are equally susceptible to the dangers of the macho attitude.
15.	Why is impulsivity dangerous to a pilot?	The tendency to deal with problems quickly can be taken too far. If the goal is to do something, anything, as quickly as possible, the chances of doing the wrong thing due to a lack of consideration before taking action increases. Impulsivity can lead to accidents that could have been prevented if more time and care had been taken when making decisions.
16.	What is the danger involved in the anti-authority attitude?	Anti-authority runs counter to the concept of cockpit resource management. Rather than availing himself or herself of all the information and assistance available to him or her, the anti-authority pilot shuts out all outside information and aid in order to handle the situation entirely on his or her own. This self-imposed isolation is not conducive to safe flight.
17.	If a pilot was taxiing out to the runway with frost on the wings and shrugged off any suggestions to clear the airplane's surfaces first, what attitude might that indicate?	That would suggest Invulnerability. The pilot knows that frost can be dangerous but has convinced himself or herself that, "It won't happen to me." In truth, frost is an equal opportunity enemy of lift. The pilot should recognize the error of his or her ways, stop, and clean the wings before attempting a departure.
18.	At the halfway point of a cross-country flight, you recognize that headwinds have caused a significantly slower groundspeed than anticipated. Your arrival time will now be 1 hour and 10 minutes later than planned. What concern might you have with that realization?	If my flight time will be extended for 1 hour and 10 minutes, I have to consider my fuel reserves. If I have enough fuel to reach my destination, I very likely would not have enough to meet my reserve needs. My best course of action would be to identify an airport along my route where I could stop for fuel, then make plans to divert to that airport. It is better to be late on arrival with sufficient fuel than to be on time with empty tanks.

19.	While flying a C-172 in high humidity, you notice your RPMs are dropping. Your fuel gauges show more than half tanks available. Oil pressure and temperature are in the green. It is 55°F. What might you do?	With a temperature of 55°F while flying in visible moisture, I would suspect carburetor ice. I would apply carburetor heat in an effort to regain normal power. But while I was waiting for the carb heat to take effect, I would identify the nearest field to divert to should that become necessary. If the carb heat worked, I would apply it periodically to prevent carb ice buildup en route. If it did not work, I would plan a diversion to the airport I had previously identified.
20.	Where should you plan to touch down when landing behind a large aircraft that has just landed on the same runway?	Stay above the preceding aircraft's flight path. Observe where the large aircraft's nose touches down and plan to touch down well beyond that point.
21.	When landing behind a large aircraft that has just taken off on the same runway?	Take note of the location of the large aircraft's rotation point and plan to land well before that point.
22.	How can a risk management assessment benefit you as a pilot?	The PAVE checklist is appropriate for every flight operation. Pilot, Aircraft, enVironment, and External Pressures all come into play when planning, conducting, and concluding a flight. Because my workload is known to rise during the approach and landing phase of flight, it is important that I use a tool that will help assure the balance of safety remains on my side throughout the flight.

2. Risk Management

23.	What are the four fundamental risk elements associated with any flight?	The pilot, the aircraft, the environment, and the type of operation.
24.	What concerns might you have about yourself, the pilot?	I have to be on guard to evaluate my competency to safely conduct the flight. This includes my health, the level of physical and mental stress I am experiencing, my fatigue level, and even my emotional state. Each of these factors has to be considered when I make my go/no-go decisions.
25.	What concerns might we have about the aircraft?	It is my responsibility to consider the limitations of the aircraft, including inoperative components that may be present. I have to be confident that the aircraft's performance capabilities exceed what will be asked of it during the flight, and that it complies with airworthiness requirements.

26.	When we think of the environment, are we considering weather alone?	Not at all. Weather is a significant factor when we consider the environment, but we also have other considerations. The term environment is all encompassing. We consider every aspect of the environment, from weather, to terrain, to ATC services available to us during the flight.
27.	Why are external pressures of significance to our planning processes?	Because external pressures can cause a pilot to make decisions based on factors that can degrade the safety margin of the flight. Meeting deadlines, pleasing people, and accomplishing secondary tasks can push a pilot to take risks that were unnecessary and may be to the detriment of the safety of the flight.
28.	A flight is scheduled for 6:00 a.m. Among the factors to consider is the fact that the pilot completed his or her previous flight at 1:30 a.m. after a full day of flying.	The Pilot element of PAVE encourages us to examine pilot fitness to fly. This pilot has not had adequate rest to safely conduct the flight. Consequently, this flight should be postponed until the pilot has had sufficient rest.
29.	A flight is scheduled for 6:00 a.m. The aircraft has been tied down on the ramp overnight. It rained until past midnight, the temperature has dropped throughout the night, and it is currently 28°F.	The Aircraft element of PAVE encourages us to consider the airworthiness and condition of the aircraft. In this case, moisture on the airframe may have frozen in areas that are difficult to see but may affect aircraft performance. The aircraft should be moved to a heated hangar where the ice can thaw and flow out of the aircraft, or the flight should be postponed until the ambient temperatures allow the ice to thaw. Trapped ice that could inhibit free movement of flaps, ailerons, rudder, or elevator could affect the safety of flight.
30.	The same flight as described in the previous question is scheduled to depart at 6:00 a.m. Light freezing rain has begun to fall. The aircraft has no deice or anti-ice capabilities.	The enVironment element of PAVE encourages us to consider all aspects of the environment that aircraft will be operating in. With no means of deicing wings or propellers, and freezing rain falling, the flight would violate regulations that prohibit flight into known icing by aircraft that are unequipped to deal with those conditions. The safety of this flight would be compromised. The flight should be postponed until more reasonable weather conditions exist.

31.	After explaining that the flight will be delayed because of freezing rain, your passenger insists that he must leave promptly, or an important business deal will fall through. He offers to pay you a considerable amount of money for making the flight.	External pressures can cause a pilot to make poor decisions that may affect the safety of the flight. In this case, neither the importance of the business deal or the money for making the flight negate the fact that freezing rain is falling and your aircraft is not capable of flying in known icing conditions. Regardless of the incentives, the flight must be postponed until conditions improve. Further, private pilots cannot legally accept compensation for performing a flight.
32.	How can a tool like the I'M SAFE checklist help pilots maintain a high level of safety?	Using the I'M SAFE checklist gives pilots a standardized approach to evaluating their fitness for flight, which provides for a more thorough self-examination of our condition.
33.	What are the elements of the I'M SAFE checklist?	Illness, Medication, Stress, Alcohol, Fatigue, and Eating.
34.	If you have had an upsetting argument with your spouse just before leaving home for the airport, what element of I'M SAFE would that fall under?	The Stress element. An upsetting argument with your spouse could cause you to be distracted, or agitated. Neither is a desirable condition for a pilot who is preparing to initiate a flight.
35.	Why is Eating an issue?	In addition to being healthy and well rested, it is equally important for pilots to be adequately nourished so that their thought processes can function normally and their motor skills are well maintained.
36.	What weather phenomenon is suggested by the approach of a fast-moving cold front?	Squall lines can lead fast-moving cold fronts by a significant margin. Although the current weather may be excellent, the squall line can bring violent weather to the area quickly.
37.	When can you expect to encounter hazardous wind shear?	Hazardous wind shear is commonly encountered near the ground during periods of strong temperature inversion and near thunderstorms.
38.	What is a microburst?	Microbursts are small-scale intense downdrafts that, on reaching the surface, spread outward in all directions from the downdraft center.
39.	What effect does encountering a microburst have on an airplane which traverses it?	First the aircraft could see an increase in airspeed (performance gained) from the tailwind. Then the wind will switch to a headwind (performance lost), which could cause contact with terrain.

40.	Under what conditions are microbursts likely?	Microbursts commonly occur within the heavy rain portion of thunderstorms, but also in much weaker, benign-appearing convective cells that have little or no precipitation reaching the ground.
41.	How long do microbursts normally last?	Microbursts seldom last longer than 15 min. from the time they strike the ground.
42.	If the winds are light and the temperature and dew point are 5° or less apart, and closing at your destination airport, what weather phenomenon might this indicate is possible?	When temperature and dew point are within 5° and winds are light, fog and low clouds may form.
43.	Why is fog particularly dangerous to pilots?	Because it hugs the ground, fog may give the appearance of being very thin and easy to see through when viewed from above. On an approach, fog may reduce visibility to near zero, however.
44.	What are the two conditions that can cause fog to form?	Cooling air until the temperature equals the dew point or adding moisture to an air mass.
45.	How can a thunderstorm be identified in flight?	Lightning flashes are an excellent indicator of a thunderstorm. However, if the thunderstorms are embedded it may be impossible to determine where the thunderstorm is specifically located.
46.	What is one way of avoiding thunderstorms when they are embedded?	The best course of action is not to fly in those conditions. Embedded thunderstorms are an extreme hazard to aircraft and should be avoided at all times.
47.	What resource will provide the most accurate indication of turbulence along your route?	Pilot reports are the most accurate indication of turbulence in flight.
48.	What is the 5P model?	The 5P model is a method of systematically assessing risk in five specific areas that are pertinent to flight.
49.	What are the five areas associated with the 5P model?	Plan, Plane, Pilot, Passengers, and Programming.
50.	How does Plan relate to the 5P model?	Plan relates to the planning of the flight. It is a reminder to take care and gather all pertinent information for the flight as it relates to the route, fuel requirements, the weather, NOTAMs, etc.

51.	How does Plane figure into the 5P model?	The airworthiness of the aircraft is critical to safety, so the Plane heading reminds pilots to verify the aircraft's mechanical fitness for flight, be familiar with its systems and their operation, and ensure that all required paperwork is in order.
52.	Other than being present, how is the Pilot aspect of the 5P model important?	Showing up for the flight is important, but the pilot also has to realistically self-evaluate his or her health, fatigue and stress levels, and any medications (s)he may have taken. The I'M SAFE checklist can be a great aid to the pilot in making these determinations.
53.	How does Passengers relate to safety in terms of the 5P model?	Passengers come in all types. Some are experienced pilots who may be able to help in an emergency. Others are noticeably uncomfortable with the idea of flying and may need to be reassured in turbulence or if an unexpected occurrence should rattle them. Knowing what sort of passengers you have on board, and recognizing how to deal with them in various flight situations can positively affect the safety of flight.
54.	The last P in the 5P model is Programming. What does Programming have to do with the flight?	As cockpits transition to glass panels, automated systems become more common, and GPS navigation becomes a primary navigation tool, the importance of verifying the integrity and currency of databases and software is increased. The Programming line item in the 5P model literally refers to the programming that runs so many of the tools that a pilot may make use of today, and the importance of verifying that it is accurate and appropriate for the flight.

3. Task Management

55.	Give me an example of where the ability to prioritize tasks might be important in flight.	If I had been cleared by ATC to proceed to a visual checkpoint, for instance, and had a map light go out while I was nearing the checkpoint. The priority would be to proceed as instructed, then deal with the map light issue. If I attempted to deal with the light first, I might miss the checkpoint and cause a safety issue to other aircraft, and increase the workload for ATC.

56.	Are there situations before the flight departs when prioritization might be important?	Yes, when acting as PIC, it is always important to recognize the need to prioritize. Even before leaving the ground, it is possible that a passenger might want to ask questions while ATC is passing along instructions. It would be my responsibility to recognize that the ATC communication is the priority task. I would indicate to the passenger that I needed to focus my attention on ATC momentarily and would be free to answer questions afterward.
57.	What about a situation in which there are no apparent problems, such as when entering the airport traffic pattern. Is there any need to prioritize your planning or your actions then?	Yes. Although everything is going according to plan, my priority is to set myself and the aircraft up for the next phase of the flight, prior to reaching that point. For pattern entry, I want to have reviewed the airport diagram and have become familiar with the airport area well in advance of arrival. I would have my radio set up for the airport early. By prioritizing the need to prepare, my flight will be less stressful and safety will be enhanced.

4. Situational Awareness

58.	What is situational awareness?	Situational awareness refers to the pilot's accurate perception of the operational and environmental factors that affect the flight. It is about being aware. That awareness includes everything from the position of the aircraft in relation to other aircraft, its position in relation to a fix or a given runway, recognition of the terrain the aircraft is flying over, current weather conditions, resources available the pilot, and even the type and use of the instrumentation available in the cockpit.
59.	Why is good situational awareness so important?	A pilot who has a high level of situational awareness can make better decisions than one who is less aware. Situational awareness allows the pilot to make better decisions, earlier, than the pilot who is struggling to see how the flight, and the available resources, fit into any given scenario.

60.	Can you give me an example of when situational awareness is beneficial to a pilot?	When entering the airport traffic pattern, a good sense of situational awareness will allow the pilot to have a sense of where (s)he is in relation to the runway and airport. That situational awareness will prevent him or her from being surprised or caught off guard when unforeseen circumstances occur. The pilot will also be more confident in his or her awareness if familiar with the physical environment (s)he is flying in, with knowledge of the current weather, obstacle heights, and the location and intention of other traffic.
61.	Can you give me an example where a lack of situational awareness could be a problem while in flight?	Perhaps the most obvious example would be the pilot who enters the approach and landing phase of flight without adequate preparation and planning. Poor situational awareness might cause him or her to violate airspace, cause a collision hazard, or result in forgotten or skipped steps that could lead to an accident. This lack of basic situational awareness can lead to tragic results.
62.	What is fixation?	Fixation is the tendency to focus on one instrument, or a single issue, to the exclusion of everything else.
63.	Why is fixation such a serious issue in instrument or visual flight?	Fixation is a potential problem for any pilot, but it is especially important for visual pilots to guard against because we need to incorporate all the information available to us in order to maintain flight safety. As an example, if I was to focus on just the altimeter, my heading would tend to wander. If I was to focus on just the GPS ground track, my altitude might vary enough to create a problem. All the while my focus would be inside the cockpit rather than outside, itself a serious hazard to flight safety.
64.	Can you give me a real world example of how serious fixation can be?	Perhaps the best known example was Eastern Airlines Flight 401. The entire crew became fixated on a burned out gear indicator light, which prevented them from noticing that the aircraft was descending over terrain with no lights. By the time they recognized the problem, there was no time left to correct it. More than 100 passengers and crew were killed in that case, in large part due to the fixation of the crew.

5. Controlled Flight Into Terrain Awareness

65.	What does the acronym TAWS stand for?	TAWS is an abbreviation of Terrain Awareness and Warning System.
66.	What does the abbreviation GPWS stand for?	GPWS refers to the Ground Proximity Warning System.
67.	Do all aircraft have TAWS or GPWS installed?	No, but it is the pilot's responsibility to understand the specific system if it is installed and be able to use it correctly in order to enhance safety.
68.	Are there similarities between the TAWS and the GPWS?	Yes, both systems are designed to give the pilot warnings meant to prevent accidents due to an excessive sink rate or flight into terrain.
69.	Can a TAWS or GPWS always prevent controlled flight into terrain (CFIT) accidents?	No, there are limitations to aircraft performance that must be understood and planned for when flying in mountainous or other potentially hostile environments. Good planning and a high level of situational awareness are necessary to ensure safe flight, regardless of instrumentation and equipment available on board.
70.	Can you give me an example of a CFIT accident scenario that could be prevented through good planning and maintaining situational awareness?	The classic example may be the poor decision to fly into a box canyon. With insufficient room to turn around, and insufficient performance to climb above the walls of the canyon, the accident becomes unavoidable as soon as the pilot enters the canyon, regardless of how long or far (s)he can fly before running out of clear airspace.
71.	Are there other circumstances where CFIT accidents can be prevented?	Yes, the Steve Fossett crash is a good example of a good pilot who suffered a serious accident due to performance issues. The NTSB found that Fossett's Bellanca was forced into the ground by winds that exceeded his airplane's ability to overcome them. His crash is a good reminder that wind and weather can cause a CFIT accident. It is for that exact reason that it is so important that pilots maintain a sense of situational awareness and plan flights in such a way that the performance of their aircraft can deal with the situations that may arise during any given flight.

| 72. | Is CFIT as much of a danger for VFR operations as it is for IFR operations? | It could be argued that Controlled Flight Into Terrain is a greater danger for VFR operations because the pilot feels more visually aware of the outside world. It is the risk of CFIT that makes it imperative that pilots maintain an awareness of risk elements like minimum altitudes, go-around procedures, and rising terrain in the vicinity of their departure/destination airports. While the see-and-avoid concept is certainly important, adherence to established information and practices is equally imperative. |

6. Automation Management

73.	How can you verify the mode of operation your autopilot is in?	The specific method differs from unit to unit, based on manufacturer, but in general there is an enunciation on the display that reads out the mode.
74.	If you were tracking a VOR with the autopilot, what mode would you be using?	NAV mode would be the appropriate choice when tracking a VOR radial.
75.	How can I manually transition from one mode to another?	The specific process varies by manufacturer and model, but in general you can manually transition from one mode to another by using a selector button located on the panel. Mode buttons are typically labeled HDG, NAV, and APR, although there may also be additional modes for reverse course and/or altitude.
76.	Can you give me an example of a situation that might surprise a pilot with an unanticipated mode change on the autopilot?	Unanticipated mode changes can catch a pilot by surprise and are often self-induced. Input errors, or misunderstanding how the autopilot works in various modes, can result in the pilot issuing a command to do something other than that which (s)he intended.
77.	How would the Garmin G1000 indicate that it was using the GPS or localizer information for navigation?	The HSI needle is magenta when the unit is using GPS information. It switches to green when it is tracking the localizer.

Single-Engine Land

Area of Operation I: Preflight Preparation

Task A: Certificates and Documents

78.	What certificates and documents must be on board the aircraft for it to be considered legal?	Remember **A.R.R.O.W. A**irworthiness certificate, **R**egistration, **R**adio station license (if you are flying outside the U.S.), **O**perating limitations, and **W**eight and balance.
79.	What are the items required to be carried with you in order to act as pilot in command (PIC)?	To act as PIC of an aircraft, you are required to carry your pilot's certificate and medical certificate or driver's license, whichever is appropriate. All pilots acting as PIC must carry a government-issued photo ID as a means of positively identifying themselves.
80.	What documents should you carry on your person when operating the airplane in flight?	A valid pilot certificate, a current and valid medical certificate, and a government-issued photo ID (a driver's license satisfies this requirement).
81.	Must you notify the FAA of a change of address?	Yes. If your address changes, you must notify the FAA in writing within 30 days, or you may not exercise the privileges of your pilot certificate.
82.	Where can pilot certification requirements be found?	Pilot certification requirements can be found in 14 CFR Part 61.
83.	What is an advisory circular (AC)?	ACs are documents used by the FAA as a means of issuing nonregulatory information to pilots, mechanics, and manufacturers.
84.	What is the definition of night?	It is the time between the end of evening civil twilight and the beginning of morning civil twilight, as published in the American Air Almanac, converted to local time.
85.	Are the currency requirements for carrying passengers at night the same as the currency requirements for carrying passengers during daylight hours?	Not quite. To carry passengers during daylight hours, a pilot is required to log three landings within 90 days in the same category and class of aircraft the passenger will be carried in. But to carry passengers at night, a pilot is required to make three night landings to a complete stop within 90 days in the same category and class of aircraft.
86.	Is there any exception for carrying passengers that requires full-stop landings during daylight hours?	Yes, if the pilot wishes to carry passengers in a tailwheel-type airplane, the three landings must be to a full stop and made in a tailwheel-type airplane, regardless of whether the flights will be made during the daylight or night hours.

87.	Define the responsibility and authority of the pilot in command.	The pilot in command is the final authority as to the operation of the aircraft. (S)he is responsible for the safety of the crew and all passengers on board the aircraft.
88.	When would you need to obtain a flight review to remain legal to act as pilot in command?	You would need to obtain a flight review within 24 months of successfully completing your commercial pilot practical test. You would then need to complete a flight review every 24 months with a certified flight instructor or a designated pilot examiner.
89.	What is the minimum age requirement to qualify for a commercial pilot certificate for a single-engine airplane?	To be eligible for a commercial pilot– airplane certificate, a person must be at least 18 years old, regardless of whether the certificate includes a single-engine or multi-engine rating.
90.	As PIC (pilot in command), what is your responsibility to your passengers with regard to safety belts?	As PIC, you must brief your passengers on the operation of the safety belts, and notify your passengers when belts must be worn.
91.	How long is a third-class medical certificate valid?	A third-class medical certificate is valid until the end of the 60th calendar month following the date of the examination if you were under 40 years of age on the day of the medical exam. If you were 40 years old or older on the day of the exam, then the certificate is valid until the end of the 24th calendar month following the date of the examination.
92.	How long is a second-class medical certificate valid?	It remains valid as a second-class medical certificate for 12 months. At that point, it reverts to being valid as a third-class medical certificate, which would allow you to exercise your private pilot privileges. For private pilots, a second-class medical certificate is valid for 60 months, provided the pilot was under 40 years old on the date of the examination. For pilots who are over 40 years old on the date of the examination, a second-class medical certificate is valid for 24 months after the month the medical examination was conducted; it is a second-class medical certificate for the first 12 months and a third-class medical certificate for the remaining 12 of the total 24-month time period.

93.	How long is a first-class medical certificate valid?	A first-class medical certificate is valid for 6 months; after that time it reverts to a second-class medical certificate. Twelve months after the date of issue, it will downgrade to third-class status and will remain so until its ultimate expiration. For pilots under 40 years old on the date of the examination, the total period of validity is 60 months after the month of the examination. For pilots over 40 years old on the date of the examination, expiration occurs at the end of the 24th month after the examination was conducted.
94.	What class of medical certificate must a commercial pilot hold?	To exercise the privileges of a commercial pilot, you must carry at least a second-class medical certificate that is valid and current.
95.	What flight experience must be entered into a pilot's logbook?	The only flight experience that is required to be entered into a pilot's logbook is that experience which is required for obtaining a certificate or rating, completing a flight review, or meeting recency of experience requirements.
96.	Are there established airworthiness requirements for pilots?	Yes, there are a number of requirements a pilot must meet in order to be considered current. These include a flight review every 24 months and three takeoffs and landings within 90 days to be current to carry a passenger. A commercial pilot is also obligated to be in possession of a current and valid medical certificate.
97.	How would a pilot show that (s)he meets those currency requirements required of pilots in order to act as PIC?	A pilot can show currency through logbook records and endorsements. Landings, and the dates they occurred, should be recorded in the pilot's logbook, and an endorsement acknowledging the successful completion of a flight review should also be included.
98.	What is a flight review?	A flight review is a mandatory period of instruction and evaluation that pilots must successfully complete within a 24-calendar-month period in order to act as pilot in command (PIC). The flight review must include a minimum of 1 hour of ground instruction and 1 hour of flight instruction.
99.	Who can provide the services required for a flight review?	An appropriately rated certified flight instructor (CFI) or a designated pilot examiner can each conduct a flight review.

100.	If you do not obtain a flight review within 24 calendar months, how can you become legal to act as PIC again?	If I do not successfully complete a flight review within 24 calendar months, I can seek out flight and ground instruction as necessary to become proficient again, and complete a flight review with a CFI or a designated pilot examiner.
101.	If you add a rating to your pilot certificate, does that satisfy the need for a flight review, or do you still need to complete a flight review without regard for the new rating?	Adding a new rating to a pilot certificate satisfies the requirement for a flight review, and the 24-month time period restarts on the date the new rating was acquired.
102.	Can the CFI you took instruction from provide you with a flight review?	Yes. A flight review can be completed with any appropriately rated certified flight instructor or a designated pilot examiner.
103.	If you have completed your flight review and are current to act as PIC, are you automatically current to carry passengers as PIC?	No. In order to act as PIC when carrying passengers, I must make three takeoffs and three landings every 90 days, in addition to completing a flight review. If the airplane is a tailwheel type, the landings must be to a full stop in a tailwheel-type airplane. To carry passengers at night, I would need to make three landings within 90 days to a full stop at night.
104.	What is required to act as PIC of a complex, high-performance, or tailwheel airplane?	To act as PIC of a complex, high performance, or tailwheel airplane, you are required to receive and log ground and flight training and obtain a logbook endorsement from an appropriately rated CFI.
105.	What is required to act as PIC of a turbojet-powered aircraft, or one with a gross weight over 12,500 lb.?	To act as PIC of a turbojet-powered aircraft, or one with a gross weight of over 12,500 lb., you are required to have a type rating.
106.	Give an example of an aircraft category.	Aircraft category is a broad classification of aircraft that includes airplane, rotorcraft, and lighter-than-air aircraft.
107.	Give an example of an aircraft class.	Aircraft class is used to describe aircraft that fall into a similar classification, such as landplane, seaplane, single-engine, or multi-engine.
108.	Give an example of an aircraft type.	Aircraft type refers to a specific make and model of aircraft. A Piper Cub is a type. A Cessna 172 is another type.

109.	Where is the registration located in your aircraft?	(NOTE: The location of the registration may vary from one aircraft to another, even when referencing aircraft of the same type. Typically, the registration is displayed in a clear plastic holder mounted in the cockpit. Be sure to cover the exact location of required documents with your instructor, using the actual aircraft in which you will be taking your practical test.)
110.	How long is an aircraft's registration certificate valid?	An aircraft's registration is valid until the aircraft is destroyed or scrapped, the owner loses his or her U.S. citizenship, ownership is transferred, the owner requests the cancelation of the registration, or 30 days have elapsed since the death of the certificate holder.
111.	Does the airworthiness certificate alone guarantee that the aircraft is airworthy?	There are inspections and maintenance requirements that must be done on a regular basis in order for the airplane to continue to be airworthy. The annual inspection or the 100-hour inspection are good examples of inspections that must be completed in order to maintain the aircraft's airworthiness.
112.	Where would I find a copy of the operating limitations for your aircraft?	The Pilot's Operating Handbook (POH) or Aircraft Flight Manual (AFM) include the operating limitations, although the placards in the aircraft that establish limits are also considered a part of the operating limitations.
113.	Give an example of a placard in the aircraft that would be considered an operating limitation.	A placard that is mounted to the instrument panel that prohibits intentional spins would be considered an operational limitation.
114.	Where would I find performance charts that are appropriate to the aircraft we will be flying today?	The POH or AFM will have the appropriate charts for takeoff and landing distances; weight and balance information; time, fuel, and distance charts; and other pertinent information specific to this airplane.
115.	Where can a listing for the best glide speed in this airplane be found?	In the POH or AFM for the aircraft.
116.	How can you determine V_A for today's flight?	V_A, or maneuvering speed, varies with the weight of the aircraft. The POH or AFM will specify what V_A is at a given weight.

117.	Which color code on the airspeed indicator shows us what maneuvering speed is?	Maneuvering speed is also known as V_A. It is not shown on the airspeed indicator because V_A changes with the weight of the aircraft. We have to look to our performance charts in the POH or AFM to find the appropriate V_A speed for the aircraft as it is loaded for that flight.
118.	What does V_A, or maneuvering speed, indicate?	V_A is the maximum speed that will allow an airplane to stall before suffering structural damage. It is often unintentionally misrepresented as the top speed that full control inputs can be applied without causing structural damage.
119.	Does V_A increase or decrease as the weight of the aircraft decreases?	V_A decreases as the aircraft weight decreases because the lighter aircraft is more susceptible to damage at a lighter weight due to sudden movements caused by turbulence or abrupt control inputs.
120.	What does the green arc on the airspeed indicator tell us?	The green arc indicates the normal operating range for the aircraft.
121.	What does the bottom of the green arc indicate?	The bottom of the green arc indicates the stall speed with flaps retracted.
122.	What does the white arc on the airspeed indicator tell us?	The white arc indicates the full flap operating range.
123.	What does the bottom of the white arc suggest?	The bottom of the white arc is the power-off stalling speed with flaps set to the landing position.
124.	What does the top of the white arc indicate?	The top of the white arc is the maximum speed that we should fly with full flaps extended. When decelerating for landing, it is the speed where it becomes safe to extend the flaps.
125.	What is V_{NO}?	V_{NO} is the maximum structural cruising speed.
126.	How can you identify V_{NO} on the airspeed indicator?	V_{NO} is identified by the airspeed at the top of the green arc, as shown on the airspeed indicator.
127.	What is V_{NE}?	V_{NE} is the maximum speed the aircraft can attain without risking structural damage.
128.	How is V_{NE} indicated?	V_{NE} is indicated by a red line at the top of the yellow arc on the airspeed indicator.

129.	What is an STC?	STC stands for supplemental type certificate. An STC allows an aircraft to be modified from its original type certificate to include a variety of modifications, such as a larger engine, vortex generators, the use of auto gas, the addition of floats for seaplane operations, or the use of non-original covering materials.
130.	How do we know if the aircraft is loaded within its CG limit when we fly today?	I calculated a weight and balance problem using both pilot and passenger weights in the aircraft, as well as our fuel load. We will be safely within the prescribed CG envelope, and our gross weight is under the maximum allowed for the aircraft. (NOTE: Show the examiner your calculations.)
131.	Where did you find the numbers (or charts) that you made your calculations with?	The weight and balance charts are included in the POH or AFM for the aircraft. I used those numbers for a starting point, then included our weights and the weight of our fuel load and baggage to calculate an accurate gross weight and CG location for today's flight.
132.	Other than CG, what other issue is of importance when doing a weight and balance calculation?	We need to verify the total weight of the loaded aircraft. We need to be sure that we do not overload the aircraft. My calculations for today's flight indicate that we are within the CG envelope and below the maximum weight for the loaded aircraft.
133.	How did you calculate the CG of this aircraft?	The POH includes weight and balance graphs, which can be used to determine the moment of each weight loaded into the aircraft. By adding together all the weights, and adding together all the moments, then dividing the total moment by the total weight, the resulting number represents the CG of the aircraft. If a Center of Gravity Moment Envelope is included in the POH, we can verify that the CG falls within limits by finding the intersection of the total weight of the aircraft with the total moment of the loaded aircraft. As long as the intersection of the two lines is within the envelope, the aircraft's CG is within limits.

134.	If there is no Center of Gravity Moment Envelope in the POH, how can you be sure we are within CG and weight limits?	The POH will list a range that the CG must fall into. If my calculated number falls within that range, we are safely within CG limits. The POH also lists a maximum gross weight for the aircraft. If our weight is below that number, and the CG is within limits, we have loaded the airplane appropriately for the flight.
135.	If the owner of the aircraft installed a new radio last week, would we have to include that in our weight and balance calculations?	No. The mechanic who installed the radio would have amended the aircraft's paperwork to reflect the new empty weight and moment of the aircraft. We can make our calculations based on the information provided in the aircraft's records, which are kept current as they are required to be.
136.	How much does aviation gasoline weigh?	Avgas weighs 6 pounds per gallon.
137.	Why does the weight of gasoline matter to us?	Because the amount of fuel we carry has a profound effect on the safety of the flight beyond just the quantity required to reach our destination. Fuel is being consumed during the entire flight. We need to be sure that our weight and CG are acceptable before taking off. But we should also calculate an estimated fuel burn for the flight, and verify that the fuel we burn during our flight is not going to cause our CG to shift forward or aft of the limits en route.
138.	Can auto gasoline be used in an airplane?	If the airplane is an older design, it can only use auto gas if an STC (supplemental type certificate) has been acquired that will allow the use of auto gas in that specific airplane. Many newer airplanes, such as those using Rotax 912 engines, are certified to use auto gas of a specific octane.
139.	Is weight and balance calculated any differently for an airplane that uses auto gas?	No, the principles are the same, and the same weight of 6 lb. per gallon is used as a reference in the calculations.

Task B: Airworthiness Requirements

140.	What instruments and equipment are required for day VFR flights?	Tachometer, oil pressure gauge, magnetic direction indicator, airspeed indicator, temperature gauge, oil temp, emergency equipment (flotation gear when over water), anticollision light, fuel gauge, landing gear indicator lights (if equipped), altimeter, MP gauge (if equipped), ELT, and seatbelts.
141.	Is there a mnemonic device to help remember the instruments and equipment required for daytime VFR flights?	Yes, I use TOMATOE A FLAMES to help remember the full list. T – Tachometer O – Oil pressure gauge M – Magnetic direction indicator (compass) A – Airspeed indicator T – Temperature gauge O – Oil temperature gauge E – Emergency equipment (flotation gear when over water, beyond gliding distance to shore) A – Anticollision lights F – Fuel gauge for each tank L – Landing gear position indicator A – Altimeter M – Manifold pressure gauge for each altitude engine (turbocharged/supercharged) E – Emergency locator transmitter (ELT) S – Safety belts/shoulder harnesses
142.	Where could I find a complete list of those required instruments for VFR daytime flights?	The complete list is included in the Federal Aviation Regulations, 14 CFR Part 91.205.
143.	When is a transponder with Mode C required for VFR flight?	A working transponder with Mode C is required any time you are above 10,000 ft. MSL, inside Class B or Class C airspace, above Class B or Class C airspace up to 10,000 ft. MSL, or within 30 NM of a Class B primary airport.
144.	When are safety belts required to be worn by all occupants?	Safety belts and shoulder harnesses, if installed, are required to be worn by all occupants during taxi, takeoff, and landing.
145.	Is the VSI a required instrument for VFR flight during nighttime hours?	No, the VSI (vertical speed indicator) is not a required instrument during VFR for day or nighttime hours.

146.	Is a radio required equipment for VFR flight?	It depends on the type of airspace you intend to fly in. If you will be flying into Class B, Class C, or Class D airspace, a radio is required. However, if your flight is entirely in Class G airspace, there is no requirement to make radio contact with ATC during your flight.
147.	Is a landing light a requirement for night VFR flight?	A landing light is only required for night VFR if the flight is conducted for hire.
148.	Can you give an example of some other equipment requirements that pertain to night VFR?	The pilot is required to have access to spare fuses of each type required to operate the systems on board. The aircraft must also have position lights installed, and the airplane must have a source of electrical power.
149.	Would it be legal to fly a small airplane that had no anticollision light system?	In some cases, yes. Small airplanes certificated before March 11, 1996, are not required to have anticollision lights installed and can be flown legally without them if the operation is limited to daytime VFR.
150.	Can an airplane operate in VFR at night if no anticollision light system is installed?	No, a requirement for VFR night operations is the installation of an approved red and white anticollision light system.
151.	Can we legally fly an aircraft if the installed VSI does not work?	It is not legal to fly in an aircraft with inoperative instruments or equipment unless the specific actions listed in 14 CFR 91.213 are performed. But the VSI is not a required instrument, so if the steps required to fly with inoperative equipment were taken, it would be legal to fly with an inoperative VSI.
152.	How would we know which steps to take under 14 CFR 91.213 should we have an inoperative instrument or equipment on board?	The remedies for inoperative equipment are broken down into a few basic options, depending on whether the aircraft operates with an approved minimum equipment list or not. We would select the appropriate option as listed in the regulations, based on that primary determining factor.
153.	What is the purpose of an MEL (minimum equipment list)?	The MEL is designed to provide aircraft owners and operators with the authority to operate an aircraft with certain items or components inoperative. Ironically, the minimum equipment list is a compendium of equipment and instrumentation that if inoperative, will not prevent the aircraft from being eligible for flight.

154.	Are all aircraft required to maintain an MEL?	No, most general aviation airplanes operate without an MEL.
155.	If your aircraft has an MEL, what are our options when confronted with inoperative equipment or instruments?	We can fly legally if the inoperative equipment or instrument is listed on the MEL. Being included on the list signifies that the FAA has approved that the level of safety of the flight can be maintained through appropriate operating limitations, a transfer of function to another operating component, or by reference to other instruments or components that provide the required information.
156.	If you have an inoperative instrument or equipment and your aircraft has no MEL, how do you know if it is legal to fly?	We can fly legally under very specific circumstances, which can be verified through a four-part test. We must confirm that the instrument or equipment is (1) not included on the mandatory VFR instrument and equipment list, (2) not included on the aircraft's required equipment list for the type of flight being conducted, (3) not required by any FAR, and (4) not required by an Airworthiness Directive (AD).
157.	If the inoperative instrument or equipment passes the four-part test, is there anything else we need to do before we fly?	Yes, provided the pilot or a certificated mechanic verifies that the inoperative instrument or equipment will not create a hazard to the flight, the item must be removed from the airplane, with the cockpit control placarded and the maintenance properly recorded, or the item must be deactivated and placarded as "inoperative."
158.	Are there requirements for operating an aircraft when an item or items on the MEL are inoperative?	Yes, the pilot must observe appropriate operating limitations, or the function of the inoperative item must be transferred to another instrument or component that will provide the required information or operational function.
159.	Can you give me an example of how we could legally fly an aircraft with an installed instrument that is not working?	If the pilot or a maintenance person deems that the inoperative equipment does not present a hazard, we can fly with it. The instrument/equipment must be removed, deactivated, or labeled, "inoperative" for us to fly the aircraft without violating the regulations. Using the broken VSI as an example, it would be legal to cap the vacuum inlet and placard the instrument as "inoperative." That would allow us to fly without violating a regulation or compromising safety.

160.	If we remove inoperative equipment or instruments, do we have to do anything else before flying?	Whenever a piece of equipment or an instrument is removed from the aircraft, the weight and balance information included with the aircraft must be amended to reflect the change in empty weight and the empty weight CG.
161.	If our airplane has an inoperative instrument or equipment that is required by regulation, is the airplane grounded until repairs are made?	Not necessarily. We could apply for a special flight permit that would allow us to move an otherwise unairworthy airplane to a base where the appropriate repairs could be made.
162.	When would a special flight permit be required?	If the airplane has inoperable instruments or equipment and it needs to be moved to a location where the repair work can be performed, a special flight permit would be required.
163.	What is implied when a special flight permit is requested?	The implication is that the airplane does not meet the current airworthiness requirements, but that it can be flown safely in order to get it to an airport where repairs can be made.
164.	Who would you request a special flight permit from?	The FAA issues special flight permits. I would contact my local FSDO to make the request.
165.	What information would you provide when requesting a special flight permit?	I would provide information about the purpose of the flight, the itinerary, and the crew required to operate the airplane. I would also provide information regarding how the airplane is currently deficient in meeting the airworthiness standards and any restrictions I consider necessary for the safe operation of the aircraft.
166.	Is a special flight permit requested verbally or in writing?	It is requested in writing, and all the information required to complete the request is included in writing as well.
167.	What specifically would you do to obtain a special flight permit?	I would submit a written request to the nearest FSDO that included the purpose of the flight, a proposed itinerary, a listing of required crew members, a specific explanation of why the airplane does not currently comply with airworthiness requirements, an explanation of any restrictions that would be necessary in order to conduct the flight safely, and any other information the FAA might deem necessary in order to establish operating limitations for the flight.

168.	What is an Airworthiness Directive (AD) and why is it issued?	An AD is issued by the FAA when there is a safety issue with a particular type of aircraft, engine, or appliance. ADs are mandatory and must be complied with within a certain time frame, unless the AD specifically indicates otherwise.
169.	How is an emergency AD different from a less urgent AD?	Emergency ADs may require inspection or repair before another flight can be made. Less urgent ADs often allow for a longer compliance period, which will allow the owner/operator to continue flying the aircraft until a future inspection or maintenance procedure is scheduled.
170.	Are ADs mandatory or voluntary?	ADs are mandatory. The AD is a written regulation that requires action within a specific time period, unless a specific exemption is granted.
171.	How do you know if an AD has been issued for your airplane?	ADs are listed on the FAA website, which allows for an easy search to see if any ADs exist for my airplane. An AD search is a required part of any 100-hour or annual inspection. The mechanic who endorses the logbooks for my airplane would have recorded any ADs that pertained to my airplane, along with the method of compliance that was employed.
172.	How can we tell if an Airworthiness Directive (AD) that was issued for your aircraft has been complied with?	There will be an entry in the appropriate maintenance log that reflects the work being performed.
173.	How can we be sure an AD that requires ongoing inspections will be complied with in a timely manner?	A record will be included in the maintenance logs by the mechanic doing the work. The record will include the next time or date that work is required in order to comply with the AD.
174.	If an AD does not require recurring action, how would we be able to determine that it had been complied with in the past?	A record of the AD and the method of compliance would be included in the aircraft's maintenance logs.
175.	Are there established airworthiness requirements for aircraft?	Yes, there are a number of requirements that aircraft owners and operators must comply with to maintain their aircraft in airworthy condition. These requirements include maintenance, record keeping, and compliance with airworthiness directives.

176.	What type of airframe inspections is an aircraft required to have undergone to be considered airworthy?	An aircraft must have undergone an annual inspection within the preceding 12 calendar months to be considered airworthy. If an aircraft is used for commercial operations, it is also required to have undergone an inspection within the preceding 100 hr. of operation, or it must be included in a progressive inspection program.
177.	Is the annual inspection required just for the airframe?	No, the entire aircraft must be included in the annual inspection, including the condition of the engine and propeller.
178.	How often must a transponder be tested and inspected to be considered airworthy?	You may not operate a transponder unless it has been inspected and tested within the preceding 24 calendar months.
179.	Who is responsible for keeping the airplane in an airworthy condition?	The owner or operator is responsible for making sure the airplane is kept in an airworthy condition.
180.	How do we establish a record that indicates if an aircraft is airworthy?	By maintaining maintenance logbooks that detail inspections and maintenance done to the aircraft throughout its life.
181.	Are all the inspections and maintenance recorded in the same log?	No, there are typically three maintenance logbooks for an aircraft. There is an airframe logbook, a powerplant logbook, and a logbook for the propeller.
182.	What type of maintenance records is the owner required to keep for an aircraft?	Maintenance records must be kept for the current status of life-limited parts (propeller, engine, etc.), the current status of all ADs, and any preventive maintenance done by the pilot.
183.	What are the required inspections for an ELT?	An ELT must have been inspected in the preceding 12 calendar months to be legal. Also, the ELT battery must be replaced after 1 hr. of cumulative use or after 50% of its useful life.
184.	If you hear an ELT distress signal when tuned to 121.5 MHz at 13:02, what does that indicate?	It may indicate an emergency. It may also indicate that a mechanic, aircraft owner, or pilot is testing an ELT nearby. ELTs may be tested in the first 5 minutes after the hour. To verify, it would be wise to monitor 121.5 MHz to see if the signal continues. If it does, the appropriate action would be to report the ELT signal to the authorities.
185.	How is an ELT activated?	An ELT can be activated either manually by flipping the switch on the physical unit or automatically by an impact to the airplane.

186.	What signal does an ELT emit?	ELTs emit a distress signal on 121.5 MHz. The signal itself sounds like a pulsing siren or like a laser gun in an old fashioned video game. The FAA describes the sound as a "downward swept audio tone."
187.	Must your airplane be equipped with a working ELT before beginning a flight?	Yes. ELTs are always required unless exempt under FAR Part 91.207. An example of when an aircraft is not required to have an ELT is if that aircraft is used for flight instruction within 50 NM of the home airport.
188.	What is the recommended duration for an ELT test?	The *Aeronautical Information Manual* suggests no more than three audible sweeps of the alarm when testing.
189.	Is an airplane owner who is not an A&P mechanic allowed to perform any type of maintenance on his or her airplane?	Yes. An airplane owner who is not a certificated mechanic is allowed to perform preventive maintenance, such as oil changes.
190.	Who is qualified to perform and make a logbook endorsement for a 100-hour inspection?	An airframe and powerplant mechanic (A&P).
191.	Who is qualified to perform and make a logbook endorsement for an annual inspection?	An airframe and powerplant mechanic with inspection authorization (IA).
192.	Why are some aircraft required to undergo a 100-hour inspection and an annual inspection, while others are only required to undergo an annual inspection?	Aircraft used in commercial operations are required to undergo 100-hour inspections in addition to the annual inspections all aircraft are required to undergo.
193.	Is there any other option besides the 100-hour and annual inspections?	Yes, you can enroll the airplane in a progressive inspection program that meets or exceeds the requirements for the 100-hour and annual inspections.
194.	What is the difference between a 100-hour inspection and an annual inspection?	The only difference between a 100-hour inspection and an annual inspection is the requirement for who makes the logbook endorsement. An A&P mechanic can make logbook endorsements for a 100-hour inspection. Only an A&P mechanic with inspection authorizations (IA) can make the logbook endorsements for an annual inspection.

195.	If you were 5 hours away from home when you realized that your airplane was 3 hours overdue for a 100-hour inspection, could you legally fly home to get the work done?	Yes. It is permissible to fly up to 10 hours past the point of the 100-hour inspection, provided the aircraft is being flown to a place where the inspection can be completed.
196.	If you do fly beyond the 100-hour time limit by 10 hours, when is the next 100-hour inspection due?	The aircraft would be due for inspection immediately, and the 10 hours would be deducted from the next 100-hour inspection period. The 100-hour inspection requirement is not extended by flying past the 100-hour limit. The next inspection would occur at the same number of hours it was originally intended to be performed at.
197.	Who is primarily responsible for maintaining accurate records pertaining to maintenance on the aircraft?	The owner or operator is primarily responsible for maintaining appropriate maintenance records.
198.	As the PIC, are you involved in the process of keeping maintenance records?	Yes, the PIC can be construed as one of the operators of the aircraft.
199.	How would you locate the most recent 100-hour or annual inspection in the aircraft's logbooks?	I would go to the most recent entry and work backwards until I found the endorsement for the most current 100-hour or annual inspection.
200.	Can you give me a couple of examples of mandatory inspections that we might find records for in the aircraft logbooks?	All mandatory inspections and required maintenance should be included in the aircraft's logbooks. This would include any ADs issued for the airframe, engine, or appliances; 100-hour inspections; annual inspections; ELT inspections; and transponder and static system inspections.
201.	If the aircraft has been modified in some way, how might that be recorded in the maintenance logs?	The FAA allows aircraft to be modified through the use of supplemental type certificates (STCs). The STC would be included in the logbook and would be appropriate if a larger engine were installed, floats for seaplane operations were added, or a fabric covering other than the material originally used were applied to the airframe.

Task C: Weather Information

202.	What is a METAR?	A METAR is a current weather observation that is updated at a regular interval and applies to a 5-mile radius around the observation point (usually at any airport), reporting wind, visibility, storm activity, ceilings, temperature, altimeter setting, and remarks.
203.	Are METAR observations made by human observers or machines?	Both trained human observers and machines such as an AWOS or ASOS are used to gather the information that is presented in a METAR.
204.	What is a TAF?	A TAF is a forecast of conditions expected over the next 24 hr. within a 5-statute mile radius around an airport. They report wind, visibility, significant weather, sky condition, and possible wind shear.
205.	How often are TAFs updated?	TAFs are updated four times a day.
206.	If it exists, how do TAFs indicate wind shear?	TAFs indicate forecast wind shear with the code WS after the sky conditions segment.
207.	Why is wind shear dangerous?	Wind shear is dangerous because it is unpredictable, and it can cause significant changes in heading, airspeed, and altitude, especially close to the ground.
208.	What is a PIREP?	A PIREP is a pilot weather report. PIREPs are important sources of observed weather aloft.
209.	How is a PIREP submitted?	PIREPs are submitted by pilots on EFAS.
210.	How can a pilot receive a PIREP?	PIREPs can be received from EFAS or an FSS.
211.	What type of information can be found in an area forecast (FA)?	An FA is a forecast of clouds and general weather conditions over an area that includes several states.
212.	How often is an area forecast updated?	Area forecasts are updated three times a day.

213.	What is included in an area forecast (FA)?	An FA contains four sections: the communication and product header, precautionary statement, synopsis, and VFR clouds/weather section. The communication and product header indicates the date and time of issuance, valid times, and area of coverage. The precautionary statement indicates icing, low-level wind shear, and IFR conditions (non-MSL heights are denoted by AGL or CIG). The synopsis is a brief summary of the location and movement of fronts, pressure systems, and circulation patterns. The VFR clouds/weather section contains a 12-hr. specific forecast and a 6-hr. outlook and covers possible weather hazards such as IFR conditions, icing, thunderstorms, and wind shear.
214.	What is standard sea level temperature and pressure?	Standard sea level temperature is 15°C (59°F). Standard sea level pressure is 29.92" Hg. These numbers are important for completing important calculations, such as true airspeed, current lapse rate, and density altitude.
215.	What is the standard lapse rate?	The standard lapse rate is 2°C per 1,000 ft. of altitude gained.
216.	What is the Coriolis force?	The Coriolis force is a theory that explains how wind, pressure, and general weather patterns deflect to the right in the Northern Hemisphere. The Coriolis force is the reason wind and weather patterns generally move from west to east (left to right) in the United States.
217.	What is the significance of a close temperature-dew point spread?	A close temperature-dew point spread indicates the probable formation of visible moisture in the form of dew, mist, fog, or clouds. A decrease in temperature (most frequently at night) can result in a close temperature-dew point spread and fast-forming fog.
218.	What are the characteristics of stable air?	Stable air is characterized by continuous precipitation, smooth air, and poor visibility.
219.	What are the characteristics of unstable air?	Unstable air is characterized by showery precipitation, rough air, and good visibility.
220.	What is clear air turbulence (CAT)?	CAT is turbulence not associated with thunderstorms. It usually occurs along an upper-level temperature inversion.

221.	Why is clear air turbulence (CAT) dangerous?	It is dangerous because it is often unexpected and can be severe.
222.	What are three types of structural icing?	Clear ice, rime ice, and mixed ice. Clear ice forms when drops are large, as in rain or in cumuliform clouds. It is hard, heavy, and unyielding. Rime ice forms as a result of small drops found in stratified clouds and drizzle. Air becomes trapped in between the drops and makes the ice appear white. Mixed ice is a combination of clear and rime ice.
223.	Does frost have the ability to significantly degrade aircraft performance?	It is important not to operate with frost on the wings because even a seemingly thin coating of frost can degrade aircraft performance by up to 40%.
224.	Where is in-flight weather information available?	In-flight weather information is available via any of the following services: • EFAS (En Route Flight Advisory Service) • HIWAS (Hazardous In-Flight Weather Advisory Service) • FSS (Flight Service Station) • TWEB (Transcribed Weather Broadcast) (in Alaska only) • ATIS (Automatic Terminal Information Service) • ASOS (Automated Surface Observation Service) • AWOS (Automatic Weather Observation Service) EFAS is also known as "Flight Watch" and is available almost anywhere in the country on 122.0 MHz. You can file a PIREP and obtain numerous types of weather information with EFAS. HIWAS is a recorded briefing of hazardous weather over select VOR frequencies. FSS frequencies are shown on navigational charts and are usually available for ATC. TWEB is a recorded broadcast of current and adverse weather conditions over select VOR and NDB frequencies. ATIS is recorded weather information for a terminal area. ASOS and AWOS are automated weather reporting stations found at many airports.

225.	Where is weather information available on the ground?	Weather information is available on the ground from a Flight Service Station (FSS), Direct User Access Terminal Service (DUATS), and Telephone Information Briefing Service (TIBS). You can speak to a pre-flight briefer at FSS and/or receive TIBS by calling 1-800-WX-BRIEF anywhere in the country. DUATS is a free service available to pilots on the Internet and by phone. With DUATS, you can receive weather information and file a flight plan. TIBS is recorded weather information that can be obtained by calling 1-800-WX-BRIEF.
226.	What is a SIGMET?	SIGMETs are weather advisories issued for conditions that could pose a risk for aircraft and may include severe icing not associated with thunderstorms, clear air turbulence, dust storms, and volcanic eruptions.
227.	What is a convective SIGMET?	Convective SIGMETs are issued for severe thunderstorms, embedded thunderstorms, lines of thunderstorms, and tornadoes, all of which imply severe or greater turbulence, severe icing, and low-level wind shear.
228.	What is an AIRMET?	AIRMETs are issued for moderate icing, moderate turbulence, IFR conditions over 50% of an area, sustained surface winds of 30 kt. or greater, nonconvective low-level wind shear, and mountain obscuration.
229.	What is a center weather advisory (CWA)?	A CWA is an advisory provided by ATC for potentially hazardous weather expected to happen within the next 2 hours.
230.	What are the four types of fronts and of what significance is this to aviation?	The four types of fronts are cold, warm, stationary, and occluded. Each front indicates a different type of weather.
231.	What type of weather is associated with a cold front?	Cold fronts usually contain the most volatile weather. Because cold air replaces warm air quickly, the difference in pressure is the greatest, with the potential for violent weather.
232.	What type of weather is associated with a warm front?	The weather associated with a warm front is usually relatively mild. Warm front weather is usually much more widespread and longer lasting than that of cold front weather.

233.	What type of weather is associated with a stationary front?	A stationary front is when warm and cold air masses meet but do not mix. Wind always blows along the frontal boundary of a stationary front and, in some cases, embedded storms occur.
234.	What is an occluded front?	An occluded front is a combination of cold, warm, and cool air. Thus, weather in occluded fronts is a combination of cold- and warm-front weather.
235.	What are the types of fog and how are they formed?	The fog types include radiation, advection, precipitation induced, upslope, and ice. Radiation fog forms when the air close to the ground is cooled faster than the air above it (usually at night or near daybreak). Advection fog forms along coastal areas when the water is warmer than the air around it. Precipitation-induced fog forms when relatively warm rain or drizzle falls through cool air and evaporation from the precipitation saturates the cool air. Upslope fog forms as a result of moist, stable air being cooled adiabatically as it moves up sloping terrain. Ice fog occurs in cold weather when the temperature is well below freezing and water vapor sublimates directly into ice crystals.
236.	What conditions must be present for a thunderstorm to form?	Formation of a thunderstorm requires a lifting action, an unstable lapse rate, and sufficient water vapor.
237.	What is a microburst?	A microburst is a heavy downdraft occurring within a thunderstorm.
238.	How long does a microburst typically last?	A microburst usually lasts for about 10 minutes, with the maximum intensity winds lasting for 2 to 4 minutes.
239.	Why is a microburst hazardous to aircraft?	Microbursts are hazardous to aircraft because of the extreme downward force of the winds coming from the downdraft. Downdrafts become stronger as they encounter the surface and begin to move horizontally, flowing outward from the base of the thunderstorm. The vertical speed of the downdraft may exceed the aircraft's ability to climb. Surface winds can be strong enough to cause significant degradation of performance to aircraft in flight.
240.	What type of flying weather do low-pressure systems present?	Low-pressure systems are quite often regions of poor flying weather.

241.	What type of flying weather do high-pressure systems present?	High-pressure systems are predominantly regions of favorable flying weather.
242.	What direction does air flow around a high-pressure system?	Air currents move clockwise around a high-pressure system.
243.	What direction does air flow around a low-pressure system?	Air currents move counter-clockwise around a low-pressure system.
244.	Is there a good method of remembering which way air currents move around high- or low-pressure systems?	Think of the short arm of the L as an arrow. You can use that memory aid to help remember that the air moves counter-clockwise around a low, and in the opposite direction around a high-pressure system.
245.	What does a radar summary chart show us?	A radar summary chart displays areas of precipitation, as well as information about the type, intensity, configuration, coverage, echo top, and cell movement of that precipitation.
246.	What is the abbreviation we use to identify radar weather reports?	We use the two letter abbreviation, SD, to identify radar weather reports. The radar summary chart is a collection of SDs in one graphic display.
247.	Does radar detect clouds?	No, radar primarily detects particles of precipitation in a cloud or falling from a cloud.
248.	Does the radar summary chart only show information gathered by radar?	The radar summary chart can also include severe weather watch areas, which are plotted if they are in effect when the chart is valid.
249.	What do wind and temperature aloft forecasts indicate?	Wind and temperature aloft forecasts indicate the wind speed and direction, as well as temperature at various altitudes.
250.	What can a pilot determine from these forecasts?	Pilots can make decisions regarding cruise altitudes and route selection that will make the best use of the most favorable winds and temperature inversions when planning flights.
251.	How many different types of wind and temperature aloft charts are there?	There are two types of wind and temperature aloft charts: forecast and observed.
252.	What is the primary difference between the two types of wind and temperature aloft charts?	The forecast wind and temperature aloft charts include expected conditions, while the observed wind and temperature aloft charts include information that reflects the actual conditions.

253.	How are wind direction and speed indicated on a wind and temperature aloft chart?	An arrow indicates the direction of the wind, while barbs on the tail of the arrow indicate wind speed.
254.	How is temperature indicated on the wind and temperature aloft charts?	It is printed out in Celsius, just above and to the right of the circle that indicates the reporting station.
255.	How does the wind and temperature aloft chart indicate a calm wind?	Calm winds are indicated by the number "99," which is printed to the lower left of the circle that identifies the reporting station.
256.	What major weather information is provided on surface prognostic charts?	Surface prognostic charts show high- and low-pressure centers, fronts, and significant troughs, as well as forecast precipitation and/or thunderstorms.
257.	There are two types of significant weather prognostic charts. What is the difference between them?	Significant weather prognostic charts are presented as either high-level or low-level versions. Pilots flying piston engine airplanes are primarily concerned with the low-level version because it covers the altitudes in which pilots generally operate.
258.	What is the distinguishing characteristic of significant weather prognostic charts?	They contain four panels. The lower two panels show 12- and 24-hour prognostic charts for the surface, while the upper two charts show the 12- and 24-hour prognostic charts for the surface up through 24,000 ft. MSL.
259.	Do significant weather prognostic charts show weather reports or weather forecasts?	The significant weather prognostic charts are forecasts of what weather conditions are expected to be at the valid time of the charts.
260.	How often are significant weather prognostic charts updated?	Significant weather prognostic charts are issued four times a day, based on the synoptic data at 0000Z, 0600Z, 1200Z, and 1800Z.
261.	What information do the upper panels of the significant weather prognostic charts depict?	The upper panels show forecasts for IFR and MVFR, as well as turbulence and freezing levels.
262.	What would indicate an area of MVFR weather?	A scalloped line encloses an area of forecast MVFR weather on the upper panels of the significant weather prognostic charts.
263.	What would indicate an area of IFR weather?	A smooth line encloses an area of forecast IFR weather on the upper panels of the significant weather prognostic charts.

264.	What does a number expressed as a fraction indicate on the significant weather prognostic charts?	The upper number indicates the anticipated top of a turbulent layer in hundreds of feet MSL, while the bottom number indicates the forecast base of that turbulent layer.
265.	Does the significant weather prognostic chart indicate areas of icing?	No. While it does indicate areas of precipitation and freezing levels, it does not indicate icing directly.
266.	What is the purpose of the convective outlook chart?	The convective outlook chart is a 48-hr. outlook for thunderstorm activity presented in two panels.
267.	What geographic area is shown in the convective outlook chart?	The convective outlook chart indicates possible thunderstorm and severe thunderstorm activity for the continental United States.
268.	In a convective outlook chart, what is the difference between the information presented in the left-hand and right-hand panels?	The left-hand panel covers the first 24-hr. period starting from 1200Z. The right-hand panel covers the forecast thunderstorm activity for the following 24-hr. period.
269.	What are the risk categories used to indicate the possibility of severe thunderstorm activity in an area?	The risk categories are slight, moderate, and high. There is also a note that reads, "See Text" that indicates a slight risk may exist, but the risk was not sufficient enough to warrant including the notation in the forecast with the current information. Pilots should refer to the textual convective outlook for additional information when "See Text" is included in a convective outlook chart.
270.	If a thunderstorm that does not meet the definition of a severe thunderstorm is expected, is a risk category assigned to that area on the convective outlook chart?	No. If forecast thunderstorms are not expected to be severe, there is no risk category included for that area in the convective outlook chart.
271.	What is an AWOS?	AWOS stands for Automated Weather Observing System. It is an older automated reporting system that may provide only basic weather information, or it may provide a complete automated METAR. AWOS capabilities vary from location to location.
272.	What is ASOS?	ASOS is also an automated system. The abbreviation stands for Automated Surface Observing System. The ASOS is being phased in, replacing the older and more limited AWOS.

273.	What is ATIS?	The Automatic Terminal Information Service is a continuous broadcast of recorded information pertinent to a specific terminal area. Winds and runway information are commonly included in ATIS broadcasts to inform pilots and lower the workload on controllers.
274.	How are AWOS, ASOS, or ATIS of value to a pilot in the air who is approaching an airport with the intention of landing?	By listening to the broadcast prior to entering the pattern, or prior to contacting the tower at a controlled airport, the pilot can be familiar with a wide assortment of pertinent information regarding field conditions, winds, active runway information, and NOTAMs.
275.	Do AWOS, ASOS, and ATIS have any value to a pilot on a cross-country flight whose route takes him or her near an airport where these services are available?	Even while en route, a pilot can monitor these broadcasts to be aware of the current altimeter setting and possible NOTAMs that are being broadcast.
276.	What is the limitation of AWOS, ASOS, and ATIS broadcasts that pilots should be aware of?	Because they are automated, the information being broadcast may not be current. In the case of the ATIS recorded broadcasts, the information broadcast can be as much as an hour old. Pilots should be aware of this limitation and plan accordingly.
277.	If we were at an airport with only one runway and you calculated a crosswind component of 15 knots, would that affect your decision to take off?	I would make my go/no-go decision based on the maximum crosswind component listed for my aircraft in the POH. If the crosswind were above that maximum crosswind component, I would not fly. If it were below the maximum crosswind component, I would base my decision on my level of experience, the terrain, and the existence of obstacles in the area that might cause a safety issue. If in doubt, I would not fly.
278.	If you were planning a flight on a day with light rain forecast, would that affect your plans?	If the ceiling was high enough to allow for adequate cloud clearance and the visibility was above VFR minimums, the fact that light rain was forecast would not automatically cause me to cancel the flight.
279.	If you were planning a flight on a day with light rain forecast and the freezing level was at 1,000 feet, would that affect your plans?	Yes, I would cancel the flight. Even light rain can cause a rapid and dangerous build-up of ice when flying above the freezing level.

280.	If your destination airport was reporting visibility below VFR minimums due to fog, but your navigation log suggested the flight would take 75 minutes, would you depart as planned or wait?	I would probably wait. If I had sufficient fuel, I could legally make the flight and opt not to land if the fog had not cleared. But the fog could also lift into a low layer of clouds that might prevent a safe landing. Until I had a better indication that the conditions would be above VFR minimums at my projected arrival time, I would delay my takeoff.
281.	If you had not flown in 11 weeks and intended to take a passenger flying but found the weather to be MVFR at the time of your intended departure, would you fly?	Not under those conditions. If I had flown recently and was sure my skills were sharp, I would consider MVFR weather for a local flight or a cross-country flight into improving weather. After more than 2 months away from the cockpit, I would want to fly under good, VFR conditions until I felt comfortable and competent enough to add to my work-load by flying in less than VFR weather.
282.	A pilot report from a B-737 reports moderate turbulence in your area at an altitude you intend to fly. How would this affect your decision-making process?	I would reconsider my flight, my route of flight, or the altitude I chose to fly. Pilot reports are subjective based on the type of aircraft being flown. If a B-737 is reporting moderate turbulence, I may very well experience that to a much greater degree.
283.	What are three weather conditions that would absolutely make you cancel or postpone a cross-country flight?	Without a doubt, I would not fly into an area with a fast-moving cold front, embedded thunderstorms, or reports of fog at my destination airport. Any of those conditions would make me delay my flight until conditions improved, or cancel it altogether.
284.	In the future, would you be inclined to limit your flying to days and times when the weather is clear and calm?	No. I certainly would enjoy flying under those conditions, but I would base my decision on when and where to fly on my competence, the type of equipment I would be flying with (including the aircraft and instrumentation), and the weather conditions. Over time, I expect increased experience to enhance my abilities and my judgment, allowing me to fly safely when the conditions are less than ideal.

Task D: Cross-Country Flight Planning

285.	What is the first step when diverting to a new destination?	The first step is to turn to the approximate heading of the new destination. This will allow you to fly towards the destination while you are figuring out the exact heading and distance. Moreover, in the event that the diversion is due to an emergency, it is vital to divert to the new course as soon as possible.

286.	What are the important calculations needed for a safe, successful diversion?	When diverting to an alternate airport, it is important to calculate the exact heading and distance to the alternate airfield. Then calculate ground speed, arrival time, and fuel needed to get there.
287.	What errors are magnetic compasses subject to?	Magnetic compasses are subject to northerly and southerly turning, acceleration, and compass card oscillation errors. Compasses are not subject to magnetic variation, but it is an error that must be compensated for.
288.	What is magnetic variation?	Magnetic variation is the difference in degrees between true north and magnetic north. Although the magnetic field of the Earth lies roughly north and south, the Earth's magnetic poles do not coincide with its geographic poles, which are used in construction of aeronautical charts.
289.	What is magnetic dip?	Magnetic dip is the tendency of the compass needles to point down as well as point to the magnetic pole. The resultant error is known as dip error, which is greatest at the poles and zero at the magnetic equator. It causes northerly and southerly turning errors as well as acceleration and deceleration errors.
290.	What is northerly and southerly turning error?	If the airplane is on a northerly heading and turns east or west, the compass will lag. If the airplane is on a southerly heading and turns east or west, the compass will lead the actual airplane heading. REMEMBER: North Lags, South Leads. Northerly and southerly turning error is the most pronounced of the dip errors.
291.	What is acceleration error?	When on east or west headings, acceleration causes compasses to indicate a turn to the north. Deceleration causes compasses to indicate a turn to the south. REMEMBER: Accelerate North, Decelerate South (ANDS). Acceleration error is in part due to the dip of the Earth's magnetic field. Because the compass is mounted like a pendulum, the aft end of the compass card is tilted upward when accelerating and downward when decelerating during changes of airspeed.
292.	What is compass card oscillation?	Compass card oscillation error results from erratic movement of the compass card, which may be caused by turbulence or abrupt flight control movement.

293.	What type of information do sectional charts provide?	Sectional charts provide topographical, physical (roads, railroad tracks, etc.), airport, NAVAID, and airspace information for a specific geographic location.
294.	We will be simulating a cross-country flight to KABC during our flight. How will you be monitoring our route of flight en route?	(Produce the appropriate sectional chart and indicate to your examiner the route and checkpoints you have chosen for the flight.)
295.	How can we be sure that the sectional chart we use today is current and valid?	The effective date and the expiration date are both printed on the sectional chart right under its name.
296.	Since we are making this flight under VFR conditions, is it acceptable to use a road map to assist in our navigation?	There is no rule that prevents us from using road maps as a navigational aid, but a sectional chart would be a better choice. The road map does not include much of the information we need to fly safely. Radio frequencies, the location and height of obstructions, and airport locations are generally not included on road maps.
297.	If we were flying into a satellite airport located inside Class B airspace, which VFR navigational chart would we use?	The sectional chart is a good reference for a wider area. But if we were flying into a satellite airport that is located within the boundaries of Class B airspace, we would be better off using a VFR terminal area chart. The scale is 1:250,000, which gives us much better indications of specific landmarks that will be important when operating in the confines of Class B airspace.
298.	If we were planning a flight that would traverse across several states, which charts would we use for planning purposes?	We would use the appropriate sectional charts for the actual flight, but for planning purposes, I would use a world aeronautical chart (WAC) because the scale allows for a broader, "big picture" view of my route. After picking my route based on the WAC, I would plan the flight out in greater detail using the sectional chart.
299.	How is a Class B airport depicted on a sectional chart?	Class B airspace is indicated by heavy blue circular lines. The floor and ceiling of each layer of the Class B airspace is included.
300.	How is Class C airspace depicted on a sectional chart?	Class C airspace is shown as solid magenta lines. The floor and ceiling of each layer of the Class C airspace is included.
301.	If the chart shows a number written like a fraction with 40 over 12, what does that mean?	The fraction indicates that the altitude of the depicted airspace extends from 1,200 feet MSL to 4,000 feet MSL.

302.	What does a dashed magenta line surrounding an airport located in Class D airspace indicate?	The dashed magenta line indicates Class E airspace that extends up from the surface.
303.	What does a light magenta-shaded line indicate?	The light magenta-shaded line indicates that Class E airspace extends upward from 700 ft. AGL. Outside the line, the Class E airspace extends upward from 1,200 ft. AGL.
304.	How is Class G airspace depicted on sectional charts?	Class G airspace is not depicted on sectional charts. It is implied to exist anywhere that controlled airspace does not exist, extending upward from the surface to the floor of overlying controlled airspace.
305.	Can you show me a maximum elevation figure on the sectional chart and tell me what it indicates?	The maximum elevation figure (MEF) is shown as a large, bold, two-digit number, indicating the highest elevation in a given quadrangle. The MEF indicates altitude in thousands and hundreds of feet. As an example, 12 means 1,200 ft. MSL.
306.	What steps should you take to determine your position if you suspect you are lost?	First, if conditions permit, initiate a climb. Climbing allows you to see farther so that you can identify a prominent landmark. If you cannot verify your position visually, you can triangulate using VORs, ask ATC for help, or utilize GPS if it is available.
307.	What determines a good visual checkpoint when planning a flight?	Visual checkpoints should be distinctive and easily recognizable. A large lake, a very tall or large building, an intersection of two highways, or something similarly unique makes a good visual checkpoint.
308.	What would be a less than desirable checkpoint?	Anything that can easily get lost in the ground clutter. Some buildings or landmarks that look obvious when viewed from the ground are significantly less obvious when viewed from the air. Small ponds or streams are also poor landmarks because they can be almost invisible when viewed from altitude.
309.	What is the risk when using lakes as checkpoints?	Depending on the area and the season, lakes may change size or shape, or they may disappear depending on whether the season is particularly wet or dry. When using lakes as a checkpoint in an unfamiliar area, it is a good idea to have a secondary landmark to verify your position.

310.	How far apart would you select checkpoints when flying cross-country?	I would select my first checkpoint within 5 miles of my departure point, to verify that I am on my route. Subsequent checkpoints would be approximately 10 miles apart.
311.	Define the different types of altitude.	Altitude types include indicated, true, pressure, absolute, and density. 1) Indicated altitude is read directly from the altimeter after it is set to the local altimeter setting. 2) True altitude is the vertical distance of the aircraft above sea level. 3) Pressure altitude is the altitude indicated on the altimeter when the altimeter setting is adjusted to standard pressure. Pressure altitude is indicated altitude adjusted for nonstandard pressure. 4) Absolute altitude is the vertical distance of the aircraft above ground. 5) Density altitude is pressure altitude corrected for nonstandard temperature.
312.	When flying in an area with no tall ground-based obstructions, would you rather cruise at 1,500 AGL or 3,500 AGL?	It would depend on the reason for the flight. On a local flight, I might fly lower rather than burn the fuel to climb higher on a short flight. But flying cross-country, I would rather fly at a higher altitude to take advantage of the better visibility, longer range of radio communications, and improved radio and visual navigation.
313.	Other than obstructions, what would be a consideration when selecting a cruise altitude for a cross-country flight?	I would be aware of the winds aloft and try to select an altitude that would provide me with either the most beneficial tailwind or least detrimental headwind for the trip.
314.	If flying cross-country at a higher altitude is better than flying at a low altitude, would it be reasonable to plan all our cross-country flights at 8,500 ft. MSL or 9,500 ft. MSL?	Not necessarily. The airplane's performance decreases as altitude increases. Also, for short trips, the time to climb to high altitudes is often inefficient. Planning a 50-mile flight at 8,500 feet MSL might be impractical since we would spend the majority of the flight climbing and descending. On the other hand, if the flight required a greater ground distance, flying at a higher altitude would be a better choice.
315.	What is groundspeed?	Groundspeed is the actual speed at which the aircraft is moving over the ground.

316.	How do you determine an accurate groundspeed?	We can calculate an estimated groundspeed by using the E6B (flight computer) to show the relationship between the true airspeed and any headwind, crosswind, or tailwind component. In flight, we can measure an actual groundspeed by timing ourselves as we pass two points over a known distance and by using the E6B to indicate our groundspeed.
317.	What is true airspeed?	True airspeed is calibrated airspeed, or indicated airspeed corrected for non-standard temperature and pressure. True airspeed at higher altitudes is greater than indicated airspeed due to the less-dense air at higher altitudes.
318.	How will you verify that you are completing all the appropriate steps for the various phases of flight, from takeoff through landing?	I will be using the checklists included in the POH for this specific aircraft type throughout the flight to verify that the aircraft is always configured appropriately and that I have completed all the necessary steps suggested for each phase of flight.
319.	What information do you need to have in order to accurately estimate your fuel requirements for a cross-country flight?	I would need to know the distance between my departure point and my destination, the estimated fuel burn for the aircraft, and the winds aloft. That would allow me to determine an accurate estimate of how long the flight would be and how much fuel I would be likely to use during the trip.
320.	If your aircraft burns 6 gallons of fuel per hour, would it be acceptable to depart on a 2-hour flight with 15 gallons of fuel on board?	No, that would be an insufficient fuel load. Because all fuel tanks contain a certain amount of unusable fuel that cannot be delivered to the engine, 15 gallons would not allow us enough range to complete the flight and still fulfill the required 30-minute additional fuel supply required for daytime VFR flights.
321.	How do you use VORs to triangulate your position?	First, tune in and identify a nearby VOR station (you may need to climb to pick up the signal). Center the CDI with a FROM indication. Draw a line on the chart to indicate the radial you are on. Repeat this process for neighboring VOR. The point where the lines intersect is your position.
322.	Why do we identify NAVAIDs like VORs and NDBs by Morse code when we first tune them in?	NAVAIDs can share frequencies, just like airports without an operating control tower can share common CTAF frequencies. We need to identify a NAVAID to know that it is working properly and that it really is the NAVAID we want, located in the place we expect it to be.

323.	What is one reason a VOR might not be broadcasting its identifier?	The facility may be undergoing maintenance. The identifier may not be broadcast in that case because the signal may be unreliable.
324.	Can we still navigate using a NAVAID that is not broadcasting an identifier?	If no identifier is being broadcast, we have no way of knowing if we are tuned into the correct NAVAID or if the signal being broadcast is reliable and accurate. If we cannot positively identify a NAVAID, we should not navigate by it.
325.	Is it legal to use a handheld GPS to navigate a cross-country flight?	Yes, it is legal. But in the interest of safety, it would be advisable to work out a navigation log and use pilotage and/or dead reckoning to verify our position throughout the flight.
326.	What is one advantage of navigating with a GPS unit as opposed to another type of navigational aid?	The GPS allows the pilot to navigate directly to the destination. There is no need to navigate in a zig-zag pattern from one NAVAID to another in order to reach your destination.
327.	Can you give me an example how a GPS might be an asset if the weather suddenly worsened or mechanical difficulties occurred in flight?	The GPS offers a "nearest" function that can be very helpful in an emergency situation or when the conditions of flight change significantly. Pressing a single key will provide me with the course and distance to the nearest airport, which lessens the workload while providing important information quickly.
328.	Why is it a good idea not to rely too heavily on a GPS unit, or any single NAVAID, for navigation?	The unit in the aircraft could fail, obstructions may interrupt the signal, or the ground-based NAVAID could fail or go down for maintenance. We should always have a backup plan when flying, especially when flying cross-country.
329.	Are weather updates on your GPS unit always available?	XM weather updates are available for many GPS units on a subscription basis.
330.	How would you make use of weather updates on your GPS, if they are available?	If an active subscription allows for accurate weather updates on the unit in my aircraft, I would use the weather information for avoidance only, by altering my route to skirt thunderstorms that are indicated to exist on my route of flight.
331.	How will you find the appropriate radio frequencies for your departure airport?	Radio frequencies are listed on the sectional chart, as well as in the *Airport/Facility Directory (A/FD)*.

332.	If the *A/FD* lists a tower frequency and a CTAF for your destination airport, which would be the appropriate frequency to use?	The *A/FD* would list the hours of operation for the tower. If I had any doubts, I could monitor the frequency inbound to determine whether the tower was operating or pilots were self-announcing on the CTAF. And I could always call the airport to confirm the tower's hours of operation before departing.
333.	How could you get pertinent weather and airport information prior to arriving at your destination airport?	I could tune to the ASOS, AWOS, or ATIS frequency before making my initial call to the destination tower or CTAF, depending on which service the airport offers.
334.	What information does an *Airport/Facility Directory* provide?	An *Airport/Facility Directory (A/FD)* provides all the information needed for an airport or radio navigation aid (NAVAID). *A/FDs* also provide published NOTAMs and areas of parachute and aerobatic activity.
335.	What information does the *Aeronautical Information Manual (AIM)* provide?	The *AIM* provides information regarding airport operations, navigation aids, flight operations, airspace, and ATC procedures.
336.	Where can regulatory information such as fuel requirements, airspace, and flight rules be found?	All flight rules that apply to general aviation are in FAR Part 91.
337.	How can we be sure that the runway at KABC is long enough for us to land on safely?	(Produce an *A/FD* and show the examiner the information pertinent to your destination airport. Also assure the examiner that you have used the landing distance performance chart included in your POH to verify that the runway at your destination is sufficiently long to accommodate your aircraft based on the current weather conditions for that airport.)
338.	Which publication would I go to if I needed to be sure fuel would be available at my destination?	The *A/FD* would tell us what types of fuel are available at the airport. If the airport symbol included on the sectional chart includes ticks, that would indicate that fuel is available, too.
339.	What is a NOTAM?	NOTAM is an acronym that stands for Notice to Airmen. NOTAMs are aeronautical information that could affect the decision to make a flight.
340.	How would you become aware of a NOTAM that might affect your flight?	The NOTAM information would be available through a standard weather briefing.
341.	Can you request information regarding a specific NOTAM from a weather briefer?	Yes, the database is available to weather briefers, and I could request specific NOTAM information using the appropriate airport or NAVAID identifier.

342.	How would you file a VFR flight plan?	I would file a VFR flight plan with the FSS by phone, using the information pertinent to my specific flight, as filled out on the FAA Flight Plan Form. I could also file by radio, or via the Internet with DUAT.
343.	What is a NASA Aviation Safety Reporting Program (ASRP) report?	The NASA ASRP is a voluntary program designed to gather information about deficiencies in the aviation system.
344.	When should a NASA Aviation Safety Reporting Program report be filed?	When a Federal Aviation Regulation is violated inadvertently and does not involve a criminal offense, filing a NASA ASRP report within 10 days may prevent an enforcement action.
345.	Should we always complete a navigation log for a cross-country flight?	Yes. It is important that pilots do not become overconfident and embark on cross-country flights without doing the necessary cross-country flight planning.
346.	Is filing a VFR flight plan mandatory?	No, but it is a good idea. Filing a VFR flight plan is the only way to be sure that search and rescue crews will be dispatched if we do not show up at our destination as expected.
347.	When will a search begin for a flight that has filed a VFR flight plan?	A search will begin 30 minutes after your scheduled arrival time at your destination. This is why it is important to close a VFR flight plan: to prevent an unnecessary search from being launched.
348.	How can you close your VFR flight plan?	It can be closed in flight by contacting FSS using the radio, or it can be closed on the ground by contacting FSS by phone.

Task E: National Airspace System

349.	What are the minimum VFR cloud clearance and visibility requirements for Class A airspace?	VFR minimums do not apply in Class A airspace because VFR is not normally permitted. However, there are exceptions if approval is granted prior to flight.
350.	What are the minimum VFR cloud clearance and visibility requirements for Class B airspace?	The minimum VFR cloud clearance and visibility requirements in Class B airspace are clear of clouds and 3 miles visibility.
351.	What are the minimum VFR cloud clearance and visibility requirements for Class C airspace?	The minimum VFR cloud clearance and visibility requirements in Class C airspace are identical to those that affect Class D airspace. They are as follows: 500 ft. below clouds, 1,000 ft. above clouds, 2,000 ft. horizontally from clouds, and 3 miles visibility.

352.	What are the minimum VFR cloud clearance and visibility requirements for Class D airspace?	The minimum VFR cloud clearance and visibility requirements in Class D airspace are identical to those that affect Class C airspace. They are as follows: 500 ft. below clouds, 1,000 ft. above clouds, 2,000 ft. horizontally from clouds, and 3 miles visibility.
353.	What are the minimum VFR cloud clearance and visibility requirements for Class E airspace below 10,000 ft. MSL?	The minimum VFR cloud clearance and visibility requirements in Class E airspace below 10,000 ft. MSL are 500 ft. below clouds, 1,000 ft. above clouds, 2,000 ft. horizontally from clouds, and 3 miles visibility.
354.	What are the minimum VFR cloud clearance and visibility requirements for Class G airspace below 1,200 ft. AGL during the day?	The minimum VFR cloud clearance and visibility requirements in Class G airspace below 1,200 ft. AGL during the day are clear of clouds and 1 mile visibility, regardless of MSL altitude.
355.	What are the minimum VFR cloud clearance and visibility requirements for Class G airspace below 1,200 ft. AGL at night?	The VFR minimums are 500 ft. below clouds, 1,000 ft. above clouds, and 2,000 ft. horizontally from clouds, with 3-statute mile visibility, regardless of MSL altitude.
356.	What are the minimum VFR cloud clearance and visibility requirements for Class G airspace above 1,200 ft. AGL but below 10,000 ft. MSL?	The VFR minimums are 500 ft. below clouds, 1,000 ft. above clouds, and 2,000 ft. horizontally from clouds. During daylight hours, 1-statute mile visibility is required. At night, 3 statute miles visibility is the minimum.
357.	Are there any other VFR minimums that pertain to Class G airspace?	Yes, if we are more than 1,200 ft. AGL and at or above 10,000 MSL, the VFR minimums increase to 5-statute mile visibility with cloud clearances of 1,000 ft. below clouds, 1,000 ft. above clouds, and 1 statute mile horizontally.
358.	What is the base and the ceiling of Class A airspace?	Class A airspace ranges from 18,000 ft. MSL up to and including 60,000 ft. MSL (FL 600).
359.	Does Class A airspace end at the coastline of the continental United States?	No, Class A airspace includes the airspace above Alaska, as well as the waters within 12 NM of the coastline of the 48 contiguous states and Alaska.
360.	What are the requirements to act as PIC in Class A airspace?	A pilot must be instrument rated to act as PIC in Class A airspace.
361.	What equipment is required to operate in Class A airspace?	Two-way radio communication, appropriate navigational capability, and a Mode C transponder are required.

362.	What class of airspace requires a clearance prior to entry?	Class B airspace requires a clearance prior to entry.
363.	What constitutes a clearance?	When air traffic control (ATC) responds to my radio call and uses the word, "cleared" to describe an action, such as "November-123, cleared into Bravo airspace."
364.	If the controller in Class B airspace responds to your call with a vector that will put you into the Class B airspace, does that constitute a clearance to enter Class B?	No, if the controller does not use the word, "cleared" in his or her call, I am not cleared and must not enter the Class B airspace until the clearance is received.
365.	Can you fly an aircraft into Class B airspace without a working transponder?	No, the aircraft is required to have an operating Mode C transponder when within or above the lateral limits of Class B airspace and within 30 NM of the primary airport.
366.	To what altitude does Class B airspace typically extend?	Class B airspace surrounds the nation's busiest airports and can be modified in size and shape to accommodate the unique needs of the traffic and the geographic area. However, Class B airspace generally extends from the surface up to 10,000 ft. MSL.
367.	How many layers are generally included in an area designated as Class B airspace?	There are generally three layers that expand in size as the altitude increases. It looks a bit like an upside-down wedding cake.
368.	Is a Mode C transponder required only when you are within the boundaries of the Class B airspace?	No, Mode C is required within 30 NM of a Class B airport. The Mode C ring is depicted on sectional charts as a magenta circle surrounding the Class B airspace.
369.	What are the dimensions of Class C airspace?	Class C airspace normally includes two layers. The lower layer extends from the surface to 4,000 ft. above airport elevation. That lower layer, which is known as the inner circle, has a 5-NM radius. The shelf area has a 10-NM radius and extends from 1,200 ft. to 4,000 ft. above airport elevation.
370.	When should you contact ATC after leaving from an uncontrolled satellite airport located inside Class C airspace?	After departing an uncontrolled satellite airport in Class C airspace, contact ATC as soon as practicable.

371.	Can you fly into or out of that satellite airport located within Class C airspace without an operating Mode C transponder?	No, a Mode C (altitude encoding) transponder is required equipment when within or above Class C airspace.
372.	What is required before entering Class C airspace?	The requirement is for the pilot to establish two-way radio communication prior to entering into Class C airspace.
373.	Does making a radio call constitute establishing two-way radio communication?	No. Two-way radio communication has been established when ATC responds to your call, using your correct call sign.
374.	What is required before entering Class D airspace?	The requirement is for the pilot to establish two-way radio communication prior to entering into Class D airspace.
375.	Are you authorized to enter Class D airspace if the controller does not respond to your call using the word, "cleared" in their response?	Yes, the only requirement prior to entering Class D airspace is that I establish two-way radio communication. If I call and ATC answers, two-way radio communication has been established and I can legally enter the airspace.
376.	What are the typical dimensions of Class D airspace?	Class D airspace typically extends upward from the surface to 2,500 ft. AGL and outward to a 5-SM radius from the primary airport. Airspace dimensions may vary according to local requirements, however.
377.	When should you contact ATC after leaving from an uncontrolled satellite airport located inside Class D airspace?	After departing an uncontrolled satellite airport in Class D airspace, contact ATC as soon as practicable.
378.	Can you fly into or out of that satellite airport in an aircraft not equipped with an operating Mode C transponder?	Yes. There is no requirement for a Mode C transponder in Class D airspace.
379.	Is it ever permissible to enter Class D airspace without a radio?	Yes. The pilot of an aircraft that does not have a radio can telephone the tower prior to the flight to arrange for arrival at an airport that lies within Class D airspace. Light gun signals allow for communication from the tower to the aircraft.
380.	How is Class E airspace that extends to the surface depicted on sectional charts?	Class E airspace that extends to the surface is depicted on sectional charts by a dashed magenta line surrounding the airport. Class E airspace that extends to the surface of an airport signifies that the airport has instrument approach procedures.

381.	How is Class E from 700 ft. AGL depicted?	Class E that begins at 700 ft. AGL is indicated by a shaded magenta ring. Class E airspace that begins at 700 ft. AGL is used for transitioning aircraft operating under IFR to/from the terminal or en route environment.
382.	What airspace designation do federal airways have?	Federal airways are an example of Class E airspace.
383.	What are the dimensions of a federal airway?	A federal airway extends upward from 1,200 ft. up to, but not including, 18,000 ft. MSL.
384.	Victor airways are federal Airways. What NAVAID might you find defining a Victor airway?	Victor airways lead to and from VORs.
385.	How are Victor airways depicted on sectional charts?	Victor airways are shown as light blue lines that radiate out from VORs. They are identified by the letter V followed by a number.
386.	Is there a general rule about the vertical dimensions of Class E airspace?	Class E airspace generally extends upward from the surface or a specified altitude to the overlying controlled airspace. If no Class B or Class C airspace overlies the Class E airspace, it would extend upward to 18,000 ft. MSL where Class A airspace begins.
387.	What equipment must your airplane be equipped with to operate in Class E airspace?	There are no equipment requirements to operate VFR in Class E airspace.
388.	What are the radio communication rules when operating in Class G airspace?	Radio communications are not required in Class G airspace. However, if the aircraft has an operational radio installed or the pilot has access to a handheld radio, it is advisable to monitor the appropriate frequency and make position calls in the interest of the safe and expedient flow of traffic.
389.	What constitutes Class G airspace?	Class G airspace is any airspace that is not designated as Class A, Class B, Class C, Class D, or Class E airspace.

390.	What procedure should a pilot use to depart the traffic pattern of a nontower airport?	At an airport without an operating control tower, you should depart the pattern straight out or with a 45° turn in the direction of traffic after reaching pattern altitude. You should state which departing procedure you intend to use when you make your takeoff call on the CTAF.
391.	What procedure should a pilot use to enter the traffic pattern of an airport that does not have an operating control tower?	Inbound pilots are expected to observe other aircraft in the pattern to conform to the traffic pattern in use. If there is not any traffic in the pattern, the pilot should overfly the airport at least 500 ft. above pattern altitude to observe traffic and wind indicators on the ground. All entries to a nontower airport's traffic pattern should be a 45° turn to the downwind entry.
392.	What is a TRSA?	TRSA stands for Terminal Radar Service Area. TRSAs are established around Class D airports that have radar service capability but do not meet all of the criteria to be designated as Class C airspace. Participation in TRSA service is voluntary (though recommended), but two-way radio communication must still be established prior to entering Class D airspace.
393.	What is a prohibited area?	Prohibited areas are established for reasons of national security. Flight is prohibited at all times within them.
394.	What is a restricted area?	Restricted areas are established to contain unusual, often invisible hazards to aircraft, such as aerial gunnery or missile tests. Flight is restricted within a restricted area when that area is active.
395.	What is a military operations area?	Military operations areas (MOAs) are established to separate IFR and military traffic. VFR flight is always permitted within MOAs.
396.	What is an alert area?	Alert areas are established to notify pilots of unusual aerial activity, such as a high volume of flight training, but flight is always permitted within them.
397.	What is a warning area?	Warning areas are located offshore and are established to alert pilots of activity that may be hazardous to nonparticipating aircraft. A warning area can be thought of as a restricted area that is located outside the borders of the United States and the U.S. airspace system.

398.	What is a military training route (MTR)?	Military training routes are depicted on sectional charts to establish flight paths used for military training, usually occurring at high speeds and low altitudes.
399.	What type of airspace is often surrounded by large temporary flight restrictions (TFRs)?	Prohibited areas are often surrounded by large TFRs.
400.	Why are TFRs put into effect around prohibited areas?	Prohibited areas protect areas where the President often visits. TFRs are in place when the President is present at these locations.
401.	Are TFRs only put into effect places where the President is located?	No. TFRs can be put into effect for reasons of national security or national welfare. They may also be put into effect in the vicinity of any incident or event that may result in a high degree of public interest and cause hazardous congestion of air traffic.
402.	How are TFRs different from other forms of airspace?	Unlike other forms of airspace, TFRs are often created, canceled, moved, or changed.
403.	How can you become aware of the existence of a TFR?	A NOTAM will be created when a TFR is implemented. The NOTAM will contain a description of the area where the restrictions apply.
404.	Can aircraft operate in a TFR?	Only with a waiver or permission obtained in advance from the FAA.

Task F: Performance and Limitations

405.	How does weight affect aircraft performance?	The airplane is designed to use a specific wing with a specific engine and propeller to produce a known amount of thrust and lift. That design is based on the airplane's ability to lift a given amount of weight. Loading the airplane outside the CG limits or beyond the maximum weight allowances will adversely affect aircraft performance regardless of weather or other variables.
406.	What structural danger is a result of overloading the airplane?	When loaded properly, the airplane will stall before the load factor can increase enough to do damage to its structure. When the airplane is overloaded that is not the case. Structural damage may result from steep turns or encounters with turbulence that would not have occurred if the airplane had been loaded properly within published weight limits.

407.	What is a "maximum ramp weight?"	Maximum ramp weight is the maximum weight allowed for ground operations. Essentially, the heaviest the airplane can be while it is still on the ground.
408.	Define "maximum takeoff weight."	The maximum weight allowed for takeoff.
409.	What is a "maximum landing weight?"	The maximum allowable weight for landing.
410.	Why are the maximum takeoff weight and the maximum landing weight different?	The maximum landing weight is determined based on structural load limits. Manufacturers determine max landing weight based on the aircraft's ability to withstand structural loads during landing. Thus, a max landing weight is generally lower than the max takeoff weight because the forces applied to the aircraft during landing are greater than those applied during takeoff.
411.	What is "zero fuel weight" and why is it an important number?	Zero fuel weight is the maximum amount the airplane can weigh prior to the addition of usable fuel. It is used to determine how many people and how much cargo can be put on an airplane. If the zero fuel weight exceeds the maximum zero fuel weight, you will have to leave people or cargo behind to allow room for fuel.
412.	How does the condition and length of a runway factor into your flight planning?	The performance charts in the POH assume a paved, flat runway. If the performance charts suggest we have sufficient length to take off or land safely, we can operate out of runways that allow for that amount of distance plus a reasonable amount of extra length for safety. However, if the runway is grass or loose dirt, if it runs uphill, or if the pavement is broken and rough, all these factors will lead to a longer takeoff roll than the POH indicates.
413.	Why might you want to choose a runway that is longer than the POH indicates you need for takeoff or landing?	Safety is the primary responsibility of the PIC. I would be disinclined to put myself into a position where I have to be perfect, the weather has to be perfect, and the airplane has to perform perfectly in order to conduct a successful flight. I would much rather select runways that will allow me a reasonable margin for error when landing or taking off.

414.	Define V_R.	Rotation speed.
415.	Define V_{MU}.	Minimum unstick speed. Used when it is important to get the airplane off the ground as quickly as possible, e.g., takeoff from a grass runway with an obstacle at the end.
416.	What is the leading cause of general aviation in-flight accidents?	Fuel starvation.
417.	How can you prevent yourself from being a victim of a fuel starvation accident?	By visually checking the fuel before every flight, establishing reasonable minimums for myself, and monitoring my fuel burn on all flights, I can increase my level of safety significantly. It is important that I adhere to VFR minimum fuel requirements and do not exceed the length of time in flight that is appropriate for the amount of fuel I departed with.
418.	If headwinds cause your groundspeed to be considerably lower than expected, and your cross-country flight time to your destination has expanded to much longer than you anticipated, what caution might you take?	I would plan a diversion from my destination for a fuel stop. It is better to have a safe flight that is longer, due to an unanticipated fuel stop, than it is to try to stretch my fuel reserves to reach my original destination and potentially run my tanks dry in the process.
419.	When preparing for a cross-country flight, what special considerations would you have pertaining to weight and balance computations?	I would compute weight and balance for our takeoff and for our anticipated weight and CG at landing. This is especially important on a longer flight when fuel will be burning off, changing the weight and CG of the airplane. I would do the extra calculations to be sure that I wasn't taking off within weight and CG limits but inadvertently allowing the airplane to shift out of CG limits as the fuel burns off.
420.	Why is knowing your estimated landing weight important?	Some aircraft list a maximum landing weight in the POH. If we were to land at a weight above the listed limit, we would risk damaging the aircraft.
421.	Is it still necessary to compute a full weight and balance and calculate the CG if you are just going on a short local flight?	It is necessary to compute a full weight and balance and calculate the CG for any flight.
422.	What effect does an aft CG have on stall recovery?	An aft CG will make stall recovery more difficult. In a multi-engine aircraft an aft CG makes flying on one engine more difficult because the aircraft will be less stable.

423.	What effect does a forward CG have on the airplane?	A forward CG will increase stall speed, takeoff roll, and takeoff speed. The pilot may also experience reduced pitch authority and may not be able to lift the nose off the ground on takeoff.
424.	Which of the performance charts will you use for today's flight?	I will use all the appropriate charts for every flight. In the interest of safety, I want to calculate weight and balance and need to estimate takeoff and landing distances based on my current loading of the airplane. I also need to consider the time, fuel, and distance chart as I calculate fuel use in order to be sure that I have a sufficient fuel supply for every flight.
425.	What tools do you need to use in order to accurately use the performance charts and tables in your POH?	A sharp pencil and a straight edge are helpful with some of the more intricate charts. I often use a calculator, too, as a means of making some of the calculations more expedient.
426.	If you found that your POH was missing a performance chart, would that keep you from flying?	It would keep me from flying until I could find a replacement book or an accurate replication of the chart that I could include in my POH until I could obtain a new replacement book.
427.	Why is density altitude a factor in aircraft performance?	Density altitude is a description of how dense the air is that the aircraft is operating in. More dense air can improve aircraft performance. Less dense air can decrease aircraft performance.
428.	Can you give me an example of how weather can adversely affect airplane performance?	Density altitude is weather dependent. A high density altitude will degrade performance by slowing the airplane's rate of climb and limiting the maximum power output of the engine (assuming a non-turbocharged engine).
429.	Why are turbocharged engines not affected as negatively as non-turbocharged engines in high density altitude conditions?	Turbocharged engines can maintain their rated power as density altitude increases, to a point, because they have the ability to increase air pressure on the intake side of the engine. Non-turbocharged engines do not have that ability.
430.	Can you give me an example of how weather can positively affect airplane performance?	Colder denser air will improve the airplane's performance. In very cold air, the airplane will have a higher rate of climb than the same plane at the same weight on a hot day.

431.	Flying from a low temperature area to a higher temperature area, would the density altitude increase or decrease?	As air temperature increases, density altitude increases. A higher density altitude indicates less dense air, which degrades airplane performance.
432.	If you fly from an area of low pressure to an area of higher pressure, how would that change affect density altitude?	Moving from a lower pressure area to an area of higher pressure would cause a decrease in density altitude. This denser air would improve aircraft performance somewhat.
433.	What specific performance is affected by air density?	Lift, power, and thrust are all affected by air density. In less dense air, the wing produces less lift, the engine produces less power, and the propeller produces less thrust. In higher density air, all three aspects of aircraft performance increase.
434.	If there is no automatic leaning control on the aircraft's engine, why do we need to manually lean the engine when in cruise flight at altitude?	As the air becomes thinner at altitude the fuel/air mixture becomes richer. We need to lean out the mixture to prevent it from becoming excessively rich.

Task G: Operation of Systems

435.	Can you name three primary flight controls?	Ailerons, rudder, and elevator.
436.	What is the function of the ailerons?	The ailerons are the primary flight controls that affect the aircraft's ability to roll. One aileron deflects upward while the other deflects downward. The down aileron creates more lift by affecting the chord line of the airfoil. As the wing with greater lift rises, the opposite wing, which is producing less lift, descends. The ability to roll, when used in conjunction with the rudder, allows the airplane to make coordinated turns.
437.	Which axis of control do the ailerons affect?	The ailerons affect roll, around the longitudinal axis. But it is equally correct to say that ailerons effect roll along the lateral axis.
438.	What effect does the elevator have on the airplane?	The elevator controls pitch. By pulling back on the stick (or yoke), the elevator deflects upward. This movement changes the chord line of the airfoil and decreases lift. As the tail loses lift, the aircraft pivots around the CG, raising the nose. The opposite is true when pitching the nose downward.

439.	Which axis does the elevator affect?	The elevator affects pitch around the lateral axis, although that same effect can be described as the elevator controlling pitch along the longitudinal axis.
440.	What does the rudder do?	The rudder controls yaw, which allows the nose to move from side to side. Pushing on the left rudder pedal will move the nose of the aircraft to the left. Pushing on the right rudder pedal will have the opposite effect.
441.	Which axis does the rudder affect?	The rudder controls yaw about the vertical axis.
442.	What does the term "coordinated" mean in reference to flight controls?	All three primary flight controls (aileron, elevator, and rudder) should be used together in order to keep the aircraft in coordinated flight. To initiate a turn, pressure is applied to both ailerons and rudder in the same direction, while the elevator pressure is increased slightly to maintain altitude. That is a coordinated use of the flight controls.
443.	What is the purpose of trim?	Trim devices are commonly used to relieve the pilot of the need to maintain continuous pressure on the primary controls.
444.	How can you tell if your aircraft is properly trimmed?	A properly trimmed aircraft can be flown hands-off.
445.	How many flight controls have trim devices installed?	Typically small general aviation aircraft only have trim installed on the elevator. But trim devices can be installed to relieve control pressures in all three axes.
446.	What is the purpose of flaps?	Flaps have two functions. They allow for a decrease in stall speed, and they allow the aircraft to descend at a steeper angle.
447.	Aerodynamically, what effect do flaps have?	When deployed, flaps can increase lift, but they also increase drag.
448.	How are flaps deployed?	Flaps are usually deployed incrementally, using a lever with stops that represent specific flap settings. Each setting is generally identified by the number of degrees of flap being deployed, but pilots often refer to these settings as "first notch," "second notch," and so on.
449.	Can you give me an example of when flaps might be employed?	Most commonly, flaps are used on landing, where they can be deployed incrementally, depending on the conditions. But flaps can also be used on takeoff to enhance lift and shorten the takeoff distance.

450.	Would it be advisable to attempt a takeoff with full flaps?	No, full flaps creates too much drag to make that position useful during takeoff.
451.	Would it be advisable to attempt a landing with full flaps?	Depending on the conditions, that might be a normal landing. Full flaps would create additional lift to steepen our approach and enough drag to help slow the aircraft. But flaps positions have to be evaluated based on the conditions. In a strong headwind, the use of full flaps might be counter-productive, requiring a considerable amount of power in order for the aircraft to make it to the runway threshold. In that case, a lesser quantity of flaps would be preferable.
452.	What are spoilers?	Spoilers are devices that can be deployed to spoil lift. They are used in some high performance airplanes to allow them to descend while maintaining a relatively high speed. Gliders also make use of spoilers.
453.	What are leading edge devices?	Leading edge devices like slats, or slots, accelerate air over the wing, increasing lift. Some aircraft have full-span leading-edge slats. Others have slots that affect airflow over the ailerons. Most general aviation aircraft do not use slats or slots.
454.	What are the four cycles of a reciprocating engine?	Intake, compression, power, and exhaust.
455.	How do air-cooled and liquid-cooled engines differ?	Air-cooled engines rely on air flowing over the cylinders to carry away heat. Oil flow aids in cooling air-cooled engines as well. Liquid-cooled engines utilize a coolant system that pumps fluid through the cylinder heads and back to a radiator to dissipate the heat generated by the engine. Air flow and oil circulation also aids in the cooling of liquid-cooled engines.
456.	What is the purpose of a magneto?	A magneto provides electrical current to the spark plugs.
457.	Why are there usually two magnetos in airplane engines?	Most general aviation engines have two magnetos for redundancy. There are also two spark plugs per cylinder. Each magneto provides current to one set of spark plugs, ensuring that the engine will continue to run even if one magneto fails.

458.	What is the risk of idling for extended periods of time on the ground, or idling with the carburetor heat in the "on" position?	The risk is that running such a rich mixture at low RPM's for an extended period of time may tend to foul the spark plugs, leading to a rough running engine that is not able to produce full power.
459.	Describe the engine installed in your aircraft.	Many older aircraft use four-cylinder, four-stroke, opposed, air-cooled, normally aspirated, direct drive engines, manufactured by Continental or Lycoming. Many newer aircraft have Rotax 912 engines installed. The Rotax 912 is a 100-HP, four-cylinder, four-stroke, air-and-liquid-cooled, geared drive engine.
460.	What does the term "direct drive" mean in reference to an aircraft engine?	The propeller is attached directly to the engine's crankshaft on a direct drive engine. This means the propeller turns at the same speed as the engine's crankshaft.
461.	What does the term "geared drive" mean in reference to an aircraft engine?	The propeller is connected to the engine via a gearbox on a geared drive engine. This design is normally used to allow the propeller to turn at a lower, more efficient speed than the engine's crankshaft. The Rotax 912 is a good example of an engine that develops power at an RPM that would be too high for the propeller to operate effectively if it was connected to the crankshaft directly.
462.	Why is it important to verify oil capacity before flight?	Low oil capacity can lead to engine damage or failure. The oil provides necessary lubrication for the internal workings of the engine and plays an important role in the cooling of the engine, regardless of whether it is an air-cooled or liquid-cooled engine.
463.	What does the term "normally aspirated" mean when used in reference to an engine?	A normally aspirated engine is not turbocharged or supercharged.
464.	What is the difference between a normally aspirated engine and a turbocharged engine?	A turbocharged engine uses exhaust gases to power a small turbine that compresses outside air as it enters the engine. This compressed induction air is directed to the intake manifold where it is distributed to each cylinder. The high pressure induction air allows the engine to achieve sea-level engine performance at higher altitudes.

465.	Explain how a turbocharger works.	Air enters the intake on the front of the engine and is directed to the turbocharger, which is made up of a turbine and impeller assembly. The turbine is powered by exhaust gases and spins the impeller. The impeller pressurizes the induction air before it flows into the intake manifold where it is distributed to each cylinder. The amount of exhaust gas that is sent to the turbine is regulated by a waste gate that allows excess gas to return to the exhaust system.
466.	What does the turbine inlet temperature (TIT) gauge measure?	The TIT gauge measures the temperature of the exhaust gases entering the turbocharger turbine.
467.	What else can you use the turbine inlet temperature (TIT) gauge for?	The TIT gauge can be used to adjust fuel flow and assist in leaning each engine. Refer to your aircraft POH for aircraft specific procedures.
468.	How is your engine cooled?	Older aircraft engine designs, such as Lycoming, Continental, or Franklin, are air-cooled. Air is directed over the cylinder heads to carry heat away as the airplane flies. Newer engine designs, such as the Rotax 912, are oil-and-air-cooled. Air cools the cylinder heads as it does on the older engine designs, but oil is routed through a radiator that helps discharge engine heat into the atmosphere.
469.	What are cowl flaps and what do they do?	Cowl flaps allow air to enter the engine compartment and cool the engine. These should be open during extended ground operation and during climbs.
470.	What is the purpose of the propeller on your aircraft?	The propeller is an airfoil that converts the power produced by the engine into thrust that propels the aircraft.
471.	What is a constant speed propeller?	Unlike a fixed pitch propeller, the constant speed propeller can change pitch in flight to maintain a specific RPM.
472.	What is a prop governor and what does it do?	A prop governor senses the rotational speed of the propeller and uses engine oil pressure to maintain a specific propeller pitch that is set by the pilot.
473.	Why is it important to control the pitch of a propeller?	The pitch of the propeller regulates the speed at which the propeller turns. By manipulating the pitch of the propeller, the pilot can control the speed of the propeller in order to maintain the most efficient RPM setting for a particular phase of flight.

474.	Explain how a prop governor works.	High-pressure oil enters the cylinder through the center of the propeller shaft. A hydraulic piston in the propeller hub is attached to each propeller blade by a rod. The oil pushes the piston forward and, as a result, moves the rods and the propeller blades because the blades are twisted towards the low pitch (high-RPM) position. Either a nitrogen charge or mechanical springs will counteract the oil pressure and allow the blades to return to a high pitch (low-RPM) position. Counterweights inside the propeller hub also assist in moving the blades to the high and low pitch positions. Your aircraft POH will provide further details specific to your aircraft.
475.	What causes the pitch of the propeller blade to vary in flight?	The pilot sets the RPM with the propeller control on the throttle quadrant. The propeller governor then uses engine oil pressure to regulate the pitch of the propeller to maintain the set RPM.
476.	When increasing power in an airplane with a constant speed propeller, are there any special concerns?	As a general rule, we increase RPMs with the propeller lever before we increase manifold pressure using the throttle. We do this to keep the RPMs higher than the manifold pressure when making throttle adjustments.
477.	When reducing power does it matter whether you reduce the throttle or RPM first?	We would reduce manifold pressure with the throttle first, then reduce the RPM with the propeller control. It is a general rule that the RPMs should remain higher than the manifold pressure throughout the flight. Although it is worth noting that some flight manuals may include procedures that contradict that rule of thumb.
478.	If the checklist included in the POH disagrees with the rule of thumb regarding throttle and propeller control movements, which should you follow?	The checklists included in the POH are always the primary reference. Those procedures are designed specifically for the aircraft as it was certified. If there is any doubt, go with the procedure listed in the checklist included in the POH.
479.	How do hydraulic brakes work on your aircraft?	Toe brakes activated with the rudder pedals allow me to apply pressure to the brake system, which actuates independent brake assemblies on each wheel. This allows me to apply brakes to one or both wheels as necessary.

480.	What is the advantage of conventional landing gear?	Conventional gear is lighter than tricycle gear because the tailwheel can be much smaller and lighter than a nosewheel would be. The conventional gear also has less drag, which allows the aircraft to cruise faster using the same power.
481.	What is the disadvantage of conventional gear?	Ground handling takes more care. Because the center of gravity is behind the main wheels, the aircraft will have a tendency to want to ground loop (the tail rotates toward the direction of travel) which requires the pilot to take much greater care and make constant rudder adjustments to control the aircraft on the ground.
482.	When taxiing, does a conventional gear aircraft present any other problems?	Visibility can be difficult because the nose is higher than it would be for a similar aircraft with tricycle gear. If visibility is restricted, the pilot can perform a series of S turns while taxiing to allow him or her to see out one side window, then the other, to verify a clear path.
483.	What are the advantages of tricycle gear on an aircraft?	The center of gravity is ahead of the main wheels on a tricycle gear airplane. This tends to make the aircraft track straight when on the ground.
484.	What are the disadvantages of tricycle gear on an aircraft?	The parts for a tricycle gear aircraft are heavier and more complex. The nosewheel has to be able to swivel freely or have a steering mechanism installed, and it requires a damper to prevent shimmy when the wheel touches down at high speed.
485.	Why is taxi speed important in reference to steering?	A tricycle-gear airplane may tend to develop a potentially damaging shimmy in the nosewheel if taxied too fast with excessive weight on the nosewheel. Both conventional- and tricycle-gear airplanes can suffer from control issues in taxi turns if entered at too high a speed.
486.	What does the term "fixed gear" mean?	Most general aviation airplanes have fixed gear. The term means that the landing gear cannot be retracted during flight.
487.	What potential danger does retractable gear present to a pilot?	The obvious risk is that you might not extend the gear before landing, and cause significant damage to the aircraft by inadvertently landing on the belly.
488.	How can you prevent an accidental gear-up landing from happening?	Always use the checklist.

489.	Would the aircraft provide any indication that you were descending for a landing without the gear being down?	Most aircraft with retractable gear have an alarm system that will sound if the throttle is retarded to near idle while the gear is still up. It is important to heed that alarm, should it sound.
490.	What powers the landing gear system in your airplane?	Most general aviation aircraft with retractable landing gear have a hydraulic system. This system is either run by engine-driven hydraulic pumps or electrically driven hydraulic pumps. System configuration varies by aircraft make and model.
491.	What indication do you have that your gear is down and locked?	There is a series of three lights on the panel that indicate whether the individual gear legs are down and locked. Three green lights tell me that I am good to go for a landing, with my gear down and locked.
492.	If your gear fails to extend as expected, do you have any options?	Yes. Depending on what type of gear retraction system the airplane uses, it may have a manual crank to mechanically extend the gear, a hand pump that can produce sufficient hydraulic pressure to extend the gear, or a pressure dump system that relieves hydraulic pressure and allows the gear to fall into the dock and hopefully locked position using gravity.
493.	When operating in snow or slush conditions, what precautions should be taken with the landing gear after takeoff?	The landing gear should be cycled up and down a few times to knock off any excess slush or snow. This will prevent the slush from freezing to the landing gear and causing further problems.
494.	What type of emergency gear extension does your airplane have?	There are several types of emergency extension systems in use. Some common types include a manual hand crank, nitrogen bottle(s), and a free-fall system. Check your aircraft POH to see what your airplane is equipped with.
495.	What is a "squat switch" and what does it do?	A squat switch, or landing gear safety switch, is used to prevent the landing gear from being retracted while the airplane is on the ground. Also referred to as a "weight on wheels" switch.

496.	How does the fuel system work on your airplane?	High-wing airplanes tend to have gravity feed fuel systems. Low-wing airplanes require an electrically driven fuel pump to push fuel uphill from the wing tanks to the engine so that the engine can be started, at which point the mechanically driven fuel pump takes over. Many manufacturers recommend using the electrically driven fuel pump when the engine is run at low RPMs, too.
497.	Is using all the fuel from one tank before switching to another a good practice?	Using all the fuel from one tank is not a good practice because it may cause vapor lock in the fuel line. It also tends to cause an imbalance as one wing lightens as the tank is emptied, while the tank in the opposite wing remains full.
498.	What is a risk of using all the fuel in one tank before switching to a tank that is full of fuel?	Draining a tank may result in engine failure due to fuel starvation. With air in the fuel lines, it may be impossible to restart the engine inflight in the limited time available as the aircraft descends to the ground.
499.	What is the function of the mixture control?	On Lycoming and Continental aircraft engines, the mixture controls the amount of fuel going to the carburetor or cylinders. It makes for better fuel efficiency, less buildup on the spark plugs, and a more efficient engine. Rotax engines adjust the mixture automatically and do not include a manual mixture control.
500.	What does the throttle control?	The throttle controls the amount of air being allowed into the intake system. The fuel is automatically metered to be in a proper proportion to the amount of air the throttle is allowing into the intake.
501.	What is the purpose of a carburetor?	The carburetor is where the fuel mixes with the air before it is sent to the cylinders.
502.	What is one of the limitations of a carburetor?	It is subject to carburetor induction icing, which can starve the engine of fuel and cause an engine failure if the icing isn't addressed in a timely manner.
503.	What does applying carburetor heat do to the fuel/air mixture?	Applying carburetor heat causes the fuel/air mixture to become enriched. This is because the hot air being routed to the carburetor intake is less dense than the colder, ambient air.

504.	What is fuel injection?	Fuel injection systems inject fuel directly into the cylinders or the induction manifold at high pressure through nozzles.
505.	What is the advantage of fuel injection?	Fuel injection systems are less susceptible to induction system icing than carburetor installations are.
506.	What is the disadvantage of fuel injection systems?	They can be difficult to start when the engine has been heated up and then shut down for a short time. This can cause vapor lock, where the fuel in the lines has vaporized from the heat and cannot be delivered effectively to the cylinders.
507.	How can you monitor the oil system in flight?	The oil temperature and oil pressure gauge give me a good indication of the oil system's operation while in flight.
508.	How can you tell if your oil level is low in flight?	The oil temperature will tend to rise and the oil pressure will tend to fall if the oil level is too low. If this occurs, it is a good idea to land in order to fill the oil reservoir and verify that the aircraft does not have an oil leak.
509.	What major components are included in a typical aircraft electrical system?	A typical training aircraft would have a battery, a starter, an alternator or generator, a voltage regulator, an ammeter, and various electrical devices including lights, radios, and perhaps an electric fuel pump.
510.	What does the battery do during the start procedure?	The battery stores the electrical energy necessary to start the engine. Once the engine starts, the battery becomes a back-up electrical source and is used to excite the magnetic field in the alternator.
511.	What does the master switch do?	The master switch brings the electrical system online, providing power to the system for engine starting and running the electrical loads of the aircraft.
512.	If the alternator or generator on your aircraft fails, what will happen?	The battery will take up the electrical load and supply power for a period of time. I would turn off all non-essential electrical devices to extend the amount of time the battery could supply power, and make a decision on whether to land at the first possible opportunity or continue to my home airport.

513.	How can you monitor the condition of your electrical system while in flight?	You can monitor the electrical system with the ammeter, to be sure the electrical power being supplied is greater than amount of electrical power being consumed.
514.	What is the advantage of an alternator over a generator?	An alternator will produce power even at idle speeds, while a generator requires a higher RPM in order to produce power.
515.	What is a disadvantage of an alternator as compared to a generator?	The alternator requires power from the battery to excite the field which allows it to produce power. A generator does not require an outside power source to produce power.
516.	What does the term "avionics" refer to?	Avionics refers to electrical devices used in the aircraft. Normally it is used in reference to communication and navigation aids.
517.	How do hand-held avionics differ from panel mount avionics.	They are used for the same functions and often have similar levels of functionality. The only real difference is that hand-held avionics are easily portable, while panel mount avionics are fixed in the aircraft.
518.	What are the benefits of avionics to the commercial pilot?	Safety primarily. They allow for communications with facilities on the ground and they provide important options for navigation that can help keep me out of airspace I do not want to stray into or to find a nearby landing spot in an emergency.
519.	What is GPS?	The global positioning system (GPS) is a satellite-based navigation system operated and maintained by the U.S. Department of Defense. GPS allows for point-to-point navigation with great reliability and accuracy.
520.	Can you tell me how GPS navigation works?	The GPS receiver in the aircraft determines its position using a constellation of satellites in orbit. The receiver computes the distance from each satellite based on signal travel time. With input from three satellites, the unit can determine its lateral position on the globe. With input from four satellites, the unit can approximate its altitude above sea level.
521.	How is GPS typically used to navigate?	Most commonly, pilots use GPS to navigate from point to point, plotting a direct route to their destination without the need to fly a zig-zag pattern from one NAVAID to another that lies near their route of flight.

522.	What is a concern that pilots using a hand-held GPS unit would have that users of panel-mount GPS units do not have?	Pilots using a hand-held GPS unit need to be sure they have an adequate power supply. Whether that means carrying extra batteries or having an electrical source supplied by the aircraft itself, the unit is only a useful tool when it has sufficient power.
523.	What does the term "EFIS" relate to?	EFIS is an acronym that stands for electronic flight information system. These units combine the information provided by analog flight instruments into a single electronic display.
524.	What is an engine monitoring system (EMS)?	An EMS provides a digital display of a variety of engine parameters to the pilot. This allows a single screen to provide important information like RPM, cylinder head temperature, oil temperature, oil pressure, and fuel flow.
525.	If navigating by VOR, with the CDI centered on 090 and a TO indication, are you east or west of the station?	I would be west of the station. If I fly 090° (with a wind correction if necessary), I would eventually fly over the station.
526.	If navigating by VOR, with the CDI centered on 090 and a FROM indication, are you east or west of the station?	I would be east of the station. If I were to continue to fly a course of 090°, I would travel farther from the station. However, if I were to fly the reciprocal of the radial indicated on the VOR (270°), I would close the distance and eventually fly over the station.
527.	What is a major training issue when pilots transition to an airplane with a glass cockpit?	Each manufacturer's system works differently. It is important that pilots who are transitioning into an airplane that has a glass cockpit obtain specific training in the use of the primary flight display and the multi-function display installed in that particular airplane.
528.	How can moving from one glass cockpit system to another cause problems for a pilot in flight?	The actual tasks required to fly remain the same. But the tasks required to operate the panel and obtain accurate information that allow the pilot to maintain situational awareness change with the menu systems provided by various manufacturers. It is important that the pilot doesn't devote so much of his or her attention to the operation of the panel equipment that (s)he neglects the task of maintaining a collision avoidance scan or other necessary responsibilities that come with being PIC.

529.	How can a pilot with a glass panel function effectively in the event of an electrical failure?	The number of options available to the pilot vary, depending on the make and model aircraft (s)he is flying and the type of glass panel that is installed. In Cessnas, for example, a power failure causes the automatic activation of a standby electrical system that will power the displays for at least 30 minutes, allowing the pilot sufficient time to find an airport for a precautionary landing or some other remedial action.
530.	If there is a total power failure that causes the loss of the primary flight display and the multi-function display, how would the pilot access the necessary information to complete the flight safely?	While flying under VFR conditions, navigation can still be performed with reasonable accuracy using pilotage and dead reckoning. Standby analog instrumentation would be sufficient to allow the pilot to maintain control of the aircraft and make a decision whether the flight should continue to the original destination or whether (s)he should land as a precaution to make repairs.
531.	Which flight instruments are part of the pitot-static system?	Typically, the airspeed indicator, vertical speed indicator, and altimeter are the flight instruments in the pitot-static system.
532.	Which instrument uses air pressure from the pitot tube?	The airspeed indicator is the only instrument that makes use of the air pressure taken from the pitot tube.
533.	If the pitot tube became blocked, what would the airspeed indicator read?	Zero. With no ram-air pressure to compare to the static pressure, the airspeed indicator would stop working and read zero until the blockage was cleared.
534.	What will the airspeed indicator read if the static port becomes blocked?	With the static pressure trapped in the system, the airspeed indicator will show a higher airspeed as the aircraft descends and a lower airspeed as the aircraft climbs, regardless of the aircraft's actual airspeed.
535.	Which instruments are driven by a vacuum pump?	Typically, the gyros in the attitude indicator and heading indicator are driven by the vacuum system.
536.	What is indicated airspeed?	Indicated airspeed is what is read on the airspeed indicator.
537.	What is calibrated airspeed?	Calibrated airspeed is indicated airspeed corrected for installation and instrument errors. These errors are generally greatest at low speeds. At cruise speeds, calibrated airspeed and indicated airspeed are approximately the same.

538.	What is true airspeed?	True airspeed is calibrated airspeed or indicated airspeed corrected for non-standard temperature and pressure. True airspeed at higher altitudes is higher than indicated airspeed, due to the less-dense air at higher altitudes.
539.	How does the vertical speed indicator (VSI) work?	The VSI is a sealed case with a calibrated leak and a diaphragm inside it. Slight difference in air pressure expands or contracts the diaphragm that is linked to the needles on the face of the instrument.
540.	Where do the VSI and altimeter get the information they base their readings on?	From the static air pressure provided by the static port.
541.	How does the altimeter work?	As the plane ascends or descends, the changing atmospheric pressure allows the aneroid wafers inside the altimeter to expand or contract. This expansion/contraction is mechanically geared to rotate the needles on the face of the instrument.
542.	How would the altimeter be affected if the pitot tube became blocked?	It would function normally. The altimeter does not use pitot pressure to display accurate altitude information.
543.	How would the altimeter be affected if the static port became clogged?	With static pressure trapped in the system, the altimeter will show a fixed altitude, regardless of whether the aircraft climbs or descends.
544.	How does the airspeed indicator work?	The airspeed indicator takes the difference between the ram air pressure from the pitot tube and the static pressure from the static vents and converts this pressure difference into indicated airspeed.
545.	What does the vacuum pump installed in your aircraft do?	The vacuum pump provides airflow to pneumatically powered gyroscopic instruments by drawing air through the pneumatic system.
546.	How do the gyroscopic instruments work?	Gyroscopic instruments work on the principle of rigidity in space. A vacuum pump or electrical power source spins a gyro in the instrument at a high rate of speed, thus keeping it rigid in space. If a force is applied, then precession happens 90° ahead of the force.
547.	Can you give me an example of a gyroscopic instrument?	The turn and bank indicator, the attitude indicator, and the heading indicator are all gyroscopic instruments.

548.	Why do some gyroscopic instruments run on electrical power while others are powered by the vacuum pump?	By using two different power systems, the aircraft benefits from a level of redundancy. That increases the margin of safety. If the electrical system fails, the vacuum-powered gyro instruments will still work. If the vacuum pump fails, the electrically powered instruments will continue to work.
549.	How does cabin heat work in your airplane?	In most general aviation training aircraft, either there is no cabin heat system or the cabin heat is provided by a muff surrounding the exhaust system. Heat radiated from the exhaust is routed into the cabin.
550.	What is the risk of using cabin heat?	Because the heater muff in most general aviation aircraft surrounds the exhaust system, there is a risk of carbon monoxide poisoning if the exhaust system has a leak. It is important to use a carbon monoxide detector in the cabin to warn of impending CO poisoning.
551.	What is the difference between anti-icing and deicing systems?	Anti-icing systems are designed to prevent ice from accumulating on the leading edge of the airplane wing. Examples of anti-ice systems include TKS or a heated pitot tube. Deicing systems, such as pneumatic boots, are designed to combat ice that has already accumulated on a leading edge surface. Aircraft that are equipped for flight into known icing conditions will have ice protection on most leading edge surfaces, including wings, propellers, horizontal stabilizers, and in some cases, the vertical stabilizer.
552.	Does your aircraft have any deicing or anti-icing systems installed?	Most general aviation aircraft have carburetor heat, which is a deicing system.
553.	How does your carburetor heat work?	A control in the cockpit closes off the cold, fresh air source and routes hot air into the carburetor to melt ice that has formed in the intake.
554.	Does it have to be below freezing for carburetor ice to form?	No. Carburetor ice is possible in humid conditions when temperatures are as high as 70°F.
555.	How do deice boots installed on wings work?	The boots can be switched on to expand and crack ice to a certain thickness as it forms, so that it is blown off the wing.

556.	If icing conditions are being reported and your airplane has no deice or anti-ice system installed, how much ice can you accumulate before you have to terminate your flight?	Flight into known icing conditions without appropriate deice or anti-icing systems is not permitted. With no way to prevent the formation of ice or rid the aircraft of ice once it begins forming, the airplane will gain weight and lose lift in icing conditions. If an airplane persists in flying through icing conditions with no means of combating it, the aircraft will eventually be unable to maintain level flight and may become uncontrollable.

Task J: Aeromedical Factors

557.	What is a good rule for flying if taking medication?	DO NOT fly if you are taking medication unless the medication is approved by the FAA or you are certain that the medicine will NOT impair your abilities.
558.	What if the medication is a common, over-the-counter drug?	The same rule applies. Pilots should not fly when taking medication unless the medication is approved by the FAA or they are absolutely certain that the medicine will not impair their judgment or abilities.
559.	How long must one wait after consuming alcohol before acting as a required crewmember on a civil airplane?	You must wait 8 hours after consuming alcohol before acting as a required crewmember on a civil airplane.
560.	What is hypoxia?	Hypoxia is an insufficient supply of oxygen in the body.
561.	What are the signs of hypoxia?	Impairment of night vision, judgment, alertness, coordination, and the ability to make calculations. Headache, drowsiness, dizziness, and a possible sense of euphoria or belligerence may occur. Unconsciousness may be the end result of prolonged hypoxia.
562.	How can hypoxia be prevented or treated?	Hypoxia can be prevented or treated by flying at a lower altitude or by using supplemental oxygen.
563.	Once an individual becomes hypoxic, how long after beginning treatment will it take for him or her to regain his or her faculties?	Recovery from hypoxia is almost immediate. The person suffering from hypoxia will regain his or her faculties very quickly after sufficient oxygen is made available.
564.	What is hyperventilation?	Hyperventilation is a condition that describes insufficient supply of carbon dioxide in the blood.

565.	What are some indications of hyperventilation?	Dizziness, rapid heart rate, tingling in the fingers and toes, and ultimately unconsciousness.
566.	How can hyperventilation be treated?	Hyperventilation can be treated by taking slow, deep breaths or by breathing into a bag.
567.	Why is it important that pilots not fly when they have a cold or allergic condition that causes congestion?	Pressure differences during climb or descent can cause severe pain and hearing loss due to ear blockage. Congestion can block the Eustachian tube and prevent the pressure equalization necessary to avoid this sort of aeromedical issue.
568.	Does the problem of pressure equalization only pertain to ear and hearing problems?	No. Blocked passages in the sinuses can cause pain and possibly the discharge of bloody mucus from the nasal passages.
569.	If you were scheduled to fly but had a cold, would it be advisable to take an over-the-counter decongestant to avoid ear or sinus issues?	No. Pilots should not fly when taking medication unless the medication is approved by the FAA or they are absolutely certain that the medicine will not impair their judgment or abilities. Decongestants can have side effects that can significantly impair pilot performance.
570.	What is spatial disorientation?	Spatial disorientation is a state of temporary spatial confusion that results from misleading information being sent to the brain from various sensory organs.
571.	Can you give me an example of how spatial disorientation might occur in flight?	When visibility is limited, the brain will rely on other input for orientation information. The ear may not be reliable because of fluid movement that does not correspond with the movement of the aircraft. This could cause the pilot to feel as if (s)he is in a steep turn when the aircraft is actually flying straight-and-level. It could also cause the pilot to feel as if (s)he is flying straight-and-level when (s)he is actually in a steep turn. That is why spatial disorientation can be a dangerous condition.
572.	What is the graveyard spiral?	If descending during a coordinated constant-rate turn that has ceased stimulating, the motion-sensing system can create the illusion of being in a descent with the wings level. A disoriented pilot will pull back on the controls, tightening the spiral and increasing the loss of altitude.

573.	On what sense does your brain rely primarily when it receives conflicting information from the senses?	When given conflicting information, the brain tends to favor the information provided visually.
574.	How can you recover from spatial disorientation?	The best way to recover from spatial disorientation is to focus on the flight instruments and rely on their indications.
575.	Does motion sickness come on rapidly?	Not usually. Motion sickness is often an incremental progression of symptoms.
576.	How can you identify impending motion sickness in yourself or a passenger?	First, the subject loses his or her appetite. Heavy perspiration might follow with a tendency to salivate. Nausea, disorientation, and headaches may also occur.
577.	How can you combat or prevent motion sickness?	By opening the air vents and getting air circulating in the cockpit. I would encourage passengers to loosen their clothing and avoid unnecessary head movements. I would also advise them to focus their eyes on a distant point near the horizon. While doing all this, I would be either returning to land at my home airport if it was close by or diverting to a nearby airport to land.
578.	What is carbon monoxide poisoning?	Carbon monoxide poisoning occurs when carbon monoxide enters the blood, thereby causing hypoxia. Carbon monoxide poisoning is of particular concern to pilots because this colorless, odorless gas can cause incapacitation.
579.	What is the primary source of carbon monoxide in aircraft cockpits?	The most common source of carbon monoxide in aircraft cockpits is exhaust fumes leaking from a defective heater or other source.
580.	Why is the recognition of carbon monoxide poisoning so important to pilots?	Loss of consciousness and death are very real possibilities if the exposure to carbon monoxide continues.
581.	If you suspect carbon monoxide poisoning is occurring, what would be a reasonable course of action?	Ventilate the cabin to the extent possible and land at the first opportunity to seek first aid, if necessary. After dealing with the human element, I would make sure the aircraft was inspected and the leak found and repaired before it was flown again.

582.	What other aeromedical condition can carbon monoxide poisoning mimic?	The effects of carbon monoxide poisoning are very similar to the effects of hypoxia.
583.	Can carbon monoxide poisoning be treated with oxygen, like hypoxia, resulting in a quick recovery?	No. Oxygen may be beneficial to the person suffering from carbon monoxide poisoning, but the carbon monoxide must be removed from the individual's bloodstream, which is a process that takes time. It cannot be remedied as rapidly as hypoxia.
584.	How can stress affect your flying?	Stress degrades decision-making ability and slows your reactions.
585.	When we talk about stress and flying, what kind of stress are we talking about?	Everyday stress that comes from personal interactions, job stress, family responsibilities, busy schedules in our lives. Stress can be subtle, but cumulative, building to the point that it adversely affects the individual's ability to perform normal functions reliably.
586.	How can stress affect you as a pilot?	It can cause distraction that affects my decision-making abilities and might cause my judgment to erode to the point that I take unnecessary risks.
587.	What is acute fatigue?	Acute fatigue refers to the everyday tiredness felt after a long period of physical or mental activity that leaves the individual feeling drained.
588.	How can acute fatigue be remedied?	By getting sufficient rest, sleep, exercise, and nutrition.
589.	What is chronic fatigue?	Chronic fatigue occurs when there is insufficient recovery time between bouts of acute fatigue. Performance and judgment continue to degrade. Because it is a deeper form of fatigue, the recovery period requires a prolonged period of rest.
590.	What is dehydration?	Dehydration occurs when the body is deprived of fluids. Dehydration can occur on flights of long duration in which the pilot fails to drink adequate amounts of water, or it can be a pre-existing condition that started prior to the flight.
591.	How can dehydration affect you as a pilot?	Dehydration acts as a stressor and can degrade your decision-making ability.

592.	How does flying affect dehydration for pilots and passengers?	At altitude, the atmosphere is thinner and contains less moisture. This leads to more body fluids being lost.
593.	How can you combat dehydration?	Ensure an adequate intake of fluids before and, if necessary, during flight.
594.	What is hypothermia?	Hypothermia occurs when your body is unable to maintain its normal temperature. An internal temperature of 96°F or lower signals hypothermia.
595.	What are some signs that a person is suffering from hypothermia?	Extreme shivering; stiffness of the arms or legs; confusion or sleepiness; slow, slurred speech; and poor control over body movements all suggest the possibility of hypothermia.
596.	Does it have to be extremely cold for a pilot or passenger to succumb to hypothermia?	No. A drafty cockpit, and especially an open cockpit aircraft, can cause a poorly prepared pilot or passenger to experience hypothermia in temperatures that might seem moderate when standing on the ground with no wind.
597.	How can hypothermia be prevented?	By dressing appropriately. Pilots and passengers should be aware that the temperature at altitude is usually lower than the temperature on the ground, and the wind blowing through the cockpit will cause our bodies more difficulty at maintaining a normal body temperature.
598.	What is the maximum allowable blood alcohol content while acting as a required crewmember on a civil airplane?	You may not act as a required crewmember on a civil aircraft while having .04% or more blood alcohol content by weight.
599.	How long should pilots and passengers wait to fly after scuba diving?	If a controlled ascent was required during the dive, wait 24 hr. before flying. If a controlled ascent was not required, wait 12 hr. before flying up to 8,000 ft. and 24 hr. for any altitude above 8,000 ft.
600.	Why is it important to wait before flying after scuba diving?	Just as the pressure decrease while ascending in the water can cause nitrogen gas trapped in the tissues to escape rapidly, a condition known as the bends, the same can occur when the ambient pressure decreases during an airplane's ascent. To avoid that possibility, individuals should wait before flying after scuba diving, to give the nitrogen gas time to leave the body.

Area of Operation II: Preflight Procedures

Task A: Preflight Inspection

601.	When is it necessary to perform a preflight inspection?	Pilots should verify the condition and airworthiness of their aircraft before any flight, whether it is the first flight of the day or a subsequent flight made later in the day.
602.	Where would we find the documentation required for the aircraft to be airworthy?	The location varies, but the registration, airworthiness certificate, and radio license (if required) are typically found in a plastic-covered pocket on the sidewall of the cockpit area. The operating limitations are included in the POH, as well as in the form of placards in the cockpit, and the weight and balance information will be calculated by the pilot prior to each flight.
603.	Where is the pitot tube on your aircraft?	The location of the pitot tube can vary from aircraft to aircraft, but it is generally located midway along the leading edge of the wing. In some cases, especially in small, pusher configuration airplanes, it is located on or near the nose of the airplane.
604.	Where is the static port located on your aircraft?	The exact location of the static port varies from one aircraft to the next, but the static port is usually located on the rear of the pitot tube or along the side of the fuselage.
605.	How will we verify that we have sufficient fuel for our flight?	We will verify fuel levels before flight by visually inspecting the fuel tanks. We will monitor fuel use during our flight by estimating fuel burn using the performance charts found in the POH, and we will plan the duration of the flight accordingly.
606.	If you find water in a fuel sample, what would be the appropriate course of action?	I would continue sampling fuel from that tank until I found clear fuel samples that show no indication of water or other contaminants.
607.	Why is evidence of water in the fuel tank such a consideration during the preflight inspection?	Water is heavier than fuel and sinks to the bottom of the fuel tank, where the fuel is drawn from for use in the engine. Since water cannot support combustion, it can adversely affect performance. Small amounts of water can cause the engine to run rough. Larger amounts of water can cause engine failure and make it impossible to restart the engine without draining the contaminants in the tank.

608.	What foreign matter would you be looking for in the air inlet to the engine compartment?	Birds often seek out the warmth of a cooling engine and may actually attempt to build a nest on the engine or in the air inlet to the engine compartment. These, as well as other foreign materials, should be completely removed before flight as they can limit airflow that is necessary to adequately cool the engine and might even cause a fire if they come in close contact with the exhaust system.
609.	How would you check the oil level for your airplane?	Explain the location of the oil dipstick. Explain how to remove the dipstick, wipe it clean, reinsert the dipstick, and remove it again to check the level of the engine oil accurately. Only check the oil level when the engine is turned off and has had a few moments for the oil in the engine to settle into the sump.
610.	What are we looking for when we inspect the propeller during the preflight inspection?	We are doing a general condition inspection. Our inspection is verifying that there are no cracks, delaminations (wood or fiberglass props), bends, or obvious damage. We are also inspecting for nicks to the leading edge of the prop. If we find a large or deep nick, we should postpone our flight until we can consult with maintenance about the condition of the prop.
611.	Where can we find a checklist to follow when performing a preflight inspection on the airplane we will be flying today?	A preflight inspection checklist is included in the Pilot's Operating Handbook or Aircraft Flight Manual appropriate to the specific type of aircraft. We will follow that checklist to assure ourselves that we have checked everything that needs to be checked in an organized, methodical manner.
612.	Where can we find information regarding the fuel capacity of the aircraft we are flying today?	Fuel capacity information can be found in the POH or AFM for the specific type of aircraft. We can look up the fuel capacity of the aircraft prior to our flight and visually inspect the tanks prior to flight to verify that we have a sufficient load of fuel before starting up the engine.
613.	What is meant when we talk about usable fuel as opposed to fuel capacity?	Fuel capacity refers to the amount of fuel the aircraft can carry. Not all of the fuel can be delivered to the engine, however. The small amount that remains in the tanks is referred to as unusable fuel and should not be included in endurance calculations.

614.	How do we know if we have the right amount of oil before starting the engine?	Oil capacity is listed in the POH or AFM. We can check the listed oil capacity for our aircraft based on that information and verify we have at least the minimum quantity during our preflight inspection.

Task B: Cockpit Management

615.	In the event of an emergency, what can you make use of to help you successfully and safely deal with the situation?	I can make use of every resource available to me, including ATC via the radio and you, my passenger, as an extra set of hands and eyes. If an emergency occurs, I will give you specific instructions regarding how you can be helpful. These may include finding an emergency checklist in the POH while I am flying the airplane or configuring the cockpit (such as opening a door and blocking it open with a shoe or a book at the hinge point) in the event a forced landing becomes necessary.
616.	As a passenger, is there anything I can do to help you during a normal, uneventful flight?	Yes. I would appreciate it if you would point out any traffic that you feel may be a factor for us and hold onto some of the charts and manuals I will be using, for easier and quicker access. (Follow up by explaining how the examiner can be of help when (s)he is acting as a passenger. Be specific when asking for assistance to prevent misunderstandings.)
617.	Is there anything I should not touch during the flight?	Yes. I want you to be comfortable during our flight, but I will need you to keep your hands and feet clear of the controls. I will point out the controls and switches you need to be aware of when we get into the aircraft.
618.	At what point in the flight do you take on the role of PIC?	I will be acting as PIC well before we get to the airplane. As PIC, I will take responsibility for the safety of the flight and my passengers throughout the planning phase, during the preflight inspection, and throughout the entire flight, right up to the point that we shut down the engine after landing and depart the aircraft.
619.	Is there any information the pilot should share with his or her passenger prior to start-up?	Yes, the pilot should provide a basic safety briefing to be sure the passenger understands the proper use of safety belts and harnesses. The passenger should also be shown how to open the cockpit door and the location and use of the fire extinguisher.

| 620. | Why should the pilot brief the passenger before flight? | For safety reasons. It may be difficult to get the passenger's attention focused on a briefing after start-up, so we do it beforehand. In the event of a true emergency, the passenger can be helpful in dealing with some situations, so the pilot should provide this basic level of information before the flight gets underway. |

Task C: Engine Starting

621.	What are the steps to hand-propping an airplane?	Hand-propping requires two people: one at the controls and the other at the propeller. It is vital that both people be trained and experienced in hand-propping procedures. The person sitting behind the controls should hold the brakes firmly, the throttle positioned for start, and both mags switched to "ON" when directed by the person on the propeller. The person propping the airplane should announce in a loud, clear voice, "Brakes on, throttle cracked, switched to ON." The person behind the controls should reply in kind. Then the person propping the plane should verify that the brakes are set by pushing firmly on the propeller close to the spinner. With his or her fingers positioned just on the trailing edge of the propeller, the person propping should pull forcefully down and move quickly away from the propeller arc.
622.	In what position should the mixture control be during engine starting?	At or near sea level, the mixture should be kept in the "full rich" position to allow for a proper fuel/air mixture at the surface where the air is the most dense.
623.	A Rotax 912 engine does not have a mixture control. Will that present a problem when starting the engine?	No, the Rotax 912 does not require a manual mixture control because the mixture is controlled automatically.
624.	If we are starting the engine at an airport that is not at or near sea level, what should we do with the mixture control?	At a high altitude airport, it may be necessary to lean the mixture somewhat to compensate for the less dense air at ground level.
625.	Where should the carburetor heat be positioned during engine starting?	The carburetor heat will be in the "off" position.

626.	After starting, what is the first instrument we should look at?	We will watch the oil pressure gauge to be sure that the pressure rises within a few seconds of the engine starting. Under cold conditions, it may take somewhat longer for oil pressure to reach the green range indicated on the gauge, but if the oil pressure does not register within 5 seconds of starting, it is wise to shut the engine down and investigate to verify that the engine has a sufficient oil supply and that there are no leaks in the system.
627.	What prevents the airplane from moving during engine start?	While engaging the starter, I will be holding the brakes with sufficient pressure to prevent the airplane from moving on the ramp.
628.	Where will you keep your hands during engine starting?	I will hold my hands on the controls during engine start. This is a safety precaution. In the event the aircraft's brakes fail, a pedestrian wanders in the direction of our propeller, or some other potential issue arises, I will be ready to shut the engine down quickly as a precaution.
629.	Our aircraft has only one engine, a fixed pitch propeller, and relatively simple systems. Can we start the engine using memory aids rather than a checklist?	No. Although our aircraft is simple to operate, it is important that we establish good safety practices at all times when operating an aircraft. We will use the engine start checklist taken from the POH for our airplane every time we start the engine, no matter how familiar we are with the process.
630.	How do higher horsepower engines differ from lower horsepower engines when starting?	Higher horsepower engines are often more susceptible to vapor lock than lower horsepower engines. This tendency can make them more difficult to start, especially when the engine is hot or has been recently run.
631.	What is vapor lock?	The heat of the engine actually vaporizes fuel in the lines. The vaporized fuel cannot be pumped through the intake system effectively. Vapor lock is the primary cause of hard starting in higher horsepower airplane engines.
632.	What specific precaution should we take immediately before starting the engine?	We should announce in a loud voice that we are about to start the engine by yelling "Clear," or "Clear prop," while visually verifying that nobody is in the area of our propeller before we engage the starter.

633.	If you are ready to start the engine but notice another pilot is preparing to preflight the airplane tied down right next to yours, what should you do?	Safety is of paramount importance. I would let the other pilot know that I was preparing to start the aircraft and ask if (s)he could remain safely clear while I started the engine and prepared to leave the area. If (s)he were agreeable, I would start the aircraft and depart in an orderly manner. If (s)he were not agreeable, I would wait until (s)he finished the preflight and was no longer in any danger before continuing with my engine start procedure.
634.	If you find the aircraft you will be flying is parked in front of a hangar with the tail pointed toward the open door, what precaution would you take before starting?	I would reposition the aircraft if possible so the prop blast was not directed into the open hangar. If repositioning were not possible, I would ask to close the hangar door before I started the engine.
635.	How do we know that we are performing all the correct tasks in the correct order when starting the engine?	We use the engine start checklist included in the POH for the aircraft.

Task D: Taxiing

636.	How can you check the steering while taxiing?	Ground steering is controlled by the rudder pedals. I will verify that I have sufficient control authority as I begin my taxi. (NOTE: Some aircraft feature rudder and nosewheel controls that are interconnected, while others utilize only rudder control for ground steering. Be aware which system your aircraft uses and be prepared to explain the advantages or limitations to your examiner if asked.)
637.	Assuming our aircraft has interconnected rudder and nosewheel steering controls, how does that affect your control on the ground?	Aircraft that interconnect the rudder and nosewheel controls have much greater ground steering capability, especially at low speeds and low throttle settings.
638.	Assuming our aircraft is steered on the ground by rudder alone, how does that affect your control on the ground?	Aircraft that do not have nosewheel steering tend to have less ground control authority when taxiing, especially at low speeds and low throttle settings. I can compensate for that limitation by using differential braking. However, it is important that I use differential braking sparingly to avoid overheating the brakes.

639.	Immediately after releasing the brakes and adding throttle to get the aircraft to taxi, what safety precaution do we take?	We apply the brakes to verify that they have enough power to bring the aircraft to a stop. We do this as a safety precaution before the aircraft has built up any appreciable speed.
640.	Why is it important to check the brakes immediately?	If the brakes are spongy or weak, it is best to find out when the aircraft is just barely moving rather than when it is rolling down the taxiway with traffic ahead.
641.	If the brakes seem weak, what would you do?	I would shut down the aircraft and report the potential problem to maintenance. If a mechanic clears the airplane for service, I can continue. If the mechanic suggests maintenance is required, I will either fly another aircraft or cancel the flight.
642.	How does a pilot apply brakes when performing a brake check?	The aircraft will either have toe brakes, which would enable differential braking, or a single brake handle that applies both brakes simultaneously (usually located between the seats). The important thing is to apply the brakes with sufficient force to be sure the aircraft can be stopped and to apply differential brakes evenly to stop the aircraft without causing it to swerve in one direction.
643.	If you were to encounter a quartering headwind from the right while taxiing, what control inputs would you use, if any?	I would turn the ailerons into the wind (raising the right aileron) and apply back pressure on the elevator to spoil any lift that might be generated.
644.	Is there a memory aid you use as a reminder of how to position the controls for the winds when taxiing?	Yes, I remember to "climb into the wind and dive away from it." I position the flight controls when taxiing so the elevator is up for headwinds (to spoil lift) and down for tailwinds (to prevent the wind from getting under the tail). The same principle is true for the aileron positions.
645.	What is a safe taxiing speed?	A good rule of thumb is to maintain no more than a brisk walking speed when taxiing.
646.	Why is it necessary to maintain a low taxi speed, even if no other traffic is in view?	Aircraft are generally bulky, gawky machines on the ground. Their center of gravity is often higher than other ground vehicles, with a significant amount of that weight held in fuel tanks that are outboard of the center line of the aircraft. This tends to make aircraft prone to ground accidents if they are taxied too quickly or if heavy braking is employed in a turn.

647.	Where would you stop before transitioning from the taxiway to the runway?	I would stop at the hold short lines, which are indicated by two solid yellow lines followed by two dashed yellow lines on the taxiway. I would hold on the side with the solid lines to verify that the runway is clear (Class G airport) or to await clearance to take the runway (Class B, C, or D airport).
648.	If the controller tells us we are cleared to taxi and hold when we are at the hold short line prior to entering the runway, what is (s)he clearing us to do?	We are allowed to taxi out to the center line of the runway and hold there until (s)he clears us to takeoff.
649.	What is the difference between the terms, "position and hold," and "hold short?"	"Hold short" means that we are cleared to taxi to the runway, but to hold short of crossing the hold markings at the entry to the runway itself. "Position and hold" means that we are cleared to taxi onto the runway center line and hold there, but we are not cleared to take off.
650.	If, while holding short of the runway, we get a call from the controller asking us if we can expedite our takeoff, what does (s)he mean?	The controller is asking if we can take off immediately if (s)he clears us to take off. We may hear this call when there is an incoming aircraft on long final.
651.	If the controller instructs us that we are cleared to take off and instructs us to expedite, do we have to accept the clearance?	No. The controller is trying to help us get out without having to wait a long time while holding. But, if we are not ready to go, or if we feel rushed, we are entitled to respond that we are unable to expedite and wait at the hold short line for our next opportunity to take off at the controller's convenience.
652.	If you received an instruction from the ground controller that wasn't entirely clear, but you thought you had understood part of the message, what would you do?	I would call back for confirmation of the clearance before doing anything else. It is important that I understand all clearances completely before I attempt to comply with them. The alternative would potentially cause me to taxi onto a runway or taxiway that I was not cleared to be on, which could cause an incident or accident for which I would be at fault.

653.	If you are number two behind another aircraft that is holding for longer than you think is necessary on the taxiway ahead of you, is it permissible to pass them in order to expedite your takeoff?	The aircraft in the lead has the right-of-way because it is difficult for the pilot of that aircraft to see behind him or her. On an airport without an operating control tower, we can call them on the radio and ask for permission to pass them (provided there is ample room to do so without the risk of a collision), but if we are unable to contact them directly, we should operate as if they have the right-of-way. We will wait for them to move rather than try to slip around them on the taxiway.
654.	If you are taxiing on a wide ramp and find yourself converging head-on with another aircraft taxiing in the opposite direction, which way should you deviate your course in order to pass safely?	When aircraft are approaching head-on both aircraft should alter course to the right in order to safely pass each other.
655.	If, while on the ramp or taxiway, you encounter an aircraft that is acting erratically (or in some way that prevents you from anticipating what the pilot might be planning to do), what would you do?	I might stop and wait for them to get clear, depending on the circumstances. If it is an airport with an operating control tower, I should be able to hear ground controller instructions to them, which should give me an idea of their intentions. At an airport without an operating control tower, I could call on the radio to the other aircraft and ask their intentions. If I could not raise them, I would be inclined to wait for them to clear the area, rather than potentially cause an incident or accident.

Task F: Runway Incursion Avoidance

656.	What constitutes a "runway incursion?"	The FAA defines runway incursion as any occurrence at an aerodrome involving the incorrect presence of an aircraft, vehicle, or person on the protected area of a surface designated for the landing and takeoff of aircraft.
657.	What elements of taxiing make it more demanding than when flying the airplane?	Taxiways, unlike the sky, are one lane roads. Proper planning and compliance with ATC instructions are very important to ensure that a collision hazard is not created with other aircraft or vehicles on the ground or with aircraft that are taking off or landing at the airport. Because aircraft and vehicles can come from many different directions, you must maintain increased vigilance when operating on the ground.

658.	How can you identify areas at an airport where runway incursions may be more likely to occur?	Airport diagrams describe hot spots for runway incursions. These hot spots are usually the intersection of runways or runways and taxiways. They are areas where an increased chance of runway incursions may exist.
659.	How can you identify areas on the airport where you need to hold short?	Hold short markings are painted on the taxiway and feature two solid lines and two dotted lines. The solid lines indicate that you should stop when taxiing toward them. Hold short signs feature the same illustration as the painted markings. Red runway boundary signs are located next to the hold short markings and further indicate that you should stop and either clear the area (at a non-towered airport) or wait for ATC clearance (at a tower-controlled airport).
660.	Assume that ATC and/or a passenger is communicating with you while you are taxiing at an unfamiliar airport. What steps will you take to ensure you avoid a runway incursion?	My first priority is to ensure safety during the taxi. I must control and eliminate distractions to do that effectively. I would politely ask the passenger to wait for a better time to converse with me. I would ask ATC to standby or ask for taxi instructions to an airport holding area where I could stop the airplane and complete the necessary conversation with ATC.
661.	Some pilots expect certain instructions from ATC when operating out of a familiar airport. How will you avoid this pilot error and ensure you comply with the instructions you actually receive?	All instructions and clearances from ATC should be written down to ensure that I get the correct message. Doing so will also help me when I read back my instructions or clearance to ATC.
662.	How will you maintain situational awareness during taxi operations?	I will use proper scanning techniques, minimize head-down time, control and eliminate distractions in the cockpit, and use a taxi diagram to ensure I am taxiing safely and toward my intended destination.
663.	What special procedures will you employ at night to avoid runway incursions?	Taxiing at night requires some additional concentration because it is more difficult to spot airplanes and vehicles as well as their direction of travel. I will maintain positive situational awareness regardless of day or night operations, but I will pay special attention to airport and airplane lighting systems to determine where I am in relation to taxiways and runways as well as other traffic.

664.	What airport lighting aids exist to help you avoid a runway incursion when operating at night?	Primarily, taxiway lights are blue and runway lights will either be white or use a color-coding system. Regardless, I can easily identify what is a taxiway and what is a runway. Airport sign illumination will also help me find my way and avoid crossing onto an active runway. Other more advanced runway status lighting systems also exist, and I can easily identify what systems will be available at the airports I intend to use and research any unfamiliar systems in the *AIM*.
665.	What airplane lighting aids exist to help you avoid a runway incursion when operating at night?	My airplane is equipped with position lights, which will help other aircraft identify my direction of travel. Likewise, I will use the position lights of other aircraft to determine their direction of travel. Anticollision lights are also effective in helping pilots identify other aircraft at night. I can use my landing/taxi light(s) to help me see the area in front of me or signal to other aircraft, if necessary and appropriate.

Task G: Before Takeoff Check

666.	How can we tell on the ground if our aircraft is rigged properly?	When we turn the yoke to the right (or move the stick to the right), the right aileron should move upward, while the opposite aileron should move downward. Similarly, depressing the right rudder pedal should make the rudder deflect to the right. Depressing the left rudder pedal should make the rudder deflect left. Pulling back on the yoke (stick) should cause the elevator to move upward, and pushing it forward should make it move downward. If we see any other results, we should cancel the flight and report the issue to maintenance for repair before the aircraft flies again.
667.	When switching the ignition switch from the "Both" position to the "Left" or "Right" position, what should we expect to happen?	We should expect to see a slight drop in RPM, but not so much that power output is significantly compromised.
668.	What engine accessory are we testing when we move the ignition switch from "Both" to the "Right" or "Left" position?	We are testing the magnetos to verify that they are supplying the ignition system with an appropriate amount of electrical energy to produce a good spark at the spark plugs.

669.	Why does the RPM drop slightly when we move the ignition switch from the "Both" position to either the "Right" or "Left" position?	The RPM drops because the engine uses a redundant ignition system that makes use of two magnetos to feed two separate sets of spark plugs. When we switch from "Both" to either "Right" or "Left," we are removing one magneto or the other from the system, and using only one set of spark plugs instead of both sets. This deprives the engine of some of its potential, which results in a slight drop in RPM.
670.	Oil pressure gauges often have two red lines. Why is that?	There is one red line at the low end of the scale that indicates insufficient oil pressure is being developed, which could lead to engine damage or failure. The second red line is at the upper end of the scale and indicates that too much pressure is being developed, which can also lead to engine damage or failure.
671.	What is the risk if we were to take off with a cold engine?	The oil may not be warm enough to circulate freely through the engine, causing damage or possible engine failure when we increase power for takeoff and climb out.
672.	Does it matter in which direction we position the aircraft for the before-takeoff check?	If possible, we will position the aircraft into the wind to help cool the engine. This is especially important for an engine that is entirely air-cooled, rather than liquid-cooled.
673.	Are there any other positioning considerations when preparing to do a run-up before takeoff?	We want to be sure the aircraft is positioned in such a way that it is not likely to pick up excessive dirt, pebbles, or other foreign matter that could damage the propeller or airframe, or blow into other aircraft or hangars and cause damage.
674.	Is there any special consideration for the position of the nosewheel?	We want to be sure the nosewheel is straight. If the brakes were inadvertently released with the nosewheel turned to one side, the potential stress could cause damage to the nosewheel assembly.
675.	Will we do the before-takeoff check on the taxiway?	Some airports have a before-takeoff check, or run-up, area that allows us to perform the check without blocking the taxiway. If that option is available, we will position the aircraft there. If there is no designated area, we will use the taxiway for our before-takeoff check.

676.	Where will you be focusing your attention during the before-takeoff check?	I will be careful to divide my attention between the aircraft's instruments and controls and the environment outside the aircraft. I will be looking for the appropriate indications on the aircraft's instrumentation to be sure that the aircraft is ready to fly. But I will also be monitoring the outside environment for aircraft, vehicles, and personnel that may be moving into our area during the before-takeoff check.
677.	How can we be sure the engine is warmed up properly before takeoff?	The oil temperature gauge is our best indication of the engine's operating temperatures. EGT and CHT should both be monitored to be sure they are in the operational range, too. When the oil temperature has risen into the green arc, we can be sure the engine is warmed up sufficiently.
678.	If we see a low oil pressure indication that does not come up into the green arc, or a high oil pressure indication that stays consistently above the green arc, what should we do?	While we are on the ground, we would return the aircraft to maintenance and bring the issue to the attention of a mechanic. It would be unsafe and unwise to take off in an airplane that is indicating a potentially serious engine problem during the before-takeoff check.
679.	If the aircraft begins to move during the ignition check when you have the power at a high RPM setting, what should you do?	I should immediately retard the throttle to prevent the aircraft from lurching forward. Controlling the aircraft is my first priority. I should then resume the ignition check while holding the brakes firmly. If the aircraft begins to move again, I should return the aircraft to maintenance to check the brakes. If I am able to hold the brakes firmly and the aircraft does not move, I will continue with the before-takeoff check (including the ignition check) to verify that the aircraft is ready to fly.
680.	Where would we stop on the taxiway prior to takeoff?	On the hold short side of the hold short line.
681.	Which side of the hold short line is the hold short side?	The side with the two solid lines is the hold short side. The side with the dashed lines is beyond the point where we should be stopped and waiting for our turn on the runway for takeoff.

Area of Operation III: Airport Operations

Task A: Radio Communications and ATC Light Signals

682.	What does CTAF mean?	CTAF stands for common traffic advisory frequency. It is the frequency that pilots use to self-announce their position and their intentions at an airport without an operating control tower.
683.	What is one aspect of using a CTAF to self-announce that could cause confusion?	More than one airport within the range of our radio receiver may use the same frequency as a CTAF. To prevent confusion, we will announce the airport we are flying from at the start and conclusion of our radio calls.
684.	If we were approaching to land at an airport without an operating control tower, when would we typically make our first radio call on the CTAF?	We would announce our position and our intentions when we are approximately 10 miles from the airport.
685.	After we make that first call, what other calls would we make?	We would make a call on the CTAF to announce we are entering the traffic pattern, another call to announce we are established on the downwind, a call to announce that we are turning to the base leg, and a call to announce that we are established on the final leg of the pattern.
686.	Are we required to make radio calls at an airport without an operating control tower?	No, but for safety and the expedient flow of traffic, the FAA and common sense encourage us to make CTAF calls if we have the equipment to do so.
687.	If we intend to land at an airport with an operating control tower, when should we contact ATC to announce our intentions?	We should contact the tower to announce our intentions and our position when we are approximately 10 miles out from the airport.
688.	Is there anything we need to know before we make that initial call?	We should tune to the airport's ATIS frequency and become familiar with the information being broadcast before making our initial call to the tower.
689.	After that initial call to report our position and intentions, when would we make our next call to the tower?	The tower controller will tell us when (s)he wants us to make our next call. (S)he will respond to our first call with information like "Report right downwind for Runway 2." That tells us to enter the traffic pattern on a right downwind for Runway 2. We will call to report our position again when we are entering or established on that right downwind.

690.	If we were departing an airport with an operating control tower, who would we make our first radio call to after starting the aircraft?	We would call ground control to advise them where we are on the airport and what our intentions are (taxi to the active runway for takeoff).
691.	At that same airport with an operating control tower, when would we make our first call to the tower?	We would call the tower only when ground control advises us to contact them.
692.	If we were flying into an airport without an operating control tower, how could we find the CTAF for that particular airport?	The CTAF is printed on sectional charts and is available in the *A/FD*.
693.	What is the frequency for emergency voice communication?	ATC continuously monitors 121.5 MHz for emergency calls.
694.	After being cleared to taxi by the ground controller, how would we know which frequency we should use to contact the tower?	The ground controller will assign us a frequency to use when contacting the tower. The tower frequency is also available in the *A/FD* and on the sectional chart.
695.	What is the procedure if you have lost communication with the tower at a tower controlled field?	You should observe the flow of traffic, enter the pattern, and look for light gun signals. When you receive a signal, acknowledge it by rocking your wings.
696.	What code should you set your transponder to following a radio failure?	The transponder code that indicates radio failure is 7600.
697.	Give me an example of a CTAF radio call when departing Runway 18, at Flying Ten Airport.	"Flying Ten traffic, Cessna 123 Alpha-Bravo departing Runway one-eight, Flying Ten traffic."
698.	How will we let the tower controller know we are familiar with the information being broadcast on the ATIS frequency?	During the initial call, we say, "Cessna 123 Alpha-Bravo, with Information X-Ray (or whatever the current ATIS broadcast identifier is)." Then we report our position and intentions to the tower controller.

Task B: Traffic Patterns

699.	If we fly to an unfamiliar airport, how will we know whether the runway we use makes left-hand traffic or right-hand traffic?	If the airport has an operating control tower, they will assign us an entry to the pattern. If the airport does not have an operating control tower, we will observe other traffic to determine the pattern in use. If there is no other traffic, we will use visual indicators at the airport and windsock information to select a runway and determine the pattern.

700.	What does it mean when a given runway uses a standard traffic pattern?	It means that the traffic pattern for that runway requires left-hand turns.
701.	Which direction is the base to final turn made when you are flying a nonstandard traffic pattern?	To the right. Nonstandard traffic patterns require right-hand turns.
702.	Where would we find the CTAF frequency for an airport without an operating control tower?	The sectional chart will list the CTAF, as will the *A/FD (Airport/Facility Directory)*.
703.	As we prepare to enter the traffic pattern, what is our biggest concern?	Collision avoidance is key. We will keep our radio tuned to the appropriate frequency and monitor it for calls from other aircraft that would give us an indication of where they are and what their intentions might be. We will also keep a good visual look-out, and I will encourage my passenger to look for traffic and point it out to me.
704.	How will you enter the traffic pattern at an airport with an operating control tower?	I will enter in any way advised by the controller. The controller has the authority to give me a straight in approach, to enter in the base leg, or to fly either left or right patterns. Unless there is a compelling safety issue involved, I will fly the pattern I am assigned.
705.	How will you enter the traffic pattern at an airport without an operating control tower?	After identifying which runway is in use and whether they are using a standard (left-hand turns) or a nonstandard (right-hand turns) pattern, I will enter on a 45° angle to the downwind leg at midfield.
706.	If another airplane is on short final to the runway you intend to use for takeoff, are you allowed to taxi into position and take off ahead of that aircraft's landing?	At an airport with an operating control tower, I will not taxi past the hold short line until I am instructed to by the tower controller. At a nontowered field, I will have to make the decision about when to taxi onto the active runway myself. In the interest of safety, I would prefer to taxi and take off when no traffic is on final. If the airport was particularly busy, I would only take the runway if I was confident that I could perform my takeoff and be clear of the runway well before the airplane on final was over the fence at the approach end of the field.
707.	How would you let the airplane on final know what your intentions were?	I would be making calls on the CTAF with my position and intentions before taxiing onto the runway, regardless of whether I see any other traffic in the pattern.

708.	After liftoff, what would be a navigational concern?	I want to maintain a line straight out from the runway. If I stray from that line, it could affect my ability to fly a rectangular pattern effectively. I will apply enough right rudder to counteract the airplane's left turning tendency and monitor my ground track visually for indications of drift caused by a crosswind.
709.	If you notice you are drifting due to a crosswind, how would you deal with that?	I would crab into the wind for my climbout, correcting as necessary as I gained altitude. I would also keep that wind in mind through the various legs of the pattern, since the wind would have an effect on the aircraft for each leg of the pattern.

Task C: Airport, Runway, and Taxiway Signs, Markings, and Lighting

710.	Which light gun signal indicates that you are cleared to land?	A steady green light gun signal indicates that you are cleared to land.
711.	Which light gun signal indicates that you are cleared for takeoff?	A steady green light gun signal indicates that you are cleared for takeoff.
712.	What does a steady red light gun signal indicate on the ground?	A steady red light gun signal on the ground means to stop.
713.	What does a steady red light gun signal indicate when you are in the air?	In the air, steady red means to give way to other aircraft and continue circling.
714.	Why would an airport rotating beacon be operating during daylight hours?	If an airport's rotating beacon is on during daylight hours, it usually indicates that the prevailing weather is below basic VFR minimums, i.e., visibility of less than 3 SM and/or a ceiling of less than 1,000 ft.
715.	What is a displaced threshold?	A displaced threshold can only be used for taxi, takeoff, and a landing rollout.
716.	How is a displaced threshold indicated?	Displaced thresholds are indicated by white arrows that point to the runway threshold, which is a thick white line perpendicular across the runway.
717.	What are hold short lines?	Hold short lines indicate the active runway environment. If you are at a tower-controlled field, you cannot cross hold short lines until you are cleared to do so. At a nontowered field, you should visually scan the area for traffic, then announce your intentions before crossing hold short lines.

718.	How is a hold short position indicated?	Hold short lines are depicted by four yellow lines, two broken and two solid. The two solid lines are always on the side where the aircraft is to hold.
719.	What color are mandatory instruction signs?	Mandatory instruction signs are white letters on a red background.
720.	What color are taxiway location signs?	A taxiway location sign has a yellow character on a black background and a yellow border. The character is the identifier for the taxiway it is posted on.
721.	What color are taxiway markings and lighting?	Taxiway markings consist of a yellow centerline and yellow shoulder markings. If lights are installed on the taxiway centerline, they will be steady green. Taxiway edge lights are steady blue.
722.	What do yellow signs with black characters and arrows signify?	These are direction signs that point the way to reach each indicated runway.
723.	What color are runway markings and lighting?	Runway markings have a white centerline and white shoulder markings. Runway centerline lights are all white. The last 3,000-ft. section of runway may be identified by alternating red and white centerline lights. The final 1,000-ft. section of runway may show only red centerline lights. Runway edge lighting is white, except on instrument approach runways. Yellow edge lighting replaces white on the last 2,000 ft. or half of the runway, whichever is less, to form a caution zone for landing.
724.	What does a red sign with white numbers on it signify?	That is a runway location sign. The numbers are the identifiers for the runway that the sign indicates.
725.	What is a non-movement area?	It is a designated area where aircraft can taxi without being in contact with the tower, for example, the ramp at an FBO.
726.	What color is a civilian land airport beacon?	Civilian land airport beacons are alternating white and green flashes.
727.	What color is a military airport beacon?	A military airport beacon flashes two whites and a green.
728.	What do red lights across the runway indicate?	A row of red runway end identifier lights (REILs) may be installed across the end of the runway.
729.	If you see a row of red REILs, what color light is on the opposite side of them?	On the opposite side of the red runway end identifier lights are a series of green lights that mark the approach end of the runway.

Area of Operation IV: Takeoffs, Landings, and Go-Arounds

Task A: Normal and Crosswind Takeoff and Climb

730.	What are two speeds that we need to be aware of during a normal or crosswind takeoff?	V_R, which is the speed that we rotate the aircraft, and V_Y, which is the best rate of climb speed. (NOTE: Be familiar with these two speeds for your aircraft and be prepared to share them with the examiner upon request).
731.	What does "best rate of climb" mean?	V_Y is the best rate of climb speed. When performing a normal or crosswind takeoff, V_Y is the appropriate speed for climbout. By establishing V_Y as we climb out following takeoff, we will gain the most altitude over a period of time.
732.	What does V_R, or rotation speed, indicate?	When the aircraft accelerates during takeoff to V_R, I will raise the nose slightly to increase the aircraft's angle of attack. The resulting increase in lift will allow us to leave the runway and climb out.
733.	How do you know what the appropriate V_R and V_Y are for your aircraft?	Both V_R and V_Y are listed in the Normal Takeoff Checklist in the POH or AFM for the aircraft.
734.	After leaving the runway, what will you be focused on as the pilot in command?	I will be dividing my attention between several concerns. I will pitch and trim for V_Y (best rate of climb speed), scan the area for traffic, adjust my ground track to compensate for the effects of the wind, maintain the center line of the runway on climbout, make radio calls as appropriate, and monitor my engine and systems to be sure everything is operating as expected.
735.	How will you ensure collision avoidance after takeoff and during your climb?	Aircraft tend to congregate at the airport. There is likely to be other traffic in the traffic pattern and in the surrounding area. At a controlled airport, I should not assume the tower controller has assumed full responsibility for collision avoidance. As PIC (pilot in command), I have the ultimate responsibility for maintaining the safety of the flight. At an airport without an operating control tower, there may be traffic in the pattern, or entering the pattern, that is not in radio contact with the field or the pilots flying there. In either case, I have to keep an eye out for potential conflicts and be aware of where other aircraft are in my vicinity.

736.	Assuming a crosswind from the left, how would you position the flight controls during your takeoff roll?	I would position my ailerons into the wind with the left aileron up as the roll begins. With the left aileron up, I can prevent the wind from getting under the wing and lifting it prematurely. As our speed builds, I will gradually neutralize the ailerons to prevent a sudden roll to the left as the ailerons gain control authority. By the time we lift off, the ailerons will be neutralized and I will shift to a crab that is sufficient to maintain a straight ground track as we climb out.
737.	If you were taking off from a field with an operating control tower, would you clear the area even if the tower had cleared you to take off?	Yes. I would proceed with my takeoff as instructed by the tower while visually scanning for traffic. If necessary, I would bring traffic that may be an issue to the attention of the controller and ask for confirmation that I was cleared to take off. (NOTE: At an airport with an operating control tower, it will rarely be necessary to query the controller about potentially conflicting traffic. But the PIC should never begin a takeoff if (s)he believes that complying with the clearance will result in a conflict with another aircraft or vehicle.

Task B: Normal and Crosswind Approach and Landing

738.	What is the approach speed based on?	Approach speed is typically 1.3 times V_{SO}. However, it is reasonable to add a few knots to the approach speed to accommodate wind gusts and minimize the risk of an unintentional stall.
739.	Where would you find the appropriate approach speed for a normal or crosswind landing?	The approach speed is listed in the POH and AFM for the aircraft type.
740.	How close should the touchdown point be to the intended point of landing?	The Practical Test Standards (PTS) specify that the aircraft should touch down within 400 feet of the intended point of landing.
741.	Would it be advisable to touch down slightly before the intended point of landing?	No. Touching down before the intended point would risk hitting runway end identifier lights, the lip of the runway, or the airport fence. It is always our intention to touch down on or after the intended point of landing, while staying within the 400-foot tolerance established by the PTS.
742.	What issue would you have when landing in a crosswind that you do not have when landing without a crosswind?	The crosswind is going to tend to push me off the centerline of the runway. To maintain a straight line, I will have to either crab the aircraft or slip with the upwind wing held slightly down.

743.	If you are cleared to land on a 5,000-foot runway but the airplane that landed ahead of you has not yet cleared the runway when you are on short final, what should you do?	If an aircraft or a vehicle is on the active runway when I am on short final, I should go around rather than potentially have a conflict during the touchdown or the landing rollout.
744.	Why is it important to hold the upwind wing down?	When landing with a crosswind, I do not want the wind to get under the upwind wing and lift it unexpectedly. So whenever I slip to a landing, I should be sure to hold the upwind wing slightly low and maintain my ground track with rudder inputs.
745.	If you crab into the crosswind on approach, can you carry the crab all the way to touchdown?	No. It is risky to touch down in a crab. The side loads could damage or collapse the landing gear, and the aircraft is likely to have control issues because it is not pointed straight down the runway when it touches down. Rather than touch down in a crab, I would transition from the crab to a slip just before touchdown, holding the upwind wing slightly low and maintaining my ground track with rudder inputs.
746.	If the crosswind is strong and the runway is wide, how close to the centerline should we be at touchdown?	We should always land on the centerline, regardless of the strength of the crosswind or the width of the runway.
747.	How far from the centerline of a runway should you adjust in a strong crosswind scenario?	We should always land on the centerline, regardless of the strength of the crosswind or the width of the runway. If the crosswind is excessively strong, it might be worth considering landing at another airport that is nearby, assuming it has a runway more closely aligned with the prevailing wind.
748.	After touchdown, what control inputs might be required that would not be required after touching down from a normal landing?	The aircraft is still in motion after touchdown, so air moving over the lifting surfaces of the aircraft may have an effect. I will remain aware of the wind direction and strength and position the controls so the upwind aileron is raised to prevent the wind from lifting it. I will also position the ailerons and elevator as I taxi clear of the runway to prevent the wind from causing control problems or damaging the aircraft.
749.	After landing without a radio at a controlled field, what must you do after clearing the runway?	After landing without a radio at a towered controlled airport, you are required to stop after clearing the runway and wait for another light gun signal before you are allowed to taxi. The signal clearing you to taxi will be a flashing green light.

Task C: Soft-Field Takeoff and Climb

750.	When taxiing to takeoff on a soft field, what concern do we have that we would not have when taking off from a hard surface?	We do not want to come to a complete stop or let the power bleed off to the point that the aircraft bogs down in the soft ground.
751.	What is our power setting when taxiing on a soft field?	It may take very near full power to get the aircraft to begin rolling. From that point, we will adjust power as needed to keep the aircraft moving at a speed that is safe but will not allow the aircraft's wheels to bog down in the soft ground.
752.	Does that mean that you would not have to clear the area, as you would before a normal takeoff?	No, we always clear the area before departing the runway (especially when departing a field without an operating control tower), but when performing a soft-field takeoff, we will clear the area without stopping.
753.	(Assume a tricycle gear aircraft.) As we advance the power to takeoff power, what is different about the soft-field takeoff roll?	I will be holding the yoke (stick) back to get the nosewheel off the ground as soon as possible. This reduces friction and drag caused by the wheel rolling along the ground, lowers the chances of damaging the nosewheel as the aircraft accelerates, and will increase lift due to the higher angle of attack.
754.	What are you trying to accomplish with this technique?	During the soft-field takeoff, we want to get the aircraft off the ground and into ground effect as soon as possible. We will level off and allow the aircraft to accelerate to V_Y in ground effect, and then we will pitch up to climb out normally.
755.	What would be the biggest risk when performing a soft-field takeoff?	It is important to remain in ground effect until the speed builds up sufficiently to support a climb out of ground effect. If we were to try to climb out of ground effect as soon as we came off the ground, our airspeed would be too low and we would risk an inadvertent power-on stall very close to the ground.
756.	Is the aircraft configured the same for a soft-field takeoff as it is for a normal takeoff?	The proper configuration for the aircraft is described in the Soft-Field Takeoff Checklist found in the POH and AFM for the aircraft type. (NOTE: If equipped, it is common for aircraft manufacturers to specify the use of a specific flap setting for soft-field takeoffs. Be familiar with the specific configuration that is described for your aircraft.)

Task D: Soft-Field Approach and Landing

757.	How does the soft-field landing approach differ from the normal landing approach?	The approach is virtually identical, although airspeed control is arguably more important since we may need to plan our touchdown and rollout more carefully.
758.	Why would we potentially want to plan our touchdown and rollout more carefully for a soft-field landing?	Our goal is to minimize the distance we need to taxi on the soft field to prevent unnecessary wear or damage to the aircraft. So we will plan our touchdown point to put us closer to our destination, allowing us to taxi a relatively short distance after touchdown.
759.	After touchdown, will you handle the controls any differently when performing a soft-field landing than you would when rolling out during a normal landing?	(Tricycle gear aircraft only.) I will hold the elevator control in the full aft position during rollout and taxi to minimize the amount of weight being supported by the nosewheel, and I will avoid using the brakes unless it is absolutely necessary.
760.	What are the special considerations when braking on a soft field?	Typically, we try to avoid using brakes on a soft field. Braking increases the weight and wear transferred to the nosewheel, and it increases the risk of bogging down in the soft surface. The additional rolling resistance presented by a soft field is usually sufficient to allow us to stop by just reducing the power to idle.

Task E: Short-Field Takeoff and Maximum Performance Climb

761.	How would you position the aircraft before beginning your takeoff roll when performing a short-field takeoff?	I would be sure the aircraft was positioned to use the entire runway. To do that, I would be sure to begin my takeoff roll at the very beginning of the runway. Ideally, the tail would be hanging out over the grass with the wheels on the first foot of pavement.
762.	How would you configure the aircraft for a short-field takeoff?	The correct configuration is included in the short-field takeoff checklist in the POH and AFM for the aircraft. (NOTE: Be familiar and prepared to discuss the specific flap position, if installed, and configuration considerations for your type of aircraft with your examiner.)
763.	Will you begin your takeoff roll any differently when performing a short-field takeoff than you would for a normal takeoff?	Yes, I will hold the brakes while I advance the throttle to full power. That will allow me to be sure we have full power before we begin using runway for our takeoff roll.

764.	What speeds are we primarily interested in when performing a short-field takeoff?	We are going to rotate at V_R, then climb at V_X until we reach a safe altitude. When we are clear of obstacles, we can transition to V_Y to continue our climb to our cruise altitude. (NOTE: Be familiar and prepared to identify the specific speed that equates to V_R, V_X, and V_Y for your type of aircraft.)
765.	Can you define V_X?	V_X is the best angle of climb speed. It is the speed that will allow us to gain the most altitude over a given distance. When taking off from a short field that may have obstacles at the departure end of the runway, we would use V_X to clear the obstacles, then transition to V_Y (best rate of climb) for our climb to altitude.
766.	Assuming there are no obstacles at the airport we are operating out of, how high will we hold V_X before transitioning to V_Y during our short-field takeoff?	The Practical Test Standards specify that we maintain V_X until we clear the obstacle or reach 50 feet above the surface. With no actual obstacles to clear, we will maintain V_X until we reach 50 feet above the surface, then we will transition to V_Y.
767.	If there are obstacles on our route of flight, can we transition to V_Y at 50 feet above the surface during the practical test?	The practical test is like any other flight. Safety is our first priority. If there are obstacles on our route of flight, we will maintain V_X until we clear them and then transition to V_Y to continue our climb.

Task F: Short-Field Approach and Landing

| 768. | Can you list some of the considerations you would have when making a short-field approach and landing? | The assumption is that the field is short with potential obstructions on the approach end of the field. With that in mind, I would select the most advantageous touchdown point based on the wind and terrain while I was still in the pattern. I would evaluate any obstructions as I select that touchdown point. I would want to make my approach with minimal power and with flaps (if equipped with flaps) set to the position indicated by the short-field landing checklist in the POH or AFM for the aircraft. I would clear the obstacles on final and touch down within 200 feet of the touchdown point I selected at the minimum controllable airspeed so that I could stop the aircraft without overrunning the end of the runway. |
| 769. | How would you go about stopping the aircraft? | I would hold the nose high, making the most of aerodynamic braking (drag). As soon as the nose settles, I would apply full brakes to stop the aircraft as quickly as possible without compromising safety. |

770.	If you touch down at minimal controllable airspeed, does that mean that you will make a hard landing?	The short-field landing can be firm so that the aircraft does not float down the runway and provide an opportunity for better braking, but it should still be smooth. It should not be a bone-jarring impact when we touch down.
771.	How close to your point of intended touchdown will you land when making a short-field approach and landing?	The Practical Test Standards stipulate that I will land within 200 feet of the point of intended touchdown.

Task K: Power-Off 180° Accuracy Approach and Landing

772.	What is the purpose of the power-off 180° accuracy approach and landing?	It is designed to enhance judgment and demonstrate the procedures necessary to perform a safe and accurate landing without power.
773.	Can you give me a scenario where this maneuver might be realistic?	Engine failures tend to occur when a throttle movement occurs. If the engine were to fail on downwind right about the time the pilot retarded the throttle abeam the numbers, the situation would essentially duplicate this maneuver.
774.	Can the skills demonstrated in this maneuver come into play when away from an airport?	Absolutely! This maneuver is a very good demonstration of how to manage airspeed and rate of descent when an emergency landing field is small enough that a highly accurate touchdown is necessary.
775.	What environmental factor is most important to you when performing this maneuver?	The wind. A high wind means having a slower final leg and being able to cover less ground on final. It also means I will have to be on guard to prevent being blown long on downwind or during my turn toward final, making the emergency field unattainable.
776.	Can you define the term "downwind key position?"	That is the point abeam the intended touchdown spot.
777.	When performing this maneuver, is it better to be slightly high or slightly low on final?	It is always better to be slightly high on final. I can slip or add flaps to lose altitude if I am too high. But there is nothing I can do to regain altitude lost if I am too low.
778.	What is the "base key position?"	The base key position is defined as the point at which the airplane completes its downwind to base turn.
779.	What would you use as an approach speed during this maneuver?	Because this is a power-off maneuver, I would use the best glide speed listed in the POH. A stabilized approach is important to doing this maneuver well, so I would pitch and trim for best glide as soon as the power loss simulation occurred.

Task L: Go-Around/Rejected Landing

780.	Can you give me an example of a situation where you might consider a go-around?	There are many good reasons to go around rather than force a landing. If there is traffic or some other obstruction (including animals) on the runway, I would be inclined to go around. If I had not gotten the airplane configured correctly or stabilized my approach sufficiently to feel comfortable, I might go around. I might even choose to go around, rather than closely follow, a larger airplane that may have generated wingtip vortices.
781.	In your opinion, is the go-around an emergency maneuver?	No. The go-around is a normal operation that can be performed as a preventive measure rather than forcing yourself into a situation that you may not be ready for, or set up correctly for, or that you are just uncomfortable with.
782.	Do we need to communicate anything to the tower or our fellow pilots if we choose to go around?	Yes. We would announce that we were going around so that the tower controller and any other traffic in the area would be aware that we have not committed to a landing and will be climbing up and re-entering the traffic pattern again.
783.	After a go-around, is it necessary to leave the traffic pattern and then re-enter, or can you continue in the pattern without departing?	The go-around is a normal procedure, so it is perfectly acceptable to remain in the traffic pattern. At an airport with an operating control tower, the controller will advise us what he wants to do. At an airport without an operating control tower, we would make radio calls on the CTAF as appropriate to each leg of the pattern we fly and make our intentions clear so other traffic in the pattern is aware of us and what we intend to do.
784.	When considering a go-around, when is the best time to initiate the maneuver?	As soon as it becomes clear that a go-around may be advisable, it is reasonable to announce that you are going around and begin the process. The lower you carry the approach, the more complicated the go-around can become. It is better to decide and start the process early than to wait until you are on short final, at low altitude, and potentially slower than you would like to be when initiating a climb.

Area of Operation V: Performance Maneuvers

Task A: Steep Turns

785.	What are the parameters you will be concentrating on when performing a steep turn?	I want to be sure I roll into the maneuver and maintain a 45° bank angle throughout a full 360° turn. My goal is to maintain my altitude plus or minus 100 feet and roll out of the maneuver within 10° of the heading I rolled into it on.
786.	Besides watching your heading indicator, what can help you anticipate your rollout point?	Because we are performing this maneuver in VFR conditions, it is a good idea to pick out a prominent landmark when I roll into the bank that will help me maintain my orientation as I near the rollout point of the maneuver.
787.	What do we need to do prior to entering a steep turn?	Before performing any maneuver, we want to clear the area to verify that there is no air traffic in the vicinity, including above, below, or around us, that might conflict with our ability to complete the maneuver safely and successfully.
788.	How can you clear the area before performing a maneuver?	To get a clear 360° view of the sky, we can either make two 90° turns in opposite directions or a 180° turn, scanning the sky above, below, and around us throughout the process.
789.	If you were in the middle of a steep turn and saw oncoming traffic that you had not noticed during your clearing turns, what would you do?	If there were any possibility of a conflict, I would terminate the maneuver, steer clear of the oncoming traffic, and wait for them to clear the practice area. Then, I would clear the area and begin the maneuver again. Safety comes first, always.
790.	How would you correct for a loss of altitude during a steep turn?	I would reduce the bank slightly, increase back pressure on the elevator control, and increase power slightly until I reached my target altitude. Then, I would increase bank angle to my target bank angle, ease off the back pressure on the elevator, and evaluate whether I should maintain the higher power setting or retard it slightly.
791.	How would you correct for a gain in altitude while performing a steep turn?	I would increase the bank angle if possible, reduce some of the back pressure on the elevator, and perhaps reduce power slightly if that was warranted.

Task B: Steep Spiral

792.	How is a steep spiral different from a steep turn?	The steep spiral is a power-off, gliding turn that results in a descent. The steep turn is done with power, and maintaining altitude is one of the criteria for its successful completion.
793.	What is your goal while performing a steep spiral?	To maintain a constant radius around a point on the ground while performing at least three 360° turns, with power off.
794.	Where will your bank be steepest?	On the downwind side of each turn, where my groundspeed will be the highest.
795.	What is the maximum bank angle allowed for this maneuver?	Sixty degrees is the steepest bank angle allowed during a steep spiral.
796.	Why is your entry altitude important when performing a steep spiral?	Because the aircraft will be descending through three complete 360° turns. I need to be sure that I have allowed sufficient altitude to perform the maneuver and recover safely.
797.	What consideration do you have for your engine, even though this is a power-off maneuver?	We want to make sure we do not shock cool the engine or leave the power at idle for so long that the plugs could foul. If necessary, we will clear the engine to maintain the engine's ability to produce power when we need it.

Task C: Chandelles

798.	What is a chandelle?	The chandelle is a maximum performance climbing turn.
799.	The chandelle is a 180° turn that has different requirements for each half. What are those requirements?	The first 90° of the chandelle requires a constant bank angle of 30° while constantly increasing the pitch. The second 90° requires the pilot to maintain that maximum pitch attitude while constantly reducing the bank angle.
800.	What is an appropriate entry speed for a chandelle?	We will use the manufacturer's recommended entry speed, which will be below maneuvering speed (V_A).

| 801. | Assuming a piston engine with a propeller that turns to the right as viewed from the cockpit, will the airplane gain more altitude when performing a chandelle to the right or the left? | In a piston engine airplane with a propeller that turns to the right, the airplane will always gain more altitude when performing a chandelle to the left because of the effects of P factor and torque. Left turning tendency helps the airplane when performing a chandelle to the left, while it fights the action of an airplane performing a chandelle to the right. |

Task D: Lazy Eights

802.	When are pitch, bank, and airspeed held constant during a Lazy 8?	Never. The point of the maneuver is to demonstrate that the pilot can remain oriented and maintain control through a maneuver when the pitch, bank, and airspeed are constantly changing.
803.	When is the airplane straight and level during a Lazy 8?	The airplane is straight and level at the entry, midpoint, and exit of the maneuver. At every other point in the maneuver, the airplane is pitching and banking simultaneously.
804.	What is the minimum safe altitude to enter the maneuver?	The minimum safe altitude for entering a Lazy 8 is 1,500 ft. MSL.
805.	What is the maximum bank to use in a Lazy 8?	The maximum bank for a Lazy 8 should be approximately 30°.
806.	Why is a good reference point critical to performing the Lazy 8 well?	Because the Lazy 8 requires constantly changing pitch and bank, it is important to know exactly where you are in the maneuver at any given point. Without a solid reference point, it would be difficult to perform the maneuver with the expected precision of altitude, bank, and airspeed required by the PTS.

Area of Operation VI: Ground Reference Maneuver

Task A: Eights on Pylons

807.	What normal aspect of flying does the rectangular course approximate?	The rectangular course is very similar to the airport traffic pattern.
808.	What is a pilot's greatest challenge when flying a rectangular pattern?	Because we fly four sides of a box, the wind is a factor that the pilot has to contend with and compensate for. Just like in the airport traffic pattern, the downwind leg will have a higher ground-speed than the upwind leg. The crosswind and base legs require a crab into the wind to maintain a straight course line.
809.	Where is the steeper bank angle required, during the downwind to base turn or during the upwind to crosswind turn?	The groundspeed is higher during the downwind to base turn, so the bank angle has to be steeper in order to compensate for the amount of ground being covered with the higher groundspeed.
810.	How can you maintain orientation when flying a rectangular course?	By using a landmark like a road, a river, or a tree line, it is possible to maintain a consistent ground track during the maneuver.
811.	What is the lowest safe altitude at which we can perform the rectangular pattern?	We should be at 700 ft. AGL or above throughout the maneuver.
812.	How will you enter the rectangular pattern?	I will enter on a 45° angle to the downwind, just as if I were entering an airport traffic pattern.
813.	Is it necessary to clear the area before doing a low altitude maneuver like the rectangular pattern?	It is always necessary to clear the area before doing any maneuver, in the interest of safety.

Area of Operation VII: Navigation

Task A: Pilotage and Dead Reckoning

814.	Can you give me a definition for the term "pilotage?"	Pilotage is a method of navigation that uses landmarks, checkpoints, and visual references.
815.	What makes a good landmark or reference point?	The bigger and more obvious a landmark is, the better. A highway, a lake, a river, railroad tracks, or a ridge line are all good landmarks.
816.	What makes for a bad landmark or reference point?	Landmarks and reference points should be unique to be most useful. A mountain is a good landmark if it stands alone, but it loses its value if it is surrounded by other mountains. Similarly, a lake is a good landmark if it is the only large body of water in a wide area. If, however, there are several other lakes in the same general region, it is a less valuable landmark since a pilot could potentially mistake one lake for another, and find himself or herself lost.
817.	What is dead reckoning?	Dead reckoning is method of navigation that involves using sectional charts to select a course, and then establishing a heading to maintain that course based on current weather information.
818.	Is it necessary to use only one method of navigation?	No, it is actually preferable to use pilotage and dead reckoning together when flying cross-country. The two methods complement each other.
819.	Can you give me an example of how the two methods complement each other for cross-country flight?	By plotting a course and figuring in the current weather reports, I can have a very accurate indication of what heading I should fly as I start out on a cross-country flight. But as I fly along my route, the checkpoints and landmarks I selected can give me a good indication if the wind is affecting my course more or less than I anticipated. By using the two methods together, I can fly a more accurate route and be more confident.
820.	If I choose to fly a cross-country flight from a field with an elevation of 120 ft. AGL, on a course of 270° and a cruising altitude of 5,500 ft. MSL, have I made a good decision?	No. To fly a westerly course above 3,000 ft. AGL, you should be at an altitude of even thousands plus 500 ft. (in this case, either 4,500 ft. MSL or 6,500 ft. MSL.) The odd thousand plus 500 foot altitudes are used by flights headed in an easterly direction. (NOTE: Use the memory aid, "East is odd and west is EVEN odder.")

Task B: Navigation Systems and Radar Services

821.	How can you use ATC to your advantage when flying cross-country?	Flight following (also known as VFR radar traffic advisory service) is available to VFR pilots on a workload-permitting basis. This allows the VFR pilot to maintain communications with ATC throughout much of a cross-country flight.
822.	To participate in flight following, what must you do?	I must have the ability to communicate with ATC, be in a radar coverage area, and be radar identified by ATC.
823.	What can we expect when we request flight following from ATC?	We can expect to be assigned a squawk code to put into the transponder, and we will often be asked to press "Ident," which will allow the controller to identify us on his or her radar screen.

Task C: Diversion

824.	When flying a cross-country flight, what might cause me to divert from my destination to an alternate airport?	There are several good reasons to divert. Some reasons you might divert include unforecast weather conditions with heavy rain, turbulence, or conditions that do not allow for continued VFR flight; a sick passenger; fuel capacity concerns due to higher-than-forecast headwinds; maintenance issues such as falling oil pressure or rising oil temperature; or the closing of your destination airport for any number of reasons. All would be good reasons to divert to an alternate airport.
825.	Once the decision is made to divert, what is the first thing you would do?	I would turn in the general direction of my alternate airport. I can make radio calls as necessary, change my flight plan, and work out an exact heading based on my location after that first turn.
826.	What information would you need to gather after making the decision to divert?	After making the turn in the general direction of my new destination, I would pick a landmark to keep me oriented in the right general direction while I worked out a specific course. I would also locate the destination on my sectional chart to get field elevation, CTAF or tower frequencies, and the ATIS frequency if one is available.

| 827. | What limitations might you consider when picking an alternate airport to divert to? | My alternate airport should be one that is close enough that my remaining fuel will get me there with endurance to spare and should have a runway that is sufficiently long to handle my arrival. The weather conditions en route and at the new destination should be VFR and within the capabilities of both myself and my aircraft. |

Task D: Lost Procedures

828.	If you begin to suspect you are lost, what is the first thing you would do?	I would climb. Weather permitting, I will be able to see farther from a higher altitude, and my radio will have a more extensive range.
829.	What do you imagine your major consideration would be if you were lost?	I would have two major considerations high up on my priority list. One would be fuel quantity. If I know I have 3 hours of fuel remaining, I can reasonably expect to find a solution to my predicament before fuel becomes a serious issue. My second major consideration would be weather conditions. If the weather along my proposed route is degrading but the weather behind me remains clear, I would be inclined to either head back in the direction I came from to retrace my route to more familiar territory and regain my bearings in order to continue my flight, or else abandon my cross-country plans and return home.
830.	Once you have climbed to a higher altitude, what would you do?	Remain calm, fly the aircraft, and begin to gather information visually that would help me identify my location. I would look for large, unique landmarks that would help suggest where I am, including major highways, population centers, lakes, rivers, or coastlines.
831.	If you cannot find any landmarks to help orient you, what might you do?	I would use the radio to communicate with resources on the ground. If necessary, I would call 121.5 and set my transponder to 7600 to help ATC identify my location.
832.	What if the aircraft you are flying is not equipped with a radio or a transponder?	If I could identify landmarks behind me that I had passed on my route and was confident I could rely on them to find my way home or to a familiar airport I had passed en route, I would turn back, retrace my route, and land at the first available airport.

833.	If your aircraft is equipped with a GPS unit, what might you do to help locate your position?	If the GPS unit has power and I am confident it is working correctly, I could use the "Nearest" function to find the closest airport, turn toward it, and obtain the radio frequency for the tower or to self-announce my intentions. Once on the ground, I would take my time and find where I went wrong. This would allow me to determine my next course of action based on weather and other variables while relaxed on the ground rather than while under pressure in the air.
834.	If you were able to use the GPS to reorient yourself, would it be reasonable to continue your flight?	Yes, it would. If using the GPS allows me to find my way back to my planned route of flight and all other factors remain unchanged, it would be reasonable to use the GPS as a backup to pilotage and dead reckoning in order to continue on to my destination with confidence.

Area of Operation VIII: Slow Flight and Stalls

Task A: Maneuvering During Slow Flight

835.	What would be a good altitude to initiate slow flight?	I would be at 1,000 ft. AGL or higher before initiating slow flight. Preferably, I would be at 1,500 ft. AGL, an altitude that provides plenty of room for obstacle clearance and a safe altitude for stall recovery if that became necessary.
836.	Is it necessary to clear the area before entering slow flight?	Yes, because the aircraft will be moving at a much slower rate of speed than is typical, for our own safety as well as the safety of transitional aircraft we may encounter, we will clear the area before entering slow flight.
837.	How would you define slow flight?	Slow flight is a maneuver where the aircraft is flown at a very low airspeed, using pitch to control airspeed and power to maintain altitude. I will be attempting to fly the aircraft at a slow enough speed that any increase in angle of attack or power reduction would result in a stall.
838.	Can you turn while in slow flight?	Yes, but very slowly, with rudder inputs, not using ailerons. An increase in load factor from a bank could result in a stall, so turns are done with the rudder alone, very slowly.

| 839. | How would you recover from slow flight? | I would add power smoothly and let the nose drop as airspeed increases to maintain altitude. When we are back at cruising speed, I can bring the power back and trim for level flight. |

Task B: Power-Off Stalls

840.	What does a power-off stall simulate?	It mimics the situation on final when power is very low or off entirely. On final approach, if the nose comes up too high and the airspeed is allowed to bleed off excessively, a power-off stall may result.
841.	What is the first indication that a stall is approaching?	The controls will tend to feel mushy and sluggish. We may feel a bit of a buffet just before the stall and the stall warning system (a buzzer or a light in most aircraft) should provide a warning just before the airplane breaks as the stall occurs.
842.	If the nose falls off to the left or the right during the stall, how do we correct for that?	With rudder inputs. Since the wing is stalled, the ailerons are of minimal effectiveness to control our heading during a stall.
843.	If one wing falls during the stall, will the ailerons be able to pick the wing back up again?	Again, we would use rudder to control our heading. We want to keep the ailerons centered during a stall because they have very little control authority during the stall, and because we want to avoid inadvertently crossing the controls and turning a simple stall recovery into a stall/spin recovery.
844.	What will break the stall?	The stall can be broken by lowering the nose to reduce the angle of attack. An increase in power will allow me to raise the nose and resume level flight without slowing down further and risking a secondary stall.
845.	How much power should be added during the recovery?	I have been trained to add full power for the recovery. Once the recovery is complete, I will reduce power to a cruise setting.
846.	Would it be acceptable to raise the nose briskly immediately after the stall to prevent any loss of altitude?	After lowering the nose to break the stall, I would raise the nose smoothly as I increased the power. If I were to yank the nose upward to prevent a loss of altitude, we would enter a secondary, and possibly deeper, stall that would almost certainly cause us to lose altitude – the exact thing we want to prevent when recovering from a stall.

847.	Is it necessary to clear the area before doing a power-off stall?	I will clear the area before every maneuver, in the interest of safety.
848.	Where could I find a procedure for how to recover from a power-off stall in the airplane we will be flying today?	The POH and the AFM both include a procedure for the proper power-off stall recovery to use in the airplane we will be flying today.
849.	What is the minimum recovery altitude for demonstrating a stall recovery?	We will recover no lower than 1,500 feet MSL.
850.	What is a reasonable entry altitude when performing stalls and stall recoveries?	The recovery must be performed no lower than 1,500 feet MSL, so I prefer to give myself a large margin of error when I perform stall recoveries by entering the maneuver at 2,500 feet MSL or higher. If any terrain or obstacles are an issue, I should increase my minimum entry altitude accordingly.
851.	What is the risk when doing a forward slip to a landing?	Airspeed control is critical because the controls are crossed. A stall with crossed controls could be disastrous, so we will be sure to maintain an airspeed at or slightly above the usual approach speed while slipping.

Task C: Power-On Stalls

852.	What does a power-on stall simulate?	Power-on stalls are a good simulation of what would happen if the pilot raised the nose too high and let the airspeed bleed off during a takeoff.
853.	If you were to perform a power-on stall, what would you be using as a power setting?	I will use a power setting of 65% or higher. It is possible to use full power on some aircraft, but on others full power requires a pitch up of 30° or more. In the interest of safety, I prefer to simulate the takeoff condition without pitching the nose that high.
854.	How is the recovery from a power-on stall performed?	Lower the nose to break the stall, smoothly bring in full power, then raise the nose smoothly to level flight and regain any altitude that was lost during the maneuver.

855.	Would it be best to raise the nose into a climb immediately to recover any lost altitude?	No, it is important to raise the nose to level flight after applying full power. The aircraft needs a few seconds for the speed to increase enough to allow us to raise the nose into a gradual climb.
856.	What is the risk of raising the nose too high too quickly during the recovery?	If the nose is raised too high too quickly, it is possible to enter a secondary stall that might be deeper than the first stall was.
857.	Where could I find a procedure for how to recover from a power-on stall in the airplane we will be flying today?	The POH and the AFM both include a procedure for the proper power-on stall recovery to use in the airplane we will be flying today.

Task D: Accelerated Stalls

858.	What is the difference between an accelerated stall and an unaccelerated, or conventional, stall?	We typically think of stalls occurring at low speeds. The accelerated stall maneuver proves that the airplane can stall at any speed. In an accelerated stall, we will be operating above the airplane's normal stall speed and will increase the aerodynamic load on the airplane to the point where the wing stalls.
859.	What causes an accelerated stall?	Like any stall, the cause of an accelerated stall is exceeding the wing's critical angle of attack. The ultimate cause of our going beyond the critical angle of attack will be aerodynamic loading rather than low speed and a high pitch attitude (like we see in a conventional power-on or power-off stall).
860.	Describe the setup and configuration you will use for an accelerated stall demonstration.	The maneuver will begin in normal cruise with the flaps and gear up. I will slow the airplane below V_A but to around 20 knots above the V_{S1} speed (low-speed end of the green arc). Once that is established, I will roll into a coordinated 45° bank, and then gradually increase back pressure to cause the airplane to approach the stall.

861.	What is the appropriate airspeed at which to begin this maneuver, and how did you arrive at that value?	The airspeed we will use for the demonstration is ____. I determined this airspeed by adding 20 knots to the normal V_{S1} speed (low-speed end of the green arc). I've ensured this speed is below the design maneuvering speed of the airplane (V_A) by first referencing the published V_A for the airplane at max gross weight, which is ____. That speed decreases as the weight of the airplane decreases and according to my weight and balance calculation for this flight, we will be operating at ____ pounds. I can do a simple calculation to determine our V_A speed by multiplying the published max V_A by the square root of our weight divided by the airplane's max gross weight. That simple equation looks like this: $V_A = V_{Amax} \times$ sq.rt (current weight ÷ max gross weight). Using that equation, our effective V_A speed would be ____ knots. Our entry speed for this maneuver is below that value.
862.	What things will you attempt to avoid during the accelerated stall demonstration?	As with all stalls for this practical test, I do not want to enter a full stall, but rather recover at the onset of the stall, when the airplane begins to buffet. Also, it's important that I maintain proper coordination throughout the entry, recovery, and stall phases of the maneuver. Failure to do so could result in a sudden power-on spin.
863.	How will you recover from an accelerated stall?	As with any stall recovery, I need to decrease the angle of attack. In this case, I will simultaneously reduce back pressure, roll out of the turn, and increase power. I will attempt to minimize any altitude loss and return the airplane to a flyable state as quickly as possible. Once the airplane is back in the normal flight regime, I will return to your preselected altitude, heading, and airspeed.

Task E: Spin Awareness

864.	What must happen first in order to spin the airplane?	The airplane must be stalled to spin. If the pilot can avoid stalling the airplane, (s)he will avoid spinning the airplane.
865.	If an airplane can only be spun after it stalls, why don't all stalls result in spins?	The airplane has to be stalled and have a yawing motion for a spin to occur. By keeping the ailerons centered and using the rudder to maintain directional control during a stall, it is possible to avoid entering a spin.
866.	Which is more likely to get into a spin, an airplane with a forward CG or an airplane with an aft CG?	An airplane with an aft CG is more likely to spin than an airplane with a forward CG.
867.	Would the location of the CG have any effect on the recovery from a spin?	An airplane with an aft CG is harder to recover from a spin, and may take longer to recover from the spin than an airplane with a forward CG.
868.	What should I avoid to prevent a spin from occurring?	Keep the airplane coordinated at all times, avoiding crossed controls, and avoid trying to steer the airplane with ailerons in a stall. If you're coordinated when turning the airplane and use the rudder for directional control during stall recoveries, the airplane should not enter a spin.
869.	How can I avoid entering a spin?	By not stalling the airplane.
870.	How can I avoid entering a spin if I do stall the airplane, even if I stall it accidentally?	If you use the proper stall recovery technique, the airplane will not enter a spin after stalling.
871.	What is the spin recovery procedure for the airplane we will be flying today?	Power to idle, neutralize the ailerons, full rudder opposite the direction of spin rotation, yoke (stick) forward briskly to break the stall. When the rotation stops, center the rudder, raise the nose smoothly, and apply power as necessary. (NOTE: This is a generic procedure. The procedure published in the POH or AFM for your aircraft is the procedure you should memorize and use for spin recovery in that aircraft.)

Area of Operation IX: Emergency Operations

Task A: Emergency Descent

872.	What in-flight situations may require an emergency descent?	This maneuver is a procedure for establishing the fastest practical rate of descent during emergency conditions that may arise as the result of an uncontrollable fire, a sudden loss of cabin pressurization, smoke in the cockpit, or any other situation demanding an immediate and rapid descent.
873.	Where would you find the prescribed emergency descent procedure for your airplane?	Because the emergency descent is an emergency procedure, it would be found in Section 3 of the airplane's POH.
874.	Describe the appropriate airspeed and configuration for an emergency descent.	The airplane should be in its highest drag configuration – gear and flaps extended, propeller control at high RPM setting (if equipped with a constant-speed propeller). The throttle should be in the idle position, and the airspeed must be kept within the operating range appropriate to its configuration. For example, operating above V_{FE} with the flaps fully extended could damage the flaps and/or the wings.
875.	How should you correctly perform an emergency descent?	I would first refer to the airplane's POH under Section 3, Emergency Procedures, to determine if a specific procedure is outlined for the airplane I am flying. If not, I will use the following technique: 1) Reduce the power to idle. 2) Move the propeller control to the high RPM position (if equipped with a constant-speed propeller). This will allow the propeller to act as an aerodynamic brake to help prevent excessive airspeed during the descent. 3) As quickly as practicable, extend the landing gear (if retractable) and full flaps to provide maximum drag so that a descent can be made as rapidly as possible without excessive airspeed. 4) To maintain positive load factors and for the purpose of clearing the area below, a 30° to 45° bank should be established for at least a 90° heading change while initiating the descent. 5) Do not exceed V_{NE}, V_{LE}, or V_{FE}, depending on the airplane's configuration.

Task B: Emergency Approach and Landing (Simulated)

876.	Given an engine failure, what is the first thing you would do?	I would pitch and trim for best glide speed immediately. After that, I would attempt a restart while picking out a suitable emergency landing spot.
877.	Once you have established best glide speed and begun your search for a suitable landing spot, what will you do?	Assuming an engine failure, I will analyze the cause of the failure and, if it is appropriate, I will attempt a restart. I will be using the emergency checklist included in the POH or AFM for the aircraft to be sure that I do not miss any steps in that process.
878.	What would suggest a good field for an emergency landing?	I would be looking for someplace that is relatively flat and has enough length to allow me to put the aircraft down and roll out without hitting any solid obstacles, like trees or rocks. I want to be aware of any wires on the approach end as well as fencing or other obstacles that would make a safe landing difficult or impossible.
879.	During that process of establishing the best glide speed, selecting a field to land in, getting out your emergency checklist, and possibly attempting a restart, what will be your primary focus?	My first priority is to fly the airplane. I will be doing a number of things during an emergency, but flying the airplane remains my primary focus. It is critical to the safe outcome of the flight that I do not allow myself to become distracted from that task.
880.	When performing an emergency landing, what is your primary responsibility?	The safety of the flight and my passengers, the same as at any other point in any other flight.
881.	Is there any circumstance that would allow us to turn around and land on a runway we had just taken off from?	Yes. If we have sufficient altitude, we can potentially make the turn and get back safely. But in order to line up on the runway, the turn will be more than 180° (180° plus an intercept angle). If there is a wind, it will work in our favor since it will be helping us to reach the runway. But it will also give us a longer rollout because of our higher groundspeed when landing downwind. Unless we are above 500 feet, I would not attempt a return to the runway. Above that altitude the chances of making a successful emergency landing improve. Below 500 feet, the likelihood of getting the aircraft turned around and lined up on the runway without running out of altitude is not good.

882.	What might be a weather consideration when picking out that landing spot?	The wind is going to be my biggest weather concern. I will make my decision on where to land partly based on the direction and intensity of the wind. With no power, my glide upwind will be shorter than a downwind glide, and I will have to make a choice of where to land accordingly.
883.	Would a parking lot be a good choice for an emergency landing field?	It depends on the parking lot. If it is large and wide open with few cars and plenty of room to roll out, then it might be a good choice. If it is a crowded parking lot with light poles and other obstacles, it would be a less desirable option.
884.	Would a road be a good choice?	A wide road with light traffic and minimal trees, electrical wires, and other obstacles may be a valid option. But a busy road or a narrow road bordered by trees and light poles would be a poor choice for an emergency landing spot.
885.	If the engine were to fail on takeoff and we had reached an altitude of approximately 300 feet, could we just turn back and land on the runway we just took off from?	Not from 300 feet, we couldn't. That altitude does not allow for a successful 180-degree turn without power. At that altitude, we would have to select and commit to the best possible landing spot that lies in front of us.
886.	If you are able to get the aircraft on the ground successfully but do not have sufficient space to stop before reaching a tree line, what would you do?	I would use aerodynamic braking and whatever means available to me to slow the aircraft down before reaching the trees. If it became unavoidable that I was going to hit the trees, I would steer the aircraft to allow the fuselage to miss the trees and allow the wings to absorb the impact.
887.	Would it make sense to perform an emergency landing if you lost partial power but the engine continued to operate?	I would make that decision based on the specifics of the situation. It is difficult to answer in absolute terms. The best course of action depends on the circumstances. If I were in an area that offered me good, safe options for an emergency or a precautionary landing but the route ahead did not, then it might be a reasonable option to land rather than press on and get into a situation that is significantly less likely to have a safe outcome. On the other hand, if I were over water or inhospitable terrain but still had enough power to maintain altitude, or were losing altitude slowly, it might make more sense to work on the problem while attempting to get to a place where an emergency landing would be less dangerous.

| 888. | Why would you steer to allow the wings to take the brunt of the crash and cause a significant amount of damage to the aircraft? | My responsibility is to the safety of the flight and my passengers. As much as I would hate to damage the aircraft in an emergency landing, it is more important that I prevent harm to my passengers as well as people on the ground. |

Task C: Systems and Equipment Malfunctions

889.	If a system failure occurs in the air, what is your primary responsibility?	My primary responsibility is to fly the airplane, regardless of whether I have a system failure or not.
890.	If you suspect a system failure, how would you verify the failure and determine which system is involved?	I can perform basic troubleshooting tasks to determine which system has failed, confirm whether it is a partial failure or a complete failure, and make a determination on how that failure might affect my flight.
891.	Are there system failures that would not have a detrimental effect on your flight?	Yes. An electrical failure would be inconvenient, but when flying VFR in daylight in Class G airspace, when my destination is in Class G airspace, an electrical failure would probably not qualify as an emergency that would adversely affect my ability to complete my flight.
892.	Can some system failures be remedied in flight?	Yes. An radio failure may be the result of a popped circuit breaker or a switch that was inadvertently turned off. A fuel system issue may be remedied by switching to another tank or employing an electric fuel pump to increase fuel pressure and quantity.
893.	What is the procedure if you have an engine failure in flight?	As soon as you realize an engine failure has occurred, establish and trim for the best glide speed for your airplane. Select an emergency landing site. Then, if time permits, go through the restart checklist in an attempt to regain power. If that fails and you have no choice but to make a forced landing, be sure to leave time to make use of the forced landing checklist in a calm and organized manner.

894.	What is the necessary action if you lose a magneto in flight?	If you suspect that you have lost a magneto in flight, you can identify the bad magneto by switching from both to either left or right. The bad magneto will be evident when the engine will not run on that magneto. After you identify the bad magneto, the engine should continue to run on the good one. There is often no harm done by continuing to leave the switch in the "Both" position, even if one magneto has failed. Land and make repairs before continuing your flight.
895.	What are some common causes of a rough-running engine in flight?	There are numerous factors that can cause an engine to run rough. The most common causes are carburetor ice, a problematic magneto, or fouled spark plugs.
896.	What would you do if your engine began running rough in flight?	Carburetor ice is one of the few issues for which I have direct access to a remedy, so I would apply the carburetor heat for a few minutes to hopefully melt the ice, then turn it off to find out if the engine would return to running normally.
897.	Is there anything else you could do to correct the problem?	Yes, I could change fuel tanks. It is possible that contaminated fuel would make the engine run rough. Switching tanks could allow the contaminated fuel to clear the system and be replaced by good fuel that will return the engine to normal operation.
898.	If the engine continued running rough, what would be your next course of action?	I would turn toward the nearest airport while checking the oil temperature and pressure gauges. As long as they were in the green I would continue on to make a precautionary landing at a nearby airport. It would be appropriate to have a maintenance technician investigate the problem before I carried on with the flight.
899.	Is it necessary to make a precautionary landing when the engine is running rough?	No, but if the safety of the flight is in question, it is always better to make a precautionary landing rather than push on and create a potentially more serious problem.
900.	What indication would you expect if carburetor or induction icing is impeding the air passages to the engine?	The engine may run rough, and the RPM may drop as power is reduced.

901.	How could you prevent or correct for carburetor or induction icing?	Applying carburetor heat or opening an alternate air source may prevent or correct carburetor or induction icing.
902.	What would you expect to see after applying carburetor heat?	The engine would run rougher, and the RPMs may drop due to the less-dense heated air entering the induction system.
903.	If you suspect icing, what would you expect to see after opening an alternate air source?	The RPMs would rise to their previous level as a result of airflow being restored to the induction system.
904.	What should you do if you notice that you are losing oil pressure?	A loss of oil pressure should be viewed as an emergency situation. The engine will tend to overheat and may not continue to run with low oil pressure. If you are in the pattern, return for a full stop landing. If you are flying outside the traffic pattern, turn toward the nearest airport and plan to land as soon as possible. If you are a significant distance from an airport, be prepared for a possible forced landing and choose your route of flight accordingly.
905.	Why is fuel starvation an issue of concern for pilots?	Because it is often preventable by taking on sufficient fuel before departure, accurately estimating fuel use, and planning flights to allow for a reasonable surplus of fuel that allows us to reach our destination and fly on to an alternate if necessary.
906.	Is fuel starvation common?	It is not common, but it is a leading cause of aircraft accidents. Careful monitoring of fuel is one of the simplest ways for a pilot to prepare for a safe flight.
907.	Is running out of fuel the only cause of fuel starvation?	No, carburetor or induction icing can cause fuel starvation even when fuel is on board. If the ice chokes out the airflow to the induction system, the fuel/air mixture cannot reach the engine, even if there is plenty of fuel on board.
908.	In the event of fuel starvation in flight, do you have any options?	If icing is the cause, I may be able to restore the fuel/air mixture by using carburetor heat or the alternate air source. If the aircraft has more than one fuel tank and a selector valve, I could switch to the other tank. If there is fuel in that tank, I may be able to prevent the engine from failing, or I may be able to restart the engine if it has shut down.

909.	Is fuel starvation an emergency situation?	Yes. In the event of a real fuel starvation situation, if another fuel source and a restart is not possible, it will be necessary to make an emergency landing.
910.	What does a low voltage light indicate when it is illuminated?	A low voltage light indicates that the alternator or generator is not working and the electrical equipment is running from the battery.
911.	How would you deal with a low voltage indication in flight?	Turn off all non-essential electrical equipment to limit the drain on the battery and land as soon as practical.
912.	What is the procedure if a circuit breaker pops?	If a circuit breaker pops and it is resettable, push it back in once. If it pops out again, leave it out and determine the next course of action. Pushing the breaker in more than once may lead to an electrical fire.
913.	What would happen if the vacuum pump failed in your airplane?	A failed vacuum pump will result in the loss of the attitude indicator and the heading indicator.
914.	How is a vacuum pump failure in flight different from most equipment failures?	A vacuum pump failure is not considered an emergency situation in VFR conditions because the instruments powered by the vacuum pump are not necessary for safe flight.
915.	What would happen to the altimeter if the pitot-static system were obstructed?	If the pitot-static system were blocked, the altimeter would indicate the altitude where the system became blocked.
916.	What would happen to the VSI if the pitot-static system were obstructed?	With the pressure in the system remaining stable due to the blockage, the VSI would show no indication in a climb or descent.
917.	What would happen to the airspeed indicator if the pitot-static system were obstructed?	Without the ability to compare pitot or ram air pressure, to static pressure, the airspeed indicator would read zero.
918.	What error does the altimeter indicate if you are using an alternate static source?	Because alternate static sources are usually located inside the cockpit where the pressure is lower than it is outside the airplane, the altimeter is likely to indicate a higher altitude than normal.
919.	Is it a serious problem if the flaps cannot be deployed?	No. It is inconvenient, but not serious. If the aircraft is on the ground, it should go to maintenance for repair before flight. If the aircraft is in the air, the pilot should operate normally, albeit without flaps, through the landing phase of the flight. After landing, the aircraft should go to maintenance for repair before it is flown again.

920.	What is the most serious flap malfunction that could occur?	Asymmetric flap deployment is a serious problem. This is when one flap extends and the other does not, or when one flap extends further than its counterpart. This causes asymmetric lift, an imbalance that can be powerful enough to render the aircraft uncontrollable.
921.	If asymmetric flap deployment occurs, what can you do?	Retract the flaps immediately. This is not a problem that can be remedied in the air. The aircraft should be flown without flaps for the remainder of the flight. After landing, the airplane should go to maintenance for repair.
922.	What can cause the trim system to be inoperative?	It depends on how the trim system works. It can be the result of an electrical failure or a stuck switch. It may also be the result of a kinked cable, a loose fastener, or a broken cable or fastener.
923.	Is an inoperative trim system a serious problem?	It certainly can be, depending on the type of failure. A runway trim system is the result of a stuck switch on an electrical system that causes the trim to run fully to the stop in one direction. In some cases, this can cause control pressures extreme enough to make control of the aircraft impossible.
924.	What if your trim system is manual, but it cannot be adjusted – is that a serious problem?	No, it is not serious, but it is a reason for concern. Increased control pressures will cause pilot fatigue to occur much more rapidly than on a normal flight. While this is not an emergency situation, it does warrant a precautionary landing at the first opportunity to repair the system.
925.	What is the risk to the safety of flight with an inadvertent door or window opening?	The biggest risk is that the pilot will become so distracted by the noise and draft that (s)he stops flying the aircraft. The consequences of that distraction can be dire.
926.	What is the best course of action if a door or window opens in flight?	If the door or window cannot be closed easily, make a precautionary landing at the earliest convenience to close and secure the door or window on the ground.

927.	Will the airplane fly with the door or window open?	A door or window that pops open will rarely affect flight performance so negatively that the aircraft becomes uncontrollable. It may degrade performance to the point that it is not possible to maintain altitude, or it may have almost no effect. It is best to remain calm, fly the airplane, and find a place to land and deal with the situation on the ground, if necessary.
928.	If you were flying and noticed ice building up on your airplane, what would your best course of action be?	Since most light general aviation aircraft have no anti-icing or deicing equipment aside from carburetor heat, my first choice would be to land at the first available airport. If possible, I would get below the freezing level, while still maintaining adequate altitude above the surface, to hopefully prevent further ice buildup and possibly melt off at least some of the existing ice while en route.
929.	What causes structural ice to form?	Visible moisture and an ambient temperature below the freezing level.
930.	Can structural ice be avoided?	Yes, it can be avoided in many cases. By avoiding flight above the freezing level when moisture is present in the form of clouds, drizzle, or rain, structural ice can largely be avoided.
931.	Is it legal to fly when icing is reported?	It is legal if the airplane you are flying is equipped to deal with icing. If the airplane is not equipped for flight into icing conditions, it is neither legal nor wise to continue flight into known icing conditions.
932.	How serious is a fire in the cabin?	Very serious. That would more than likely meet the standards for declaring an emergency. I would look for a place to land immediately, shut off the master switch to prevent an electrical fire from worsening, and follow the emergency checklist in the POH for a cabin fire.
933.	If shutting the master switch off stops the fire, would you continue with the flight?	That depends on the situation. If I were in a place where no safe landing sites were available, I would continue, leaving the electrical system turned off. (NOTE: Become familiar with the appropriate emergency checklist in the POH for your aircraft and be prepared to discuss it with your examiner.)

934.	How could you troubleshoot an electrical fire in flight?	With the master switch turned off, I would turn off each device individually until all the electrical items on board were shut down. Then, I would turn the master switch back on. One by one, I would turn on only the device or devices I need to conduct the flight. If the fire starts up again, I would shut off the device that caused the fire but continue to use the other devices until landing if there is no indication that a fire would result.
935.	How would you deal with an engine compartment fire?	It depends on whether the fire occurs on the ground or in the air. On the ground, if the fire starts during engine start, it may be best to shut off the fuel supply while continuing to turn the engine over to suck the fire inside the engine. In the air, an immediate emergency landing might be in order. (NOTE: Become familiar with the specific emergency checklist in your POH and be prepared to discuss it with your examiner.)
936.	If the elevator fails in flight, what would you do?	I would control the airplane with power and elevator trim and return for landing.
937.	If the elevator fails in flight, would that qualify as an emergency?	Yes, it probably would, especially if there is heavy traffic in the area. I would declare an emergency to make it clear that I have limited control and ensure that I have a clear path to the runway without conflicting traffic.
938.	Could you still control the airplane if the rudder failed?	Yes, although my control would be limited. I could make shallow-banked, skidding turns back to the airport for a landing.
939.	If the ailerons failed, could you control the airplane in flight?	Yes, I could control the aircraft with the rudder and the elevator and return to the airport for a landing.
940.	Would you be tempted to make an emergency landing off airport due to a flight control malfunction?	No, probably not. The aircraft would be less maneuverable than usual, but it would be controllable. I would be better off landing back at the airport, or at another airport, where emergency equipment might be available and the runway would provide me with a wide, long landing area to use.

941.	Why are ballistic parachute systems installed in aircraft?	A ballistic parachute system offers an extra measure of safety to airplane operations. When deployed, the parachute allows the airframe to descend slowly to the ground, under control.
942.	How does a ballistic parachute system operate?	The pilot pulls a handle/lever that ignites a rocket motor. The rocket deploys the parachute, and the airflow opens the parachute.
943.	What precautions must be taken when operating an aircraft equipped with a ballistic parachute system?	Pilots must be careful not to hold/pull the handle/lever to avoid inadvertent deployment. Most systems employ safety pins that must be removed prior to flight. Refer to the Emergency Procedures Checklist regarding how to operate the system before you find yourself in an emergency situation.

Task D: Emergency Equipment and Survival Gear

944.	If you were planning a cross-country flight that crossed mountainous terrain, what emergency equipment might you carry?	Because the risk in mountainous terrain includes cold, I would carry blankets for myself and my passenger. I would also carry flashlights, food, water, and flares to help rescuers locate us.
945.	If you were planning to fly over a large body of water, what emergency gear would you carry?	I would be sure to have life vests for myself and my passenger, as well as a raft that would allow us to get out of the water in the event of a ditching.
946.	Is there any electronic gear you would consider carrying?	Yes, I would consider carrying a portable ELT that would send out a signal to help rescuers locate myself and my passenger on the water.
947.	If your route of flight takes you over the desert, would you carry any particular emergency equipment?	Water is the most important emergency item to have when in the desert. So I would carry drinking water, blankets, flares, and flashlights when flying over the desert, in case an emergency landing is necessary.
948.	What additional equipment might you carry if flying through an area where extreme temperature changes might occur?	If extreme heat was a possibility, I would be sure to carry drinking water and appropriate light clothing. If extreme cold was possible, I would carry blankets, a winter coat, extra socks, boots, a hat, and mittens or gloves. Exposure can be very dangerous, so carrying the appropriate emergency equipment to deal with the situation is important.

Area of Operation X: High Altitude Operations

Task A: Supplemental Oxygen

949.	What forms are aviator's breathing oxygen available in?	Aviator's breathing oxygen, or ABO, can be stored as a gas or as a liquid.
950.	Is aviator's breathing oxygen the same product as medical grade oxygen or industrial grade oxygen?	No, they are different products. In fact, only aviator's breathing oxygen is approved to be used in aircraft for the benefit of the passengers and crew. Medical and industrial grade oxygen do not meet the stringent standards set for aviator's breathing oxygen, and therefore cannot be used as a supplemental oxygen source on aircraft.
951.	What is the advantage of storing aviator's breathing oxygen in its gaseous form?	The gaseous form of aviator's breathing oxygen is more economical. It can be stored in low-pressure containers at 400–450 psi, or high pressure containers at 1,800–2,200 psi.
952.	What is the disadvantage of storing aviator's breathing oxygen in its gaseous form?	The storage tanks are heavy and bulky, which makes the gaseous form of aviator's breathing oxygen problematic for smaller aircraft.
953.	What is the advantage of storing liquid aviator's breathing oxygen (LOX)?	The liquid form of aviator's breathing oxygen has a 900 to 1 expansion ratio. This characteristic allows for a 5 to 1 weight savings over storing aviator's breathing oxygen in its gaseous form.
954.	What is the disadvantage of liquid aviator's breathing oxygen (LOX)?	Liquid oxygen is stored at 197°F below zero. Contact with exposed skin will cause severe frostbite. LOX also has a volatile nature when it comes in contact with petroleum products. Thus, great care is required when working with LOX to prevent injury.
955.	Why is the continuous oxygen flow system considered to be wasteful?	The continuous flow system is reliable and economical, but it is considered to be a very wasteful system because the oxygen flows continuously, whether you are inhaling, exhaling, or pausing between breaths.
956.	Why is the continuous flow system considered economical if it is so wasteful?	Because the continuous flow system does not require complicated masks or regulators to function properly.

957.	How does the diluter demand system differ from the continuous flow system?	The diluter demand oxygen system only supplies oxygen when the user is inhaling, while the continuous flow type delivers oxygen constantly, regardless of whether the user is inhaling or not.
958.	Where is the pressure demand system used?	The pressure demand system is designed to be used above 40,000 ft, where it is not possible to obtain 100% oxygen without a pressurized system to deliver it.
959.	How does the pressure demand system work?	The pressure demand system provides oxygen under positive pressure, which slightly over-inflates the lungs. This has the effect of pressurizing the lungs to a lower altitude where they can make more effective use of the oxygen delivered to them.

Task B: Pressurization

960.	What is the primary reason for the mandatory availability of supplemental oxygen, even in a pressurized aircraft?	In the event of decompression, it is necessary for the pilot and passengers to be protected against the effects of hypoxia, until the aircraft can descend to an altitude where supplemental oxygen is no longer required.
961.	For pressurized airplanes meeting the specific requirements of FAR Part 23 and Part 25, exceeding what cabin altitude will cause a warning system to activate?	When the cabin pressure exceeds 10,000 ft., pressurized airplanes certified under Part 23 or Part 25 of the FARs, the warning system will activate.
962.	For airplanes that are required to have them, at what cabin altitude will oxygen masks automatically be deployed?	If the cabin altitude exceeds 15,000 ft., the supplemental oxygen masks will deploy automatically.
963.	For how much time must the supplemental system provide oxygen to passengers when flying at altitudes above FL 250?	At flight altitudes above FL 250, a 10-minute supply of supplemental oxygen must be provided to all occupants of the aircraft.
964.	If one pilot leaves the flight deck while cruising at FL 350 or higher, what must the pilot who remains at the controls do?	The pilot who remains at the controls must wear and use an oxygen mask that is secured and sealed until the other pilot returns to the controls again.

965.	When above FL 350 but below FL 410, must at least one pilot wear a mask that supplies supplemental oxygen?	No. There is an exception to the rule that requires one pilot to wear a mask that supplies supplemental oxygen when flying above FL 350. The exception allows for neither pilot to be wearing an oxygen mask if the aircraft is below FL 410, both pilots are at the controls, and each pilot has a quick-donning type mask that can be placed on the face with one hand and operated within 5 seconds.
966.	As a general rule, what altitude represents the the ceiling for brain oxygen saturation that allows for normal functioning?	The rule of thumb is that 12,000 ft. is the ceiling for normal functioning. Above that altitude, the brain oxygen saturation drops to a level that could adversely affect performance.
967.	Hypoxia is a serious threat to pilots at high altitudes. How many major groups of hypoxia are there that pilots should be aware of and on guard for?	There are four major groups of hypoxia that pilots should be aware of. They are hypoxic hypoxia, histotoxic hypoxia, hypemic hypoxia, and stagnant hypoxia.
968.	What causes hypoxic hypoxia?	At high altitudes, the ambient pressure makes it difficult or impossible to obtain a sufficient level of oxygen through inhaling air normally.
969.	How can hypoxic hypoxia be remedied?	The use of supplemental oxygen will relieve the effects of hypoxic hypoxia very quickly.
970.	What causes histotoxic hypoxia?	Alcohol or drug use can impair the ability of the body's cells to use oxygen effectively. Although sufficient oxygen may be available in the ambient air, the body is not capable of processing it well enough to prevent the onset of the effects of hypoxia.
971.	Can histotoxic hypoxia be prevented?	Yes, but only by abstaining from the use of alcohol or drugs other than those approved by a flight surgeon or aviation medical examiner.
972.	What is hypemic hypoxia?	Hypemic hypoxia refers to the reduction of available red blood cells, which carry oxygen to the brain, as a result of anemia, carbon monoxide poisoning, excessive smoking, or blood loss.
973.	Can you describe stagnant hypoxia?	Stagnant hypoxia is the result of impaired circulation that does not pump sufficient blood to the tissues.

974.	Is stagnant hypoxia caused exclusively by disease?	No. Disease can be a factor, but stagnant hypoxia can also be caused by excessive G-forces or positive-pressure breathing for long periods of time.
975.	To prevent hypoxia, would it be advisable to use supplemental oxygen all the time, regardless of altitude?	No. Prolonged use of one hundred percent aviation oxygen can lead to harmful health effects, including coughing, fever, vomiting, nervousness, irregular heart beat, and lowered energy.
976.	Gases in the body can cause pain or serious physical issues due to changes in pressure. What are the two groups of gas that can lead to decompression sickness?	Trapped gas is a description of the expanding and contracting gases that are contained within the body. Evolved gas is the term used to describe the process of nitrogen coming out of solution into a gas while inside the body.
977.	Does body type make you more or less susceptible to decompression sickness?	Yes. Because fatty tissue can store more nitrogen, overweight people are more susceptible to decompression sickness.
978.	Are there physiological issues that affect your vision at altitude?	Yes. Just as hypoxia affects brain activity adversely, your vision can be adversely affected by a lack of oxygen, too. Another concern at altitude is the sun's ultraviolet rays which also can reduce your visual acuity.

Area of Operation XI: Postflight Procedures

Task A: After Landing, Parking, and Securing

979.	Where would we clear the runway at an airport without an operating control tower?	We would clear the runway at the first available taxiway after slowing the aircraft to a safe speed that would allow for the turn.
980.	Where would we clear the runway at an airport with an operating control tower?	We would turn off the runway onto the taxiway assigned by the tower controller. When we are clear of the runway, we will call ground control and request permission to taxi to our destination.
981.	When is it appropriate to start cleaning up the aircraft by retracting the flaps, turning off the carburetor heat, and so on?	For safety reasons, we only start to clean up the aircraft after we have cleared the runway and have the opportunity to stop and perform tasks in an orderly fashion without distractions.

982.	After clearing the runway at an airport without an operating control tower, when can we taxi to our destination?	We can taxi to our destination when the aircraft is cleaned up, our after-landing checklist is completed, and we have verified that the taxiway is clear for us to continue.
983.	If you are at a large, unfamiliar airport with an operating control tower, how can you navigate the taxiways to your destination?	If I am unfamiliar with the airport layout, I can request a progressive taxi from the ground controller, who will then provide me with directions that will help me taxi to my destination.
984.	What safety consideration do you have when taxiing into the ramp area at any airport?	There are several safety considerations that are all important. The ramp area contains aircraft that are tied down, aircraft that are arriving and departing, fuel trucks and other support vehicles, and pilots and passengers walking between the terminal and their aircraft. I have to be sure to carefully identify any risks so that I can evaluate and avoid conflicts with them as I taxi onto the ramp area.
985.	What concerns might you have about tie-downs on the ramp?	I will be careful not to taxi over tie-down ropes or chains while taxiing on the ramp area. I will only taxi in the designated areas in such a way that I can pull directly into the tie-down spot without putting the propeller in close proximity to any ropes or chains. If that is not possible, I will shut the aircraft down and move it into the tie-down spot manually.
986.	Once you are in the tie-down space, how will you shut the engine down and secure the aircraft?	I will be using the checklists available in the POH or AFM appropriate to the aircraft to shut the engine down and verify that the aircraft is configured and secured properly.
987.	When will your passenger be exiting the aircraft?	My passenger will be exiting the aircraft only after I have shut the engine down and verified that the aircraft is secured from rolling or being blown in a way that could cause an injury.
988.	Is your passenger allowed to help you secure the aircraft?	Yes. If the wind comes up to the point that it might cause the aircraft to move while it is being tied down, I can ask my passenger to help secure the aircraft and direct him or her specifically on what to do.

Multi-Engine Land

Only the multi-engine Tasks not covered under the single-engine Tasks are included.

Area of Operation I: Preflight Preparation

Task G: Operation of Systems

989.	What are some engine-driven accessories in your multi-engine aircraft?	A typical light twin aircraft may have some or all of the following engine-driven accessories: alternator, generator, vacuum pump, fuel pump, and hydraulic pump. Check your aircraft POH for parts specific to your aircraft.
990.	What kind of flaps are on your airplane and how are they actuated?	There are many different types of flaps used on general aviation aircraft. Some common types include split, fowler, slotted, and plain. They are usually electrically actuated in light twin aircraft. Refer to your aircraft POH for more information.
991.	What does "feathering" or "feather the prop" mean?	A "feathered" prop is a propeller that is at its highest pitch setting, which means that the chord line of each propeller blade is almost parallel to the relative wind. This condition produces the least amount of drag from the propeller blades and is primarily used in an engine-out scenario.
992.	Describe the fuel system on your multi-engine aircraft.	In general, the fuel system of a multi-engine airplane consists of at least two tanks with one tank located in each wing. These tanks can be used to cross-feed to the opposite engine or transfer fuel between each tank. They generally use engine-driven fuel pumps, boost pumps, and auxiliary fuel pumps. Some aircraft will also be equipped with fuel transfer pumps.
993.	What is the maximum fuel imbalance allowed in your aircraft?	The answer for your specific aircraft will be found in your POH. The POH will also advise you of what actions to take in the event of a fuel imbalance. Generally, depending on your aircraft, you will use a cross-feed switch or a fuel transfer pump to help balance out the fuel load.
994.	How is cabin heat produced in your multi-engine aircraft?	Some multi-engine aircraft will use heat exchangers that take heat from the exhaust manifold like in a single-engine aircraft. Many multi-engine aircraft use a small combustion heater. These combustion heaters use aircraft fuel to burn a small flame that is used to heat outside air.

Task H: Principles of Flight–Engine Inoperative

995.	If you lose an engine you only lose about 50% of your performance, right? That's why you have two engines, isn't it?	No. The loss of an engine in a light twin will usually result in an 85% penalty in climb performance. Not only do you lose the thrust generated by that engine, but you increase drag from the windmilling propeller. Drag is also increased due to the amount of rudder input required to maintain directional control. This increased rudder input coupled with asymmetrical thrust causes the vertical stabilizer and rudder to create even more induced drag, which further degrades aircraft performance.
996.	Define V_{MC}.	14 CFR 23.149(a) defines V_{MC} as: *V_{MC} is the calibrated airspeed at which, when the critical engine is suddenly made inoperative, it is possible to maintain control of the airplane with that engine still inoperative, and thereafter maintain straight flight at the same speed with an angle of bank of not more than 5 degrees. The method used to simulate critical engine failure must represent the most critical mode of powerplant failure expected in service with respect to controllability.*
997.	What are some factors that determine V_{MC}?	1) Aft CG (to the rear limit) 2) Trim in takeoff position 3) Out of ground effect 4) Max takeoff weight at sea level 5) Max takeoff power on good engine 6) Flaps in takeoff position 7) Cowl flaps in takeoff position 8) Landing gear retracted 9) Standard atmospheric conditions 10) Bank up to 5 degrees in operating engine 11) Prop windmilling 12) No more than 150 lb. of rudder pressure 13) Must be able to maintain within 20 degrees of heading
998.	Define V_{XSE}.	Best angle of climb on a single engine.
999.	Define V_{YSE}.	Best rate of climb on a single engine.

1000.	Why is it important to compute single-engine climb performance before takeoff?	Under certain weight and atmospheric conditions, it may not be possible for your airplane to climb if you lose an engine on takeoff. When flying multi-engine aircraft, you always have to consider what will happen to your performance if you lose an engine.
1001.	How do you calculate single-engine climb performance?	Your airplane's POH will have several performance tables that you will need to be familiar with. One of the more important tables is the single-engine climb performance. These tables and their names vary by manufacturer, but the information obtained from them is the same.
1002.	What is an "accelerate-stop distance?"	An accelerate-stop distance is the distance it takes an aircraft to accelerate from a standing start to a point where there is an assumed engine failure and from that point to V1 or the takeoff decision point and then come to a full stop. It answers the question, "Can the airplane accelerate from a full stop, lose an engine, and safely stop on the remaining runway?"
1003.	What is an "accelerate-go distance?"	The distance required to continue a takeoff and clear a 35-foot obstacle following an engine failure after takeoff decision speed.
1004.	Define "climb gradient."	The amount of altitude gained per horizontal distance.
1005.	Explain what a single-engine absolute ceiling is.	The density altitude that the airplane is capable of reaching and maintaining with one engine inoperative and with that inoperative engine feathered and the operative engine at full power. If the airplane is above this ceiling when an engine fails, it will begin descending until such a point where altitude can be maintained on one engine.
1006.	What will happen if an airplane reaches its single-engine absolute ceiling?	This is the point where no further climb is possible. The airplane will simply remain at this altitude.
1007.	How is single-engine service ceiling different from single-engine absolute ceiling?	At the single-engine service ceiling, the airplane should be able to maintain a 50-foot per-minute climb with the inoperative engine feathered. At the single-engine absolute ceiling, a climb is no longer possible.

1008.	What are the four factors that define the "critical" engine?	P-factor, spiraling slipstream, accelerated slipstream, and torque.
1009.	Define critical engine.	The critical engine is the engine whose failure would most adversely affect the performance or handling qualities of the airplane.
1010.	Does every twin-engine propeller airplane have a critical engine?	No. Some airplanes have counter-rotating props and therefore have no critical engine.
1011.	On a conventional twin-engine aircraft which engine is considered to be the critical engine?	The left engine is the critical engine.
1012.	On a non-conventional twin that does not have counter-rotating props, which engine is considered to be the critical engine?	The right engine would be the critical engine.
1013.	Why is the left engine the critical engine on a conventional twin?	The loss of the left engine on a conventional twin would cause the most adverse effects for several reasons. First, the p-factor of the right engine would enhance asymmetrical yaw. Second, the spiraling slipstream from the right engine would not aid in counteracting yaw like the left engine would. Third, the accelerated slipstream from the right engine would increase the rolling tendency of the airplane because it is farther away from the center of lift. Fourth, the torque from the right engine would increase the tendency to roll to the left while simultaneously causing the airplane to yaw to the left.
1014.	Define "balanced field length."	Balanced field length is where the accelerate-stop and the accelerate-go distances are equal. This means that the distances required to stop after an aborted takeoff is equal to the distance required to takeoff and climb to a height of 35 feet above the runway.
1015.	What is asymmetrical thrust?	A condition that develops when one or more engines becomes inoperative. In a light twin, this means that one engine has failed. The operating engine causes the airplane to yaw and roll in the direction of the inoperative engine.

Area of Operation VIII: Emergency Operations

Task B: Engine Failure During Takeoff Before V_{MC} (Simulated)

1016.	If an engine fails in a light twin during the takeoff roll prior to V_{MC}, what will you do?	I will close both throttles and apply the brakes in an effort to come to a stop prior to the end of the runway.
1017.	If an engine fails on a light twin during the takeoff roll after V_{MC} but with the airplane still on the ground, what will you do?	If the airplane is still on the ground, I have no choice but to close both throttles and apply the brakes, even if insufficient runway remains to come to a stop. Light twins do not have sufficient performance to rotate and climb after an engine failure.
1018.	Do all multi-engine aircraft require the PIC to abort the takeoff if an engine failure occurs while the aircraft is still on the runway?	No. Some jets and turbo props have sufficient performance on one engine to continue the takeoff roll. This ability is rarely if ever seen on piston-powered light twins.

Task C: Engine Failure After Lift-Off (Simulated)

1019.	What will you do if an engine fails after takeoff?	I will base my decision on a few factors. If I still have the landing gear down and runway below me, I may elect to close both throttles and land if sufficient runway is available to land and stop on. If the gear is up or in the process of retracting, I will carry out the appropriate engine failure checklist for the aircraft type while pitching for V_{YSE}. If performance allows, I will attempt to return to the airport and land.
1020.	If an engine fails on a light twin once airborne, are there any guarantees that the performance will be sufficient to continue to climb?	No. Many light twins do not have the ability to climb on one engine. The performance is affected by the density altitude and weight of the aircraft. A lightly loaded airplane on a cold day may be able to climb. The same airplane at maximum weight on a hot day may not be able to climb.
1021.	During an in-flight engine failure, how can you quickly and easily identify which engine has failed?	The airplane will yaw and roll in the direction of the dead engine. Applying rudder pressure towards the good engine will help you maintain directional control. Remember: Dead leg, dead engine.
1022.	Which airspeed should you initially pitch for when an engine fails in flight?	V_{YSE} or "blue-line" is the speed you should pitch for. V_{YSE} is your best single engine climb speed and will help you obtain the best performance from your airplane while one engine is inoperative.

1023.	Why is it important to verify which engine has failed before adjusting throttles, props, or mixture control?	Not correctly identifying which engine has failed and pulling back the throttle, prop, or mixture control of the operating engine could have a devastating effect on the airplane's performance. Always identify and verify before making any reductions with the engine controls.
1024.	Would there ever be a time when you wouldn't troubleshoot or try to restart a failed engine?	Yes. Adequate time and altitude are key factors when determining if an engine should be restarted. The downwind leg of the pattern would be an example of a time when restarting the engine would not be safe.
1025.	What are the emergency memory items associated with an engine failure for your aircraft?	Check your airplane's POH for the appropriate emergency checklist items. Generally the initial memory actions include: mixture, props, and throttles full forward. Boost pumps on. Reduce drag by raising flaps and landing gear if extended.
1026.	Other than yaw, what are some ways to determine which engine has failed?	Engine gauges are a good indicator as to which engine has experienced a failure. This is particularly true in the event of a partial loss of power where yaw and roll tendencies are less pronounced.

Task D: Approach and Landing with an Inoperative Engine (Simulated)

1027.	What effect will an inoperative engine have on your approach to land in VFR conditions?	The approach to land will not be greatly affected by the engine failure. However, a go-around may not be possible on one engine due to the performance loss. I will need to pay very close attention to my airspeed on final to ensure a go-around does not become necessary.

Area of Operation X: Multi-Engine Operations

Task A: Maneuvering with One Engine Inoperative

1028.	How is an engine failure in level cruise flight different from one on the upwind just after takeoff?	Typically, the power settings and pitch attitudes are lower in cruise flight, making the aircraft easier to control immediately after the engine failure.
1029.	Because the airplane is easier to control, is it still important to feather the propeller on the inoperative engine?	Yes. The plane may be easier to control, but it will most likely not have the performance required to maintain altitude. Feathering the engine may allow the plane to maintain altitude or even climb slightly.
1030.	Is maneuvering possible with one engine inoperative?	Yes, but it will be important to minimize the bank angle used in turns and to ensure that the turns are well coordinated.

Task B: V_{MC} Demonstration

1031.	Describe the V_{MC} demonstration.	The airplane, operating on one engine, will be placed in different configurations and pitch attitudes to show the effect of each configuration on single-engine performance.
1032.	Will you go all the way to V_{MC} during the demonstration?	No. Not all of the available rudder will be used. This will allow a simulation of V_{MC} while not getting down to the actual speed.
1033.	Why will you avoid going all the way to V_{MC} during the demonstration?	Going all the way to V_{MC} would most likely result in a loss of control and perhaps a spin.

Task C: Engine Failure During Flight (by Reference to Instruments)

1034.	How would you detect an engine failure during flight in IMC conditions?	The first indication would be seen on the inclinometer. The ball would deflect away from the failed engine. Next, the turn coordinator and attitude indicator would indicate a turn towards the failed engine.

Task D: Instrument Approach–One Engine Inoperative (by Reference to Instruments)

1035.	How will an engine failure affect your ability to fly an instrument approach?	The approach itself should not be greatly affected. However, I will need to pay close attention to my airspeed because a missed approach may not be possible due to the performance reduction, and large additions of power may affect my ability to maintain the inbound course.

APPENDIX A
ABBREVIATIONS AND ACRONYMS USED BY COMMERCIAL PILOTS

AC	Advisory Circular
AD	Airworthiness Directive
ADF	automatic direction finder
ADM	aeronautical decision making
A/FD	*Airport/Facility Directory*
AGL	above ground level
AIM	*Aeronautical Information Manual*
ATC	air traffic control
CFI	certificated flight instructor
CG	center of gravity
CNS	central nervous system
CRM	cockpit resource management
CTAF	common traffic advisory frequency
EFAS	En Route Flight Advisory Service
EGT	exhaust gas temperature
ELT	emergency locator transmitter
ETA	estimated time of arrival
ETE	estimated time en route
FAA	Federal Aviation Administration
FAR	Federal Aviation Regulation
FBO	fixed-base operator
FL	flight level
FMAS	Flight Maneuver Analysis Sheets
FSDO	Flight Standards District Office
FSS	Flight Service Station
ft.	foot/feet
GPS	global positioning system
IFR	instrument flight rules
IR	instrument reference
kt.	knot(s)
km.	kilometer(s)
LAA	local airport advisory
L/D_{MAX}	maximum lift-to-drag ratio
LLWAS	low-level windshear alert system
LORAN	long-range navigation
MEF	maximum elevation figure
MEL	minimum equipment list
min.	minute(s)
MMEL	master MEL
MOA	military operations area
MP	manifold pressure
MSL	mean sea level
MTR	military training route

NAVAID	navigational aid
NDB	nondirectional beacon
NM	nautical mile
NOTAM	Notice to Airmen
PAPI	precision approach path indicator
PIC	pilot in command
PIREP	pilot weather report
POH	Pilot's Operating Handbook
PSI	pound per square inch
PTS	Practical Test Standards
sec.	second(s)
SM	statute mile
STC	supplemental type certificate
SUA	special-use airspace
TRSA	terminal radar service area
V_A	design maneuvering speed
VASI	visual approach slope indicator
V_{FE}	maximum flap extended speed
VFR	visual flight rules
VHF	very high frequency
VHF/DF	VHF direction finder
V_{LE}	maximum landing gear extended speed
V_{LO}	maximum landing gear operating speed
V_{MC}	minimum control speed with critical engine inoperative
V_{MU}	minimum un-stick speed
V_{NE}	never-exceed speed
V_{NO}	maximum structural cruising speed
VOR	VHF omnidirectional range
VR	visual reference
V_R	rotation speed
V_{S1}	stalling speed in a specified configuration
VSI	vertical speed indicator
V_{S0}	stalling speed in the landing configuration
V_X	best-angle-of-climb speed
V_Y	best-rate-of-climb speed

INDEX